CARING FOR STRANGERS

NIAS – Nordic Institute of Asian Studies
New and Recent Monographs

NIAS Press is the autonomous publishing arm of NIAS – Nordic Institute of Asian Studies, a research institute located at the University of Copenhagen. NIAS is partially funded by the governments of Denmark, Finland, Iceland, Norway and Sweden via the Nordic Council of Ministers, and works to encourage and support Asian studies in the Nordic countries. In so doing, NIAS has been publishing books since 1969, with more than two hundred titles produced in the past few years.

UNIVERSITY OF COPENHAGEN

Nordic Council of Ministers

CARING FOR STRANGERS

Filipino Medical Workers in Asia

Megha Amrith

Caring For Strangers
Filipino Medical Workers in Asia
by Megha Amrith
Nordic Institute of Asian Studies
Monograph series, no. 134

First published in 2017 by NIAS Press
NIAS – Nordic Institute of Asian Studies
Øster Farimagsgade 5, 1353 Copenhagen K, Denmark
Tel: +45 3532 9501 • Fax: +45 3532 9549
E-mail: books@nias.ku.dk • Online: www.niaspress.dk

A CIP catalogue record for this book is available from the British Library

ISBN: 978-87-7694-192-5 (hbk)
ISBN: 978-87-7694-193-2 (pbk)

Typeset in Arno Pro 12/14.4
Typesetting by BookWork

Printed and bound in the United States
by Maple Press

Cover image: Nurses take an oath during induction ceremonies
of newly certified health workers in Pasay City, south of Manila,
Philippines, 14 March 2011. (EPA/ROLEX DELA PENA)

Contents

Figures

Maps

Acknowledgements

I am thankful to all of the individuals who have so generously shared their stories and their time with me, and without whom this book would not have been possible. I am indebted to them for their trust, for warmly opening their homes and lives to me and for teaching me many valuable life lessons. As with any ethnographic study, the narratives that lie ahead have been jointly created and shaped through these important relationships.

Pseudonyms for informants have been used throughout the book in keeping with anthropological conventions on confidentiality. The names of the hospitals and nursing homes where I conducted my research have also been disguised. However, original names are used for public figures, as well as to refer to broad districts or public spaces.

The Gates Cambridge Trust and Overseas Research Studentship generously funded the research on which this book is based. The Gates Cambridge Trust, The Evans Fund and Wolfson College also provided financial support for fieldwork and conference travel. For all of this crucial support, I am very grateful.

This research began as a doctoral project at the Department of Social Anthropology at the University of Cambridge. I express my gratitude to Leo Howe and Susan Bayly for their guidance and mentorship, which ensured that I would pursue my research and writing with a firm sense of rigour and honesty; and to Pnina Werbner and Perveez Mody for their invaluable feedback and for inspiring and supporting me to take this work further. I also thank my peers at the Department for the lively conversations during my time there.

Fieldwork would not have been possible without the help of many individuals and institutions in Singapore and in the Philippines. I am thankful to the Asia Research Institute in Singapore for hosting me as a Visiting Researcher. In the Philippines, Mike Muñoz was of great help in introducing me to Manila's medical world, while friends and colleagues at Ateneo de Manila University and at the University of the Philippines were always there for deeply educational and enjoyable discussions. Special thanks go to Jonathan Ong for his hospitality in the Philippines, and for his friendship, advice and company as we pursued our research paths together. I am fortunate to have carried with me enduring friendships from Singapore, London and Wolfson College, which have provided a lot of support. I have also drawn inspiration from those I have had the good fortune to meet over the course of this research who work tirelessly in solidarity with migrant workers so that they may live with dignity.

Over the years, I have presented parts of this book at conferences, seminars and workshops and have learned a great deal from the many thought-provoking conversations with scholars and mentors who have engaged with my work. For helpful conversations and advice along the way, I would like to thank Jason Cabañes, Janet Carsten, Elka Drazkiewicz, Delwar Hussain, Jessica Johnson, Mark Johnson, Johan Lindquist, Nicholas Long, Mirca Madianou, Daniel Miller, Helena Patzer, Emma Rothschild and Mika Toyota. More recently, I have much appreciated the support I received from Parvati Nair as I finalized this book in my current academic home at the United Nations University Institute on Globalization, Culture and Mobility, and the warm encouragement of my colleagues at the Institute, especially Valeria Bello, Tendayi Bloom and Janina Pescinski.

The manuscript has been much enriched by the detailed and constructive comments from the anonymous reviewers for NIAS Press. My thanks to them and to Gerald Jackson, Editor of NIAS Press, for his kind support, along with the rest of the editorial team. I acknowledge permission from Taylor & Francis to reprint passages and material adapted from the following articles: "'They Think we are Just Caregivers': The Ambivalence of Care among Filipino Medical Workers in Singapore' in *The Asia Pacific Journal of Anthropology* 11 (3–4), 2010; and 'Encountering Asia: Narratives of Filipino Medical Workers on Caring for Other Asians' in *Critical Asian Studies* 45 (2).

Last but certainly not least, I thank my family: my extended family across the world whose remarkable journeys have shaped my personal interests in migration; Frank and Monika Werner for their warmth and hospitality from São Paulo to Neustadt; Ruth for her wisdom and constant encouragement and Theodore for all the joy he brings. I am incredibly lucky to have a wonderful older brother, Sunil, who has been a true guide and inspiration to me since the very beginning of my academic endeavors until now. I am ever grateful to my loving parents, Jairam and Shantha, for their help and moral support in every way, and to Andreas, for discovering the world with me and for being my pillar from near and from far.

Abbreviations

Abbreviations are explained throughout the book. The recurrent ones are also listed here:

DH   Domestic helper (an abbreviation commonly used among Filipino migrants)

NCLEX   National Council Licensure Examination (the examination required for nurses to work in the United States)

PAP   People's Action Party (ruling political party in Singapore)

POEA   Philippine Overseas Employment Agency

OFW   Overseas Filipino Worker

PR   Permanent Resident

Terminology

The terms 'Pinoy' and 'Pinay' (male or general, and female respectively) correspond to 'Filipino' and 'Filipina' and are terms popularly used, in an informal manner, to talk about anyone from the Philippines or anything related to the Philippines.

Informants' names in this book are sometimes preceded by Filipino terms of respect, following my informants' usage of the terms. These are:

Até and *Kuya*   Elder sister and elder brother respectively. Apart from their literal usage, these are commonly used terms to address an acquaintance or a stranger who is slightly older than the speaker with respect and warmth.

Tita and *Tito*   Aunt and uncle respectively. Apart from their literal usage, these are commonly used terms to address anyone who is significantly older than the speaker with respect and warmth.

Sir/Ma'am   Often used to address teachers, employers and people in positions of authority.

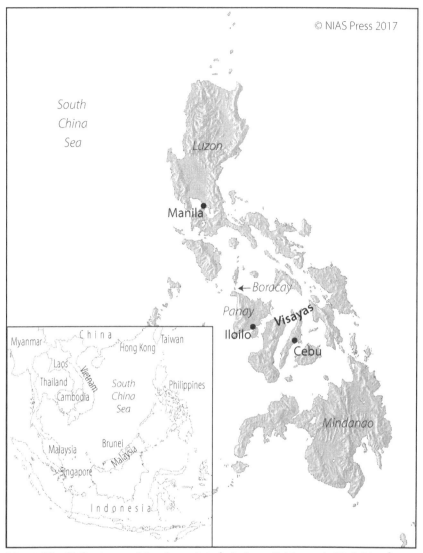

Map 1: The Philippines and Southeast Asia (relief map © Mountain High Maps)

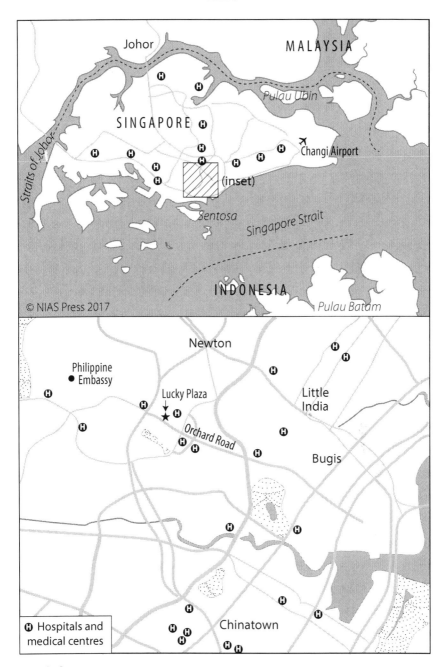

Map 2: Singapore

CHAPTER ONE

Introduction

My Filipino teacher, Ms Cherry, was one of the first people I met and got to know in the early days of this research. Ms Cherry was teaching the Filipino language at a language centre in Singapore after an eclectic career and a global journey spanning a number of countries: as a dancer in a Filipino cultural troupe that travelled the world, as a sports teacher in different schools and as lead singer in a band playing at a hotel lounge. All the while, Ms Cherry was a single mother after her marriage to her children's Pakistani father ended, and she moved between the Philippines and Singapore as her children were growing up. Soon after our classes were to end, she would be off to Texas to see relatives and meet a man she had been chatting with on an Internet dating website. Ms Cherry offered me valuable insights into the presence of Filipinos in Singapore. We went to Lucky Plaza one afternoon, Singapore's 'Filipino mall' full of stores selling goods from the Philippines, remittance agencies, beauty salons and eateries, where I was to practice what I had learned of the Filipino language. While we were there, she said, 'you are going to study nurses, right? I'm sure we can meet some here'. She proceeded to stop people in the mall, asking if they were nurses. Most of the people she stopped were indeed nurses and they chatted with us in passing. We then spotted another lady in a Filipino eatery; Ms Cherry said, 'ah, she might be a nurse'. As she walked closer, she paused and changed her mind, 'no, she's not a nurse'. 'How can you tell?' I asked. 'I just know', she said, 'you can tell who is a nurse just by how they are, how they look'.

In a separate unrelated episode about a month later, I attended a 'Philippine Idol' concert one Sunday afternoon as part of my initial explorations into the worlds of Filipino migrants in Singapore. I sat next to a couple in the auditorium and throughout the show I noticed them observing me intently for prolonged periods of time, watching my reactions to the performances. It was towards the end of the show when the man finally asked me: 'do you have the blood of a Filipino?' The question was no doubt arresting and memorable. My negative response triggered a series of other questions: 'so then why are you here?' 'do you understand?' and 'how come you know Tagalog?' These questions – mostly borne out of sheer curiosity rather than hostility – indicated surprise that someone without 'blood ties' to the Philippines might express an interest in Filipino cultural expressions and languages.

Both episodes, although I did not fully realize it at the time, foreshadowed important themes and questions in this book: that Filipino lives are often mobile, and their connections global; and secondly, that there is something unique and identifiable about Filipino nurses, that they appear to embody a certain distinctiveness in the landscape of migrant Filipinos. Yet, at the same time, my experience at the concert revealed quite explicit boundaries drawn on the basis of having or not having the 'blood of a Filipino'. What did that say about notions of identity, belonging and community among Filipinos abroad? What are the exclusions to this notion of belonging and in what ways do the ties of blood intersect or conflict with the bonds of class and with particular performances of status, style and labour? I wondered about the solidarities and tensions beneath the surface within the differentiated crowd of migrant Filipinos at the concert and sought to find out more in the course of my ethnographic explorations – and it is precisely these solidarities and tensions that now sit at the heart of this book.

The Image of the Migrant

Mobility has been central to Asia's history. The migrant in Asia has come to take on a number of meanings in the social, political and popular imagination, and today encompasses mobile people in a diversity of careers and pursuits. However, it is often the most vulnerable of migrants that harness widespread attention in the contemporary popular imagination in Asia, and in polarizing national debates about migration. They are either celebrated for their heroic sacrifices, or disparaged as necessary yet undesirable presences in a number of countries to which they migrate. At present Filipinos are often seen as the archetypal labour migrants of the world. With almost ten per cent of the Philippine population overseas, migration has become a way of life.

An article in a glossy global magazine on art, travel and culture, *Monocle*, featured a story on migrant Filipinos entitled, 'People Power – Manila' (2011). Celebrating the Philippines' 'export-industry' of labour, the article describes the country as a provider of global leaders in service: highly-trained, professionalized workers (as chefs, super nannies, call centre agents) who are flexible and adaptable seekers of adventure with an entrepreneurial spirit. As I came to discover, the article's tone parallels in many ways Filipinos' own narratives of their migration. This celebratory tone is also reminiscent of the words of Carlos Romulo, a renowned Filipino statesman and diplomat, who described the Filipino as being 'at the vanguard of progress ... a forlorn figure in the eyes of some, but not one defeated and lost' (Romulo, [1941] 1998: 4). In his writings on identity, he presented Filipinos as internationalists; civilized, assertive, and assured of their national identity. It was, after all, the establishment of an independent republic in the Philippines in 1898 from Spanish colonial rule, which made it appear to others in Asia as a 'visionary forerunner of all other anti-colonial movements in the region' (Anderson, 1998: 227).

At the other end of the spectrum from this confident narrative are stories that speak of vulnerable, downtrodden, sometimes undocumented, migrants who work in exploitative conditions. The 1995 scandal of the execution of Flor Contemplacion in Singapore, a Filipina domestic worker accused of murdering another Filipina domestic worker, led to an outcry in the Filipino public and media discourse about the lack of protection of the country's overseas migrant workers and the indignities that they, particularly the women, face on a regular basis. Meanwhile, the labelling of Filipino overseas contract workers as modern-day heroes (*bagong bayani*) of the nation who endure hardship and undergo sacrifices for the economic benefit of the nation (Rafael, 1997) continues.[1] By adding a moral underpinning to the country's explicit policy of emigration, the Philippine state attempts to legitimize such hardship.

The image of a country's migrants abroad is a key preoccupation of states, of politicians, of the public, and of the migrants themselves. It is particularly the case, as Romulo's statements have shown, for postcolonial

---

1. This was a term that the late President Corazon Aquino used in the 1980s, and is now a mainstream term in the Philippines today to refer to OFWs (Overseas Filipino Workers).

nation-states. Given that the Philippines is now one of the world's largest exporters of migrant labour – with 'few issues as important, pervasive or controversial to a globalizing Philippines as is international migration' (Tyner, 2009: 6) – these questions take on even greater importance. However, both the tone of celebration and tone of self-pity in the narratives about Filipino migrants neglect complex layers of the migrant experience. These binary narratives also overlook the sheer range of migrants who might hold very different aspirations and priorities.

This book is situated in-between the depicted confident image of Filipinos in the world and the stories of abuse and exploitation faced by contract labour migrants. It focuses on the migration of Filipino medical workers to Singapore and how they respond to the branding of global Filipino migrants in public discourses, as they sit in an ambiguous space that does not quite fit within the categories that have typically been used to understand global migration. The Philippines has now become one of the largest exporters of medical workers in the world and they constitute an increasing proportion of Filipinos abroad (POEA, 2010–2014).[2] Nursing, in particular, has become a big industry in the Philippines, with over four hundred nursing colleges in the country. Nursing and overseas migration are inextricably linked. Medical workers form a complex category of labour, which straddles the boundaries of 'professional' labour and 'unskilled' labour,[3] and of flexible and restricted regimes of migration. The category includes nurses of different ranks (from 'staff nurse' to 'nursing aide')[4] and also healthcare as-

---

2. In 2013, the stock estimate of Filipinos working abroad was 10.2 million (in permanent, temporary or irregular migration situations) (Commission on Filipinos Overseas). According to statistics published by the Philippine Overseas Employment Agency (POEA), between 2010 and 2014, Saudi Arabia, the United Arab Emirates and Singapore were the top three destinations for newly hired and rehired workers. In 2014, an estimated 19,815 nursing professionals and personnel left the Philippines, along with approximately 12,075 caregivers and caretakers, with the numbers increasing each year between 2010 and 2014. See Appendix A for detailed tables.

3. The term 'unskilled' is widely used to speak of migrants in occupations such as domestic work and manual labour. My usage of the terms 'unskilled' or 'low-skilled', however, comes with the caveat that these terms, as many have pointed out, are discursive terms that fail to acknowledge the many skills that migrants contribute, regardless of their occupation.

4. See Appendix B for an example of how nursing positions are structured in a hospital in Singapore.

sistants or auxiliaries, technicians and physiotherapists. While doctors on the one hand, and domestic caregivers on the other hand, are not the key focus of this work, their presence is always felt. The experience of medical workers is ambivalent, as their labour, their aspirations and their spatial and temporal orientations situate them in an in-between liminal space that is neither here nor there. This book tells the stories of these migrants and their journeys to Singapore, a city-state shaped by migrants, and with new arrivals of migrant workers each day. Singapore, in comparison to the United States and the Middle East, is a relatively recent destination for Filipino medical workers, even as Filipina domestic workers have been there since the 1970s. It is widely regarded as a transit city: a place to gain experience en route to somewhere else. As Singapore develops itself as a 'medical hub' within the region, while simultaneously grappling with the demands of an ageing population, it depends increasingly on contract medical workers from the Philippines (as well as China, Burma and India) to work in its government and private hospitals, and in nursing homes for the elderly and chronically ill. This ethnography of medical worker migration to Singapore is situated within a broader context of the globalization and commodification of healthcare, with Southeast Asia in particular witnessing increasing and distinctive health-related population movements that reflect the region's socio-economic inequalities.

Global Aspirations: Expectations in Limbo

This book follows the global aspirations of a new generation of migrants who seek empowerment through the professionalization of labour yet whose aspirations remain unfulfilled, as things do not turn out as they expect. Given that nursing in the Philippines is intertwined with expectations of overseas work, it is viewed by many as a lucrative international profession and has become a symbol of social and economic mobility. Yet contrary to the expectations of social mobility and professional empowerment associated with nursing, migrants arrive in Singapore to confront a widespread perception of Filipinos as coming from a 'nation of servants'. They are situated close to the boundaries of unskilled and feminized domestic work and encounter conflicting cultural understandings of medical labour that are influenced by entrenched racial, national and gendered stereotypes and hierarchies in the region. These stereotypes and hierarchies emerge in migrants' intercultural encounters with the people they work with and care for: from elderly Singaporeans of different ethnic and linguistic backgrounds in nursing homes, to migrants from other Asian countries, who all converge in Singapore's public and private hospitals. While there are opportunities for cultivating new relationships across cultural boundaries, migrants frequently come up against the deep-seated barriers of prejudice. The anxieties created by these professional and social barriers also influence whom Filipino medical workers choose to socialize with. Many distance themselves from Filipina domestic workers with whom they are conflated in public perceptions, and exclude them from their social circles.

Migrants' personal and professional experiences and aspirations therefore intersect in powerful ways. As they care for the wellbeing of strangers in Singapore's medical institutions, they are often separated in space from their own families and their children and carry out their intimate lives online. In the meantime, their experiences in Singapore often drive them to imagine and plan individual and familial life projects in other countries in Europe, North America or Australia.

This is a story of the everyday encounters, anxieties and boundaries that relate to the care for others at an Asian crossroads of global capital, medical care and transnational migrant labour. The dilemmas of migrants in the region reflect a bigger picture of unresolved dilemmas, desires and disparities that are present in a postcolonial, twenty-first century, global Asia. The narratives of Filipino medical workers in Singapore thus offer a lens onto broader debates on global migration, class, gender, race and citizenship. I shall now turn to the themes that cut across this book: the contested meanings of care and intimacy, shifting understandings of migrant labour and agency, and the specific forms that contemporary inter-Asian connection (and disconnection) takes.

Care and Intimacy

The idea of care has multiple inflections in the lives of Filipino medical workers in Singapore. The question of who cares for whom is at the heart of their migrant lives, in a professional sense, as well as in the broader sense of caring for the self, the family, the nation, the other. This book is situated in a moment where fundamental questions – within and beyond the academic world – are being asked about the new forms of

sociality and intimacy that care engender; the tensions as well as the opportunities involved in the transnational commodification of care and
the 'purchase of intimacy' (Zelizer, 2005).

Migrant workers are increasingly central to the provision of care.
While migrant care labour itself is not new, its scale, diversity and
global reach makes it unique today. The feminization of labour since the
1970s has seen Asian women migrate for domestic work, service work,
entertainment and sex work (Hondangneu-Sotelo, 2007; Anderson,
2000; Ehrenreich and Hochschild, 2003; Yeates, 2009a; 2009b;
Parreñas, 2001). More recent is the increasing contract migration of
health workers, particularly nurses (Connell, 2008; Kingma, 2005). A
range of scholarly as well as public debates have emerged in light of the
prominence of migrants in care professions across the world, especially
when considering the broader linkages this phenomenon has with neoliberal globalization. These debates focus on the structural inequalities
that motivate and perpetuate the migration of poorer women from the
'Third World' to the 'First World'; the exploitation of care labour, particularly in its intersections with gendered and racialized hierarchies that
together marginalize female immigrant care workers (Parreñas, 2001;
Ehrenreich and Hochschild, 2003; Yeates, 2009a; 2009b; Anderson,
2000); the devaluation of care and how to raise its worth (Nakano
Glenn, 2000); and the opportunities for empowerment and transformation in care work (Constable, 2009; Datta et al., 2010; Zelizer, 2005).
In relation to the last point on empowerment, recent research on care
'has been critical in providing more nuanced understandings of these
relationships which move beyond the "caring" and "careless" dichotomy
while also highlighting the complex negotiations of trust, disclosure and
vulnerability that are central to the giving and receiving of care' (Datta
et al., 2006: 7). There are many taken-for-granted assumptions about
care, that relate to who ought to provide care (most often women), what
care means (most often construed as selfless and altruistic), and which
contexts are the most authentic sites for caring relationships (most often
the family), all of which tend to obscure a more complex and layered reality. I take as an example Joao Biehl's (2005) ethnography about 'zones
of social abandonment' in Brazil, to demonstrate how the family, as well
as medical and welfare institutions, are not sites of inherent or ideal care
and that they may, in locally specific situations, rather be intricately in-

volved in processes of exclusion. Responding to similar concerns about using potentially constraining normative labels and categories when speaking about care, John Borneman (1997: 583) calls for 'a concern for the actual situations in which people experience the need to care and be cared for'.

These debates on care are exemplified in Tomer Heymann's (2006) documentary film *Paper Dolls*, about the experiences of Filipino transgendered carers in Tel-Aviv. The opening scene of the film is compelling: we see a transgendered Filipino care worker holding the hand of an elderly Orthodox Jewish man crossing the road and accompanying him to a synagogue. It is a relationship of care that immediately challenges normative ideas about gender, kinship and care. Each character in the film highlights a different aspect of this global landscape of care and its ambivalences. For instance, Sally, a transgendered Filipino care worker, and Haim, an elderly Israeli man suffering from throat cancer, have developed a close relationship based on daily co-presence, trust and intimacy. Haim depends on Sally to take care of him and pays her to do so. At the same time, Sally is like a daughter to him, as well as a friend and confidante, with whom he jokes, teases, argues and co-exists in the same everyday space. Another character, Jan, is not visibly caring in the scenes where we see him at work – he is unsmiling and non-effusive, yet professional and efficient, reminding us that care work need not necessarily be about effusive demonstrations of love (Manalansan, 2008). In the film, we also see the relationships of care amongst the migrant workers themselves, as they gather nightly to perform in the *Paper Dolls* dance troupe. However, all of them live in precarious conditions as migrant workers without documents in Tel-Aviv and in a volatile political context. The film highlights in multifaceted ways, the different affective dimensions and tensions that accompany the migration of care workers: friendship and intimacy in cosmopolitan landscapes, 'disaffection', professionalism and distance in the labour of care and the questioning of gender normative understandings of care. It also demonstrates the importance of care for the self in a context where migrants experience specific vulnerabilities (Manalansan, 2008; Foucault: [1984] 1997).

Engaging with these conversations on care, this study asks what forms the new intimate relations that develop between migrants and those that they care for take? What roles do qualities such as trust and reciprocity, or responses such as hostility and fear play in these relationships? How do migrants understand the labour of care and the intimate relations they develop in the distinctive context of a global Asian city?

I am concerned here with intimate relations as 'social relationships that are – or give the impression of being – physically and/or emotionally close' in their broadest sense, including nursing and hospice care (Constable, 2009: 50). These intimate relationships may be based on close affective bonds of friendship, love and interdependence, at the same time as they may be marked by tension and transience. In the emerging field on transnational intimacies, we see how intimacy, care and commercial practices are increasingly intertwined. In this perspective, doing intimate labour for a wage still involves complex subjective negotiations of intimacy; while intimate relationships typically seen as 'authentic' are also 'linked in new and evolving ways to commercial practices and material desires' (Constable, 2009: 56). While studies on the commodification of intimacy must recognize the prevalence of new power relationships within the spaces of global capital, research agendas could productively engage with the potentially empowering dimensions of this process rather than seeing commodification as exclusively linked to exploitation, an absence of agency and a loss of something authentic (Constable, 2009: 58–59).

The contradictions that Filipino migrant nurses experience subjectively – both in their journeys abroad and in the work that they do – reveal themselves powerfully in the multiple inflections that care takes in their lives. The idiom of care – both analytically and ethnographically – is salient, yet deeply contested. My informants are medical workers who leave the Philippines to care (most often distantly) for their families, to care for themselves and their own futures, while caring for strangers in Singapore. They debate the nature of care regularly in their daily lives; the questions of who ought to care for whom and how, are omnipresent. Care, in such reflections and discussions also takes on a nationalistic character, as my informants speak about how one ought to treat strangers, neighbours and family and develop social critiques of a hyper-capitalist ethic that they witness abroad and its impacts on caring relationships. However, when care is linked to labour, it becomes more divisive, often evoking a sense of shame. The intersections of care and labour in the global service economy are relevant, particularly when situated within the recent history of Philippine labour migration and the consequences of the branding of Filipinos as a particular type of labour migrant.

Global Filipinos and Their Labour

Domestic workers have come to represent the Filipino migrant worker, or the 'OFW' ('Overseas Filipino Worker', as they are known in the Philippines), in the public imagination, both at home and abroad. The image of the OFW has been shaped by the increasing feminization of the labour force travelling overseas. Their presence in the world has, in part, produced a characterization of Filipinos as 'servants of globalization' (Parreñas, 2001), raising troubling questions about the gendered and devalued nature of Filipino migrant labour in the globalized world, particularly in the spheres of intimate labour and service work. For this reason, the relation between nurses and domestic workers, both falling under the ambiguous rubric of care labour, is central to this book.

Nurses attempt to differentiate themselves from the 'servants of globalization' characterization. They aspire to find greater freedom, respect and possibilities in the world than those typically given to Filipino labour migrants (including the right to residence or citizenship in other countries, which domestic workers typically lack). That said, these processes of differentiation are not so clear-cut and my focus on nurses as 'semi-professionals' illuminates the complexity of what constitutes migrant care labour and the precarious boundaries that separate the different occupational labels within it. This manifests itself not just in discussions about work, but also in social interactions among migrants, as also called migrant socialities. Care labour is a key site for the negotiation of social mobility and for understanding how one is perceived as a Filipino migrant in the world. [5] This is firstly because of the sheer number of Filipino migrants employed under the broad category of care labour, and secondly because the tensions between nurses and domestic workers are sharper given that they are more proximate in the work that they do.

---

5. The experiences of the Philippine 'elite' complicate this picture, as they too participate in discussions about Philippine citizenship and politics, however, these experiences are beyond the scope of this study (see Ong and Cabañes, 2011; Cabañes, 2009).

Filipino medical workers have been internationally mobile for a long time, yet it is only since the 1990s that they have come to have such a visible presence within the broader profile of Filipino migrants. The majority of the foundational works on Philippine migration have focussed on Filipina domestic workers, sex workers and entertainers. This literature has been crucial in bringing to light the experiences of Filipina migrant women since the 1970s.[6] A number of analyses have been influenced by Michel Foucault's (1977) work on disciplinary modes of power and 'docile bodies', where disciplinary techniques of surveillance, as well as the training and internalization of bodily gestures, behaviours and practices, work to '[increase] the forces of the body (in economic terms of utility) and [diminish] these same forces (in political terms of obedience)' (1977: 138). Beyond the individualized opera-tion of power, these techniques work at a collective 'biopolitical' level, concerned with regularizing societies and populations (Foucault, 1976 [2003]). A number of scholars have taken Foucauldian approaches in their analyses of the suffering of vulnerable Filipina migrant women. For example, Rolando Tolentino (2001: 3), in his work on mail-order brides, demonstrates how 'on the one hand, the [Filipina] body be-comes a tool for (limited) economic empowerment, placing the Filipina in the non-traditional role of "wage earner" or "head of the family"'. On the other hand, the Filipina's body becomes the very requisite for being positioned in this "new" economic situation. Her supposedly nimble fingers and perfect eyesight, her youth, and her unmarried status all add up to a stereotypical performative body in transnational circuits'. These discourses are regularly used by migrant recruitment agencies and through the Philippine state's own promotion of its workers as 'good, disciplined workers' and of hardworking, caring and meticulous migrant heroes (Tyner, 2004; Rodriguez, 2008a: 799). This body of research has also been shaped by the afore mentioned feminist scholars Rhacel Parreñas (2001) and Arlie Hochschild and Barbara Ehrenreich (2003), who have analysed from a sociological perspective the global migration of women from lower-income countries to higher-income

---

6. These studies have marked a departure from earlier voices in Philippine history. Reynaldo Ileto (1998: 205–206) writes that, 'certain social classes have been fa-voured by the written word. Colonial officials, friars, explorers and travellers, il-lustrators, the native clergy, revolutionary officers, mestizos, *principales,* and as a whole, men, are the principle subjects of our archival records'.

countries in socially reproductive labour. A prominent critique in these works is the commodification of female bodies, and the ways in which this is being encouraged and reproduced through the Philippines' use of 'labour brokering as a developmental strategy' as a part of the country's insertion into processes of neoliberal globalization (Rodriguez, 2008a; 799; Guevarra, 2009). They are critical of the ways in which the state profits from this commodification and export of bodies, overlooking the human and social costs of this process that migrant workers have to bear. Underpinning this strand of research is a feminist-Marxist critique of the current global order and the global exploitation of migrant labour. The implications of female migration on mothering and on children left behind, as well as the suffering that separated families have to endure have frequently been flagged up, most notably in Parreñas's work on the *Children of Global Migration* (2005). This also mirrors a wider narrative among migrants themselves and civil society groups advocating for migrant rights who critique the state's migration regime for the breaking up of families when mothers go to work abroad. However, as Rodriguez (2008b) highlights, such narratives, while critical of the government's labour export policy, tend to uphold gendered norms that construct women exclusively as mothers, and thus perpetuate patriarchal notions of femininity. Yet local examples from the Philippines have revealed more nuanced constructions of family life when a mother goes to work abroad. These include, for example, recognition of alternative care arrangements that involve the extended family playing a significant role (Aguilar *et al.*, 2009); or localized interpretations of family intimacy that are not necessarily based on long-term face-to-face contact but on the sharing of narratives and stories (McKay, 2012). These interpretations complement the spread of new media technologies, which have offered migrants novel ways of keeping in contact and sharing stories with their families at home (Madianou and Miller, 2012). Migrant mothers, moreover, may have other motivations to go abroad, beyond the 'socially acceptable' public narrative, which represents their journey solely as one of sacrifice for the family (Madianou and Miller, 2012: 5-6). In short, there is a sense of ambivalence in both public and research debates on the subject.

While debates continue on the implications of these overseas labour arrangements on gendered and family roles and on migrant women's wellbeing, all of these works share a common critique of the poor treatment that a number of female migrant workers are subjected to in the countries to which they go. The scholarship also goes beyond simply accepting the existence of disciplinary modes of power by examining how migrants resist or subvert such forms of power rather than accepting their ill-treatment passively as victims. They focus on the agency of migrants in negotiating the structures of domination in which they find themselves. To take a few examples, Constable (1997) examines the forms of popular protest and the political organization of domestic workers in Hong Kong as they fight for their rights as workers, whilst also illuminating the practices of simultaneous resistance and accommodation in their daily routines as workers in their employers homes.[7] Meanwhile, Yeoh and Huang (1998: 599) explore how migrant domestic workers express themselves and make claims to public spaces on their weekly day off, even as dominant discourses seek to exclude them from these spaces; the authors argue that subversions of public norms are 'not necessarily deliberate acts of defiance, but are inscribed in habitual practice'. Connecting these acts and practices to a larger structural level, Aguilar (2002: 12) reiterates that the 'collective efforts of individual migrants sometimes with valuable support from advocacy groups, transform in due course the mechanisms, institutions and concomitants of migration'. Such examples importantly demonstrate the agency of migrant women as they attempt to resituate the margins.

Recent scholarship has given further attention to the subtler aspects of migrant social and cultural life beyond resisting exploitation. It has been driven by the concern that, in exploring migrant lives purely through the lens of how certain power structures are resisted, negotiated and subverted, we often overlook aspects of their lives that are not directly concerned with such questions. Here Saba Mahmood's (2004: 15) words are illuminating: 'binary terms of resistance and subordination ... ignores projects, discourses and desires that are not captured by these terms'. She argues that, 'agentival capacity is entailed not only in those acts that resist norms but also in the multiple ways in which one inhabits norms' (Mahmood, 2004: 15). Agency can also be understood

---

7. Beyond the Asian context, Mary Romero's (1992) work on Chicana household workers' in the US and their strategies to improve their working conditions in the face of oppressive and demeaning conditions of work is notable.

through migrants' pursuits of new moral engagements and forms of sociality, which in turn provide a more encompassing picture of migrant lives. In the case of Asian migrant women, Pnina Werbner and Mark Johnson (2010: 205, 213) 'challenge a dominant view that construes women international migrants from Asia as docile bodies shaped and constrained by their transnational (re) productive labours', as 'not all Asian migrant women always and everywhere live on the margins, falling through the cracks'. Rather, they argue, a move away from a political economy approach could allow us to understand 'the moral and ethical considerations and dilemmas that shape people's affective relationships because these are performatively reworked and transgressed within and across discrepant diasporic spaces' (Werbner and Johnson, 2010: 207). There is thus a shift towards studying the new modes of sociality, conviviality, as well as the cultural practices and creative engagements of migrants. This includes the experiences of religious conversion and religious pilgrimage as salient aspects of migrant lives (Liebelt, 2010; Constable, 2010) and the desires for new consumption possibilities and lifestyles (Silvey, 2006).

In light of these recent scholarly discourses on Asian migrant women, this study on migrant medical workers contributes to understanding the shared, overlapping and divergent aspirations that migrants hold, putting forward a story of migration as a journey of self-reflection. It also traces how these practices and processes are shaped in and through the perceptions that migrants have of each other. For instance, while nurses perceive domestic workers as belonging to an inferior social class, domestic workers find creative ways to respond to and redefine this characterization. Occupational labels, even if they are often used to define the contours of sociality and mobility, are not the sole determinants of migrants' identities; 'less tangible qualities' of taste, conduct and 'habitus' influence interactions on the ground and shape a politics of status at home and abroad (Bourdieu, 1986; Brenner, 1998: 140; Pinches, 1996).

Inter-Asian Encounters

This is a story situated in the plural, urban milieu that is contemporary Singapore, which sees the convergence of migrants, past and present, into its national space. Many of these migrants come from other parts of Asia. In focussing on the aspirations, expectations and identifications of Filipino migrants, as well as several other migrant groups that they encounter in Singapore, this book is also an exploration of what being 'Asian' means and how citizens of different Asian nation-states regard one another in the context of regional inequality.

The 'Asian values' discourse emerged in the 1980s and 1990s as a political-ideological discourse, its main proponents being the former leaders of Singapore and Malaysia, Lee Kuan Yew and Mahathir Mohamad, alongside a number of public intellectuals. It emerged in East and Southeast Asia during a particular period of capitalist growth and development in the region, wherein the economic successes of the 'Asian Tiger' economies were explained in part by the role of these so-called Asian values. These values are based upon a Confucian ethic of hard work, thrift, communitarianism, a strong family orientation and a respect for political leadership (Milner, 2001; Chua, 1999). In this framing, Asian values are posited as fundamentally different to 'Western' values, which are perceived to hold an individualistic orientation and a lack of social discipline. The Asian values discourse has of course been critiqued for upholding authoritarian regimes at the expense of human rights and for essentializing a highly diverse region that has been shaped by a multiplicity of religious traditions and practices, ethnicities, histories and expressions of cultural pluralism. If anything, Asia is a region defined through this very diversity and difference rather than any immutable or inherent values.

The Philippines is positioned ambivalently in this discourse. Benigno Aquino, Corazon Aquino's late husband, once suggested that 'the Filipinos were an Asian people not Asian in the eyes of their fellow Asians, not Western in the eyes of the West' (cited in Sheridan, 1999: 19). There has been growing interest to engage with the Asian region in certain circles, as well as a renewed orientation towards pre-colonial idioms, and the use of Filipino over English by certain political figures in resistance to a hegemonic 'West' (Milner, 2001); however, in other perspectives the Philippines is seen as distant, in political, economic and socio-cultural terms, from the Asian values discourse. Moreover, the legacies of its Spanish and American colonial past remain visible in the contemporary Philippines in many cultural expressions and institutions (the Catholic Church being one), albeit in a hybrid and localized manner. In this ambivalent framing, it is important to ask how its citizens and overseas migrants engage with these discourses in their everyday lives. How do they position themselves as Filipinos in the Southeast Asian region? How do they relate to the citizens of other Asian nations when they travel as migrants within the region – do they understand and belong to Asia in geographical terms, or also in terms of particular shared values, ethics or ways of life? This ethnography demonstrates that, on one level, migrants often refer to 'Asia' and the 'West' as opposed categories in their narratives and in their expectations. At the same time, the diversity of their encounters when they cross borders within Asia – and the surprise, novelty and the unexpectedness that such encounters bring – provoke new reflections, questions and critiques among migrants. Their everyday practices and interactions are revealing of heterogeneous ways of being, interacting with and seeing the world, rather than a simplistic reflection of an essential Asian way of life.

While my focus is on the particular experiences of Filipinos in Singapore, I imagine that the actual complexity of identities and interactions on the ground is not unique to this study, but relevant to other experiences of intra-Asian migration, particularly given the vast history of cultural encounters within Asia. Examining interactions on the ground enables us to think about Asia in novel ways, through the eyes and words of those who cross borders within the region, and who see their encounters with other Asians as culturally familiar, yet alien.[8] Migrants' shifting understandings and reflections of the Asian region challenge a taken-for-granted notion of Asian values. Studies of migration from the Philippines so far have tended to focus on Filipinos in Europe and North America (with some notable exceptions such as Nicole Constable's *Maid to Order* (1997) on Filipino domestic workers in Hong Kong, and Lieba Faier's (2009a; 2009b) work on Filipina women in Japan). Other Asian cities are important in Filipino migrations: for medical workers,

---

8. Resil Mojares (1994, cited Sears, 2007: 46) says: '"Southeast Asian Studies" is itself an imaginary field to the extent that it takes as its object of study a region that is a recent, externally defined political intervention, one that is not an exclusive, internally bounded entity, geographically, ethnically, or culturally. Yet, there exists within the region such a range of cultural affinities, such historical depth of exchanges, and such a body of equivalent experiences and interests, as to make of the region something not wholly fabricated or arbitrary'. This idea is mirrored in academic debates about the region, as well as debates that migrants engage with when they arrive in a new place.

Singapore is a valuable stepping-stone en route to other destinations in the 'West'. Not only is it a place to wait until visa and examination requirements for these other destinations are met, it is also a place which makes the risk of migration appear less dramatic ('it's so close to the Philippines', my informants say) and it has a reputation for being a place to gain rigorous experience. The particular dynamics of intra-Asian migration involve moments of both recognition and familiarity, of mis-recognition and shock, of expectations and assumptions reinforced or challenged about different Asian economies and moralities. Proximity to other Asians unsettles, and sees the emergence of deep-seated preju-dices and the formation of new hierarchies and distinctions. This is a process which migration accentuates.

Contests for distinction among Asian citizens thrive, while nar-ratives of pan-Asian identification simultaneously place Asia as a distinct cultural entity apart from the 'West', which is constructed and imagined in homogenous terms by my informants. The West, however, remains a point of reference – a desired destination and the location of future stability – for many of the people in my study. My Filipino informants see Singapore as remarkably modern; but because it is Asia, it is not seen as different enough. Ironically, they simultaneously perceive it as not Asian enough in its values. The lure of America still prevails, even if the codes of America and its colonial and postcolonial presence are domesticated within local idioms and modes of performance (Cannell, 1999). [9] Meanwhile, Singapore is uncomfortably neither here nor there.

Migrants are thus not moving directly between fixed places of origin and destination, but undertake journeys that include one or more other locations. Singapore is a place that embodies a sense of temporal and spatial uncertainty. This is therefore also an account of how migrants make sense of what they expect to be transient encounters. On the one

---

9. Fenella Cannell (1999), speaking of Filipino cultural practices that are legacies of American colonialism such as beauty pageants or karaokeing Frank Sinatra songs, writes that people are not necessarily: 'thinking consciously about the problems of "post-colonialism" ... they are thinking about getting the song right, and enjoying themselves in ways which have in many senses become domesticated as part of the Filipino scene and which therefore appear banal. Nonetheless, the songs belong ... to codes of behaviour associated with the American colonial and post-colonial presence in the Philippines.'

hand, Singapore is a liminal place: migrants do not actively cultivate enduring connections to it, as can be seen in the profound moments of disorientation they experience and how they cope with it. This disorientation exists also in part because the Singapore state does not actively produce the conditions for migrants to feel a sense of belonging here. There is often an anxious craving to move on. As Johan Lindquist (2009: 8) writes, 'temporal insecurity and open-endedness' generate a sense of anxiety; anxiety 'arises in ill-defined conditions' and 'attaches to what might happen' (Sennett, 2006, cited in Lindquist, 2009: 8). On the other hand there are interruptions to this notion of transience, as certain nurses develop, unexpectedly, enduring connections in Singapore: to their work, their neighbours and churches. The barriers to migration, which involve restrictive visa policies and often prohibitive financial costs, also mean that nurses' onward journeys are often halted or delayed. The journeys of Filipino nurses are linked to a search for a new home with a future and being in Singapore sharpens their discussions about where they can go, how they can realize their aspirations, what kinds of connections they develop to other places, and what their prospects are in this search for a home. Migrants also face questions and dilemmas of citizenship, both in practical terms – devising strategies to move to other countries with the hope to settle, while also acquiring permanent residence in Singapore as a safety net – and also in terms of belonging. Does a transit mentality disable a sense of belonging to Singapore? Running through this story are the anxieties of transience, as well as the unexpected transitions that migrants make.

In this sense, Singapore is a place where migrants work through ethical questions about how one should conduct oneself in the world and how one should relate to others (Johnson, 2010). Mark Johnson's (2010: 428) work on Filipinos in Saudi Arabia similarly emphasizes that Saudi Arabia 'is not simply a temporary stopping point to a better future elsewhere, but is also a place where the middle-class aspirations of Muslim Filipinos may be realized and where their religious affiliations as Muslims may be seen as enhancing rather than detracting from those dreams and imaginings'. In Singapore, migrants question what it means to be an Asian, a Filipino, a Christian, and a professional nurse in the world. The stepping-stone is more important in shaping migrants' identifications and subjectivities than it might initially appear.

This book is therefore about transit in a broader sense. Filipino medical workers are situated in the spaces between many of the categories that we have used for understanding global mobility. Being in-between places and categories, and straddling boundaries, medical workers' experiences allow us to see how boundaries are formed, negotiated, dissolved and realigned (Barth, 1969).

Histories of Medicine and Mobility

Migration and travel are deeply embedded in the histories of both the Philippines and of Singapore. Both countries have been at the intersection of global trade and political networks, leading to numerous cultural encounters over centuries. 'Diasporic worlds' are 'an old phenomenon in Southeast Asian history' (Harper, 1997: 264) and ideas have moved across the region along with people.

Reflecting the wider experience of the region, Manila too has been shaped by 'an amalgam of cultural encounters' as it stood at the heart of a vast transpacific trading network; as early as the late 1500s, Manila was the 'world's first global city' (Irving, 2010: 44). Continuing this global orientation, in the 19th century, men from the Philippines, who were known as 'Manilamen' in the English-speaking world, sailed across the world through transnational maritime networks, working in multi-ethnic and multi-lingual vessels and developing far-reaching connections between the Philippines and other places further afield (Aguilar, 2012). Nowadays, Filipinos continue to be out in the world as one of the world's largest labour diasporas, albeit through different kinds of arrangements, institutions and routes. Vicente Rafael (2000: 9) argues that 'the Philippines and Filipinos are thus permeated with foreign origins, their historical realities haunted by the ghosts of colonialism', under the Spanish, Americans and Japanese. This complex colonial history combined with political and economic crises in the post-colonial Philippines have been fundamental in shaping the Philippines' role as one of the primary senders of labour migrants across the world.

Of particular interest here is the history of colonial medicine in the Philippines under American rule, which was inextricably bound to the racial politics and hierarchies of empire (Kramer, 2006). Medicine was intrinsic to a civilizing mission of 'benevolent assimilation' that the Americans undertook to reform Filipinos, their 'little brown brothers'

(Rafael, 2000; Kramer, 2006). Warwick Anderson (2006: 1, 5) explores the 'medico-moral vision' held by American colonial authorities, which put hygiene reform at the heart of their attempts to '[forge] an improved sanitary race'. They sought to 'transform' Filipino inhabitants from a 'weak and feeble race … into a strong, healthy and enduring people' (Heiser, cited in Anderson, 2006: 1). Anderson investigates how American military and health officers undertook this 'civilizing project', albeit in ways that were always contested by Philippine inhabitants, as colonial discourse was never entirely hegemonic. This was accompanied by the development of a public health infrastructure of hospitals and training colleges for Filipinos in Western medicine (Anderson, 2006; Arnold, 1993). Catherine Choy (2003) illuminates the contradictions of these medical training institutions. She highlights how American nursing training in the Philippines oriented Filipino nurses towards careers abroad – in the United States – rather than at home. Moreover, the 'nurturing' of Filipina women, was never separate from the racialization of these women, nor were close relationships between trainers and students matched by any sense of professional solidarity (Choy, 2003: 5, 19). Similarly, Anderson (2006: 10) investigates how, in the gradual Filipinization of the medical service under the tutelage of Americans, Filipinos were continually seen as flawed, inferior imitations of Western health professionals. Yet this 'uncanny sense of the copy' was unsettling and even served, in some cases, to reaffirm American power (Anderson, 2006: 10).

Following on from earlier migration to the US under American colonial rule, Filipino medical workers continued to migrate to the US in the post-colonial context. However, the beginning of mass Filipino migration has its roots in the political and economic crises of the 1970s, when overseas migration became an official state policy under the government of Ferdinand Marcos.[10] With declining real wages, high levels of unemployment and growing political authoritarianism, overseas migration appeared a promising alternative to careers at home, particularly in light of new employment opportunities in the Gulf States and parts of Asia (Anderson, 1998; Tyner, 2004). Filipinos went abroad 'in search of alternatives – economic, political, cultural – to the pressures of uneven developments

---

10. In fact, before the 1970s, migrating medical workers were discouraged from leaving the Philippines and creating a 'brain drain' (Tyner, 2004).

and unrealized desires that they face[ed] in the Philippines' (Rafael, 2000: 2). It was during this period in the 1970s that the state officially established institutions to govern and regulate migration. Migration was a new strategy for national development relying heavily on remittances. As Rafael (2000: 205) suggests, overseas Filipinos 'take on the semblance of spectral presences whose labour takes place somewhere else but whose effects command, by their association with money, a place in the nation-state'.[11] This recognition of migrants' political and economic clout led to the proliferation of state-driven narratives of migration to legitimize and solidify migration as a central part of the national imaginary. Large numbers of Filipinos left to work abroad, including nurses who comprised one of the largest groups of migrating medical and technical workers from the Philippines.[12] Today, the main destinations include the USA, Canada, the UK and Australia, while many migrants stop off first in Singapore and in cities in the Middle East (Riyadh, Doha, Dubai).

The importance of migrants to the Philippines is accompanied in many countries by a lingering derogatory image of the Filipino as the hardworking, yet inferior service worker. This has its roots in colonial constructions of race in which the Filipino was continually stuck in positions of inferiority (Halili, 2006). An example is how Filipino navy stewards were not permitted to move up the ranks despite their high levels of education and skills, a stark contrast from the masculinist dreams that many Filipinos had of the honour and courage of navy work (Espiritu, 1995; 2002; Kramer, 2006). Rafael (2000: 69–70) also writes about male servants in colonial households, wage labourers 'who lived in the house were referred to by the infantalizing and desexualized Spanish term muchachos or "boys" in English, regardless of their age'. In the postcolonial period, Filipino migration since the 1970s was initially dominated by men in the construction sector, but for the past three decades the largest numbers of Filipinos migrating overseas have been women who go abroad for domestic work (Ball, 2008: 32). By 2001, Filipina women constituted 72% of migrant workers leaving the

11. Remittances from OFWs to the Philippines in 2015 were estimated at over $US 25 billion (BSP, 2015).

12. By 1988, Filipino overseas nurses outnumbered those in the Philippines (Eviota, 1992: 142). In 2003, figures estimated that almost 85% of *employed* Filipino nurses were working abroad (based on data that was recorded on nurses' employment locations) (Lorenzo, F.M.E, Galvez-Tan, J. Icamina, K. and Javier, L, 2007).

Philippines (Ball, 2008: 33). Contemporary Filipino migrants continue to be overrepresented in occupations that entail feminized service work (Parreñas, 2001).[13] However, the stories in this book demonstrate that the structural location that Filipinos tend to occupy in the global economy is not static.

In terms of religion, the majority of my informants were Roman Catholic, with a few exceptions. This reflects the religious make-up of the Philippines, which is about 83% Roman Catholic (Abinales and Amoroso, 2005: 11). Mindanao, in the Southern Philippines, however, resisted colonial practices of conversion to Catholicism, and has the largest concentration of Muslim Filipinos in the archipelago. There are also branches of charismatic Christianity and non-denominational Christian movements, which have gained a number of followers in recent years (Wiegele, 2005; Aguilar, 2006). Compared to neighbouring countries which are largely Muslim or Buddhist, the Philippines is unique in Southeast Asia.

A historical perspective is equally important to an understanding of Singapore's position in Asian networks of migration. A 'child of diaspora', Singapore has experienced a strong culture of migration throughout its history, making it a meeting point for diverse migrant populations (Harper, 1997). The early nineteenth century saw 'thousands of traders, mariners and adventurers' arrive from places all over the region and beyond (including Chinese, Malays, Indians, Javanese, Filipinos, Acehnese, Siamese, Cambodians, Burmese, Armenians, Parsees, Arabs and Jews). Such pluralism was characteristic of port polities across maritime Asia (Trocki, 2006: 40; see also Frost and Balasingamchow, 2009), and this polyglot character of the population was reminiscent of a longstanding tradition of mobility and cultural circulation in the region that encompassed not only Southeast Asia but also its wider connections with the maritime worlds of the Indian Ocean, South China Sea and Bay of Bengal (Trocki, 2006: 40; Tagliocozzo, 2013; Amrith, 2013). In the late nineteenth century, migration reached an unprecedented scale and was driven, among other factors, by 'uneven economic development' (a pattern still observable today), and 'the expansion in the reach

---

13. However, in nursing, there are also a significant number of male nurses. As we shall see later, their experiences of work as nurses in Singapore recall some of the earlier characterizations of male domestic servants in the Philippines.

and capacities, and the ambitions of colonial and post-colonial states' (Amrith, 2011: 4-5, 18).

Singapore now defines itself as a multiracial nation-state and is perceived as a 'Chinese enclave in the Malay sea' (Chua and Kuo, 1995: 108). The early post-colonial period, after Singapore's independence in 1965, was a period of managing Singapore's diversity for the project of nation-building and fostering a sense of national belonging among a diverse population. 'The social engineering of ethnicity has seemingly ended the tendency of racial strife that seemed imminent in the 1960s', yet beneath this rhetoric of multiracialism, or living together in harmony, there remain 'ripples of disquiet' (Trocki: 2006: 157; Chua and Kuo, 1995). Singapore is thus a nation defined discursively by its government, and by many of its inhabitants, in terms of its ethnic make-up – a population of Chinese, Malays, Indians and 'Other', a categorization that is so taken-for-granted and ingrained in everyday language in Singapore, that it is rarely questioned. This categorization of the population according to ethnicities – already a simplification of more dynamic interaction[14] – is being undermined by new waves of migration. The category of 'Other' is a catch-all devised initially to accommodate the country's Eurasian population, but now refers to all manner of others, including newer migrants (such as Filipino nurses) who have acquired permanent residence.[15]

Singapore's history of migration saw a period of relative standstill between 1930 and 1980 (Trocki, 2006: 159). This was part of wider restrictions on international migration within Asia, where borders, passports and visas came to determine the nature of mobility and the entry and exit of people in and out of particular states (Amrith, 2011: 8). The more recent waves of migration thus picked up again in the late 1970s and have been governed in different ways. The Singapore government's deliberate strategy to attract foreign labour as it went through rapid development brought migrants from other Asian countries (Yeoh, 2004b). The social and cultural fabric of Singapore became yet more heterogeneous. The country continues to be a 'mini-laboratory for the study of

14. Of course, within these categories of national origin were the distinctions of locale and class (Trocki, 2006). An example is how immigrants from China would more often identify themselves as Hokkien, Teochew or Cantonese rather than as Chinese.
15. 'Eurasians' in Singapore refer to people of mixed descent.

globalism and its ambiguous belongings', although this must also take into account the degree to which the state has defined the 'parameters of the political community' which exclude many working-class temporary contract labourers (Harper, 1997: 286). Skilled and unskilled labourers from India, China, Bangladesh, Indonesia, Burma, Thailand and the Philippines arrived in Singapore to work in construction and shipbuilding, in domestic work, and in medical work. Singapore's 'non-resident' population in 2015 stood at over 1.6 million out of a total of 5.53 million (SDS, 2015).

Female domestic workers have come from the Philippines to Singapore in large numbers since the 1970s (CIIR, 1987). Singapore has now become a popular destination for migrant medical workers, and their presence is needed by health institutions in Singapore as a result of its ageing population and a shortage of local workers in these jobs. The demand for medical workers is also linked to Singapore's public and private investments in internationalizing its medical sector, a project encouraged by its heavy-handed state. Filipinos are one of the largest migrant groups among medical workers – nurses, nursing aides, technicians and therapists – working in Singapore's healthcare institutions.[16] Certainly, economic disparities influence contemporary migration flows. Singapore's national income and wage levels are greater than that of the Philippines; Singapore's 'economic miracle' has put it at the very heart of global capitalism and of Southeast Asia's economy. While acknowledging the strength of these global structural interconnections, it is important also to have a nuanced understanding of their contingencies and limits (Cooper, 2005). It is here that I believe an anthropological contribution is imperative in drawing attention to the personal narratives of migration that make sense of these broader structural forces.

Reflections on Fieldwork

Ethnographic research took place primarily in Singapore between 2008 and 2009, with two additional months in the Philippines. As I recounted, the fact that I did not have 'the blood of a Filipino' was surprising to

---

16. According to the Singapore Nursing Board (SNB) in 2014, Filipino nurses were the most numerous of migrant nurses (in 'registered' and 'enrolled' nursing categories) in Singapore. More than 65% of the nurses who registered with the SNB in 2014 were from abroad. These figures, however, exclude the many Filipinos who also work in Singapore as nursing aides, auxiliaries and caregivers.

the couple I met at the 'Philippine Idol' concert. I subsequently found that people frequently asked me 'why Filipinos?' while beginning this research. My own background as a Singapore-born researcher of Indian origin interested in the specific experiences of Filipinos was initially puzzling to some of the people I met during my time in the field. Moreover, the fact that I was living in the UK at the time was also intriguing to them, given that many had migration aspirations to eventually move to the UK. I encountered curiosity, endearment (a few people said it was an 'honour' that someone wanted to listen to their stories) and also suspicion that I might be trying to expose something negative about Filipinos abroad. I thus had to explain my own curiosity in this subject as someone with a family history of migration; as well as my professional interest in their particular stories and experiences as people from a country with large numbers of migrants abroad, and whose presence in Singapore has been fundamental to sustaining the society in so many respects. These explanations helped to ease the sense of insecurity that I was sometimes faced with. After such conversations, I followed my informants in and around various spaces in Singapore where they worked, gossiped, relaxed, ate, danced, sent money home, bought groceries, prayed and met friends, as a way to get a sense of the rhythms and concerns of their everyday lives. Many of my meetings with nurses were at fast-food restaurants such as McDonalds or KFC, food courts, outdoor parks, malls across Singapore and in nurses' apartments, which were mostly apartments in HDB blocks ('Housing Development Board' blocks, Singapore's public housing).

Most of these locations were chosen by the nurses themselves, and were often locations that form a mundane part of the lives of many Singaporeans. Rarely, and perhaps contrary to my initial expectations, did I meet nurses at Filipino restaurants or in Singapore's 'Filipino mall', Lucky Plaza. I also met and accompanied nurses to Catholic churches or to a non-affiliated independent church. The other significant location for fieldwork was in the working environments of medical workers – in hospitals and nursing homes. The experiences of domestic workers are also a part of this book and my meetings with them took place at Lucky Plaza, events for the Filipino community, as well as in weekend skills classes.

There were challenges doing fieldwork in a transit city, with medical workers whose schedules are hectic and uncertain. Carrying out

Figure 1: A typical HDB residential estate (author's photo)

ethnographic work with people who work extremely long hours, who generally have just one day off per week, and who undertake shift work, I had to adjust to the irregular and highly-strung rhythms of their lives. The rhythms of my own fieldwork began to mirror the unpredictable schedules of my informants. Moreover, the Internet was an important space for understanding my informants' lives, given the amount of time they spent on it making future plans, sustaining old connections and developing new ones. I once asked a domestic worker to write a letter about her experiences, since she did not have a proper day off to meet me. Working as an anthropologist also meant migrants asked for my help with practical concerns. Hence, being 'on call' became a part of my routine just as it was for the medical workers themselves. I recall one evening at 10pm, one nurse, Alyssa, called me in a panic after work. She urgently had to scan her work visa needed by her husband for his immigration requirements before he was due to arrive in Singapore the next day. She called me in the hope that I would have access to a scanner, which fortunately, I did. It was precisely in such unplanned, fleeting encounters that I carried out the research for my ethnography and learned much in the process about the anxieties permeating migrants' lives in Singapore.

Fieldwork also involved getting to know migrants' working environments in hospitals and nursing homes. I focused my attention on two institutions specifically. One was a flagship government hospital hiring nurses in specialist fields. It is an example of a rapidly expanding hospital, which is constantly hiring new medical staff. It attracts local patients of all income levels, as well as medical tourists. In this hospital I was granted access weekly as a volunteer mobile librarian. This enabled me to wander in and out of the wards, while observing routines of work, care, structure and practice. However, conversations with staff had to be kept to a minimum and in this fast-paced, highly-strung environment, my role was more that of a passive observer. The other institution was a Buddhist nursing home and community hospital for the long-term care of chronically ill and elderly patients. Here the pace of work was slower and I had more chance to speak to medical workers in a very different setting from the fast paced government hospital. The onset of 'Swine Flu' (H1N1) in the middle of my fieldwork period presented obstacles to having the hospital as a primary field site, as hospitals and nursing homes imposed stringent restrictions on who could visit and enter their premises. In this already restrictive context of research access, I continued conversations with medical workers outside of these institutional spaces.[17]

The majority of my informants were nurses of different levels from the Philippines, and a handful of other medical workers including physiotherapists, radiographers, a phlebotomist and an optometrist. They came from all parts of the Philippines and from a range of socio-economic backgrounds; most were women, both single and married

---

17. Other scholars have also reflected on 'hospital ethnography' and its challenges, particularly on negotiating access and the extent to which one can truly participate in a hospital setting as an anthropologist doing participant observation (see Long, Hunter and van der Geest (2008) and Wind (2008)). I empathize with Wind's (2008: 83) comments that at times the activities that one does as a researcher in a hospital (hanging around, asking questions, taking notes, chatting) 'are seen at best as trivial, and at worst as time wasting or even interfering with the real work of the health workers'.

and many of the married women had children left in the care of relatives in the Philippines. However, increasingly male medical workers also migrate and I had the chance to speak with a few. The majority were Roman Catholic and spoke Filipino, English and often one other local language in the Philippines. Interviews and discussions were also held with hospital administrators, government officials, church leaders, family members, community health workers, NGO activists as well as a handful of Filipino migrants in teaching, IT and executive professions, and migrants of other nationalities.[18]

Different kinds of Filipino migrants related to me as an anthropologist in noticeably varied ways, something I observed when I started to talk to a number of domestic workers, whose stories are intertwined with the themes of this book. I spent much time cultivating relationships with nurses who were often initially distrustful or too busy. I was therefore struck when I first walked into a Sunday class for domestic workers, by the sheer excitement that almost every student in the large class expressed in talking with me. Their self-initiative and willingness to share their life stories without much hesitation was quite surprising. My reflections on such differences, which emerged during my research, gave me an early sense of the distinctions that exist between the two categories of migrants.

Visits to the Philippines were also crucial to the ethnography. I made two trips to the Philippines: the first trip was to Manila, where I spoke to nurses and nursing students in hospitals and colleges across Metro Manila, recruitment agencies, the Philippine Overseas Employment Agency and other spokespeople involved in the migration of medical workers. For the second trip to the Philippines, I accompanied a nurse, a key informant, home on an annual visit for two weeks. It so happened that this trip home was to involve a special reunion that would bring together a large number of her family members from across the world, to her village in Iloilo province in the Visayas region of the Philippines. During this short and intense period of village ethnography, I observed family life, the activities during a village *Fiesta* (celebration) and the dynamics between migrants and those at home. These visits to the Philippines illuminated some of the key sentiments that migrants in

---

18. Fieldwork interviews and conversations were recorded in the form of handwritten and typed field notes.

Singapore shared with me and gave me a sense of where they had come from in their journeys, and where they wanted to go.

Tracing Migrant Trajectories

This book narrates the stories of this new generation of migrant medical workers in a globalizing Asia, their migrant trajectories, career possibilities and aspirations. It is a multi-sited ethnography that follows aspiring migrants from Manila's vibrant nursing schools where they dream of glamorous lives abroad, to the mundane routines and stresses of Singapore's multicultural hospitals and nursing homes where they confront misrecognition as semi-professional workers. Away from work and the melancholic life of high-rise housing blocks, they find moments of respite in shopping malls and churches; they also retreat into online spaces searching for future jobs in small towns in Texas, Ontario or northern England, negotiating immigration policies and connecting with friends and family around the world. The account finally follows them back to Filipino village life on a vacation that brings together the hopes and frustrations of transnational and multi-generational families.

The chapters follow a structure that mirrors the trajectories of my Filipino migrant informants, from the Philippines to Singapore and to hopeful futures ahead. Chapter 2 contextualizes the contemporary migration of medical workers from the Philippines, examining the political and economic structures which govern the flows of migrants to particular places, as well as the wider forces configuring the global and regional economy of health and care. Chapter 3 begins in the Philippines among potential migrants in nursing colleges and hospitals. It explores the state of the 'nursing industry' in the Philippines today and the culture of migration that is inextricably linked to it. The chapter zooms into the narratives of potential migrants and on their desires to go abroad, while also looking at familial and state discourses on the migration of medical workers. Chapter 4 meets the migrants in Singapore in their working environments and in the ambiguous arena of care labour. It explores the everyday rhythms and textures of the institutional workspaces of migrants, as well as exploring different cultural understandings of care labour, its worth and its boundaries. Chapter 5 looks more closely at the relationships that medical workers develop with those they care for, as well as with the other Asians they meet in and around Singapore. It is concerned with questions of care and morality, everyday engagements with cultural pluralism and contested 'Asian values'. Chapter 6 moves on to explore migrant socialities and the boundaries operating in migrant social life. It draws attention to how tensions among Filipino migrants in the sphere of care labour are manifest in urban space through the tastes, social networks and activities of different groups of migrants. Chapter 7 then raises the question of home, the spatial and temporal orientations migrants hold in a transit city, and how this ties in with their relation to their Philippine homes and their plans for future homes further afield. Chapter 8 reflects on the distinctive features of migrant medical workers' lives in transit, while pointing towards the broader implications of their migrations to urban communities, questions of citizenship, experiences of cultural diversity and a globalizing care sector.

CHAPTER TWO

The Political Economy of Care and Migration

T he globalization of health and the increasing mobility of medical workers across borders forms part of significant economic, social and demographic transformations across the world. Medical workers might migrate for demographic reasons, to respond to shortages in health personnel and to care for increasingly ageing populations; for the fulfilment of personal and professional aspirations; as part of state-led development and humanitarian projects that provide technical expertise; or for religious-oriented purposes and in response to epidemics. These movements are often a response to, or symptom of, vast inequalities in public health systems and resources. They are thus of global relevance, yet each case is specific and dependent on a particular constellation of global, regional and micro-level factors.

This chapter examines the political economy of migration, taking into account the political and legal frameworks which govern the flows of migrants, and regulate mobility and citizenship in a specifically Southeast Asian context. The Southeast Asian region is significant here because of its current large-scale population movements, changes in the labour market and developments in the health sector. This discussion will be situated within the wider political economy of care, looking at the reasons for the expansion and the diversification of transnational care arrangements, and outlining how states, institutions and informal networks configure the contemporary landscape of care and migration.

The Political Economy of Migration

My anthropological focus on the narratives of Filipino medical workers as they cross borders must be explained as part of the macro political-economic structures which govern the mobility of the hundreds of thousands of labour migrants across Asia and the world. Without intending to put forward a deterministic understanding of such political-economic structures, it is nonetheless important to acknowledge that individual and family aspirations, decisions and dilemmas operate within a broader field of global and regional inequalities, even as migrants accommodate and subvert such structures in multiple ways. I therefore start this chapter looking at how migration features in the contemporary economies of both the Philippines and Singapore and at the conditions that shape these migrations.

The movements of migrants within Asia are linked to the different economic trajectories of its states. Unequal capitalist development in the region has set up the conditions for accelerated labour migration in Southeast Asia. As a result of state-driven economic policies, countries such as Singapore and Malaysia, for instance, have seen a movement towards high-technology economic activities, leading to shortages in the manual labour sectors of the economy. These states have thus turned to their neighbours to provide a supply of cheap labour and to fill jobs that are often thought to be '3D' (dirty, dangerous, and demeaning). These neighbouring countries meanwhile often have strong labour export policies that are driven by states and private agencies, with their national economies unable to absorb the labour force in the national (and in particular, urban) job markets (Cheah, 2006: 185-186). As Pheng Cheah (2006: 185) notes: 'for each case of state-sponsored globalization, there seems to be another case of state-driven exportation of labor'.

Such are the economic conditions that set the structural foundation for labour migration within Asia, particularly for those in domestic or manual labour. The migration of medical workers is in part determined by these economic disparities, but is also structured by other factors, including changes in population and health needs. The medical journal *The Lancet* (2011) did a feature on 'Southeast Asia: An Emerging Focus for Global Health', highlighting that its increasing international health-related population movements[1], alongside 'accelerating movements in trade, especially of health services', makes the region distinctive in

---

1. This includes medical workers from certain countries in Southeast Asia, such as the Philippines, Indonesia, Burma (while for other countries such as Cambodia and Laos, the movement of medical personnel is limited by language and qualifications barriers), as well as patients seeking treatment in other Southeast Asian countries, particularly Singapore, Malaysia and Thailand.

the world today. Health is also an area where the region's diversity, its 'sociopolitical contrasts and contradictions' are most evident (Lancet, 2011: 534). The move towards regional integration within the ASEAN region may also mean greater mobility and recognition of qualified workers between states, including nurses and medical workers (Guinto et. al, 2015: 1–2), though as this book highlights, in practice there are still a number of barriers and challenges to this plan for 'harmonization'.

The Philippine state has had an explicit policy of labour migration since the 1970s, with the aim that the revenue gained from remittances would act as an impetus for economic development and as a source of foreign exchange. In the 1970s, the domestic economy faced high rates of unemployment, debt and a fiscal crisis under the Ferdinand Marcos dictatorship and a period of martial law. Many Filipinos saw overseas migration as a solution to the day-to-day problems faced at home (Cheah, 2006; Tadiar 2004; Tyner, 2009). Domestic economic problems persisted in the following decade, with the Philippines experiencing the impacts of structural adjustment loans, which required the country to move towards an export-oriented economy, accompanied by the privatization of social services and a prolonged dependency upon foreign donors (Parreñas, 2005: 14–15). State funds were directed to servicing a large external debt, and the economic stagnation ensured that overseas migration continued to gain pace (Bello, 2004; Guzman, 2003). [2] Labour emigration has been matched in this context with 'aggressive institutionalization through national state policy with the sanction of international bodies' (Cheah, 2006: 186). The export of labour in the Philippines is driven largely by the overseas remittances coming into the country. In 2015, remittances were estimated at over US $25 billion (Bangko Sentral ng Pilipinas, 2015). A culture of remittances is important not only on a national level, but also at household level, as these crucially depend on remittances for economic and social mobility (Porio, 2007: 217, 240; Aguilar et al., 2009). Rochelle Ball (2008: 33) writes that, 'by the mid-1980s, a combination of several key factors increased global demand for and employment of Filipino women: escalating economic decline in the Philippines; a rise in labour demand in

---

2. Though during Corazon Aquino's term there were temporary bans in deployment of women overseas as domestic workers in an effort to better protect workers from exploitation (Guzman, 2003).

the international service sector in both Asia and the Gulf; declines in (male) labour demand in the Gulf construction sector; and aggressive global labour marketing campaigns by the Philippine state'.

The Philippines Overseas Employment Agency (POEA) is the archetypal case of an institutionalized state agency for the 'export' of labour acting as an intermediary between labour migrants and the global labour market. The POEA governs all aspects of the migration process from influencing the formulation of migration policies, to accrediting recruitment agencies, posting advisories on migrant destinations, and being a necessary stop for most migrants to get documents stamped and accredited. Whether explicitly institutionalized, or implicitly promoted, many Asian states have a specific discourse regarding overseas migration. For instance, Sri Lankan labour migration has been institutionalized by the Sri Lanka Bureau for Foreign Employment since the 1980s (Tyner, 2009, Cheah, 2006). In the case of Indonesia, the state's gendered discourse permitted women to leave their families and go abroad as transnational migrant workers, for the sake of the 'national family's broader economic development agenda' (Silvey, 2006: 30). However, the Philippines with its 'highly developed transnational migration apparatus' is distinctive in the way it acts as a 'labour broker'; as Robyn Rodriguez (2008a: 794–796) argues, it plays 'a critical role in producing, distributing, and regulating Filipinas as care workers across the globe'. James Tyner (2009: 3) furthermore highlights that 'for millions of Filipinos, the POEA is the portal to the world's labour markets. For others, however, the POEA constitutes much that is wrong with globalization: the commodification and exploitation of labour and the sacrifice of people for profit. Statistics tell part of the story'[3], with over ten million Filipinos living and working in countries all over the world. Migration has become a highly politicized issue, which sees debates about its positive and negative aspects occurring at all levels: in personal and familial circles, civil society spaces and at a national and global level. The state, individual migrants, their families and localities have different interests at stake. Even at the state level, there are different views put forward. Public health policy (which generally encourages health professionals to stay in the Philippines), migration policy (which

---

3. See Appendix A for a table indicating where Filipino migrants are deployed across the world.

encourages people to leave and send remittances home), and personal and familial aspirations for migration are all intertwined in overlapping and contradictory ways.

Singapore's Migration Hierarchy

I now turn to one of the key destinations of Philippine migrant labour: Singapore. The labour market for service work in Singapore has long depended on labour from neighbouring Asian countries, the Philippines constituting one of the largest migrant groups.[4] Singapore has set itself up as a central meeting point for many migrant workers in the Asian region. Though Singapore is itself a nation constituted by immigrants, Singapore's migrant population now refers to recent migrants. Recent migrants are those who have been arriving since the 1970s, not long after Singapore's independence. Numerically, it has been temporary contract labourers who have dominated the profile of Singapore's 'new migrants', including construction workers from India and Bangladesh and domestic workers from the Philippines, Sri Lanka, Burma and Indonesia. In recent years, there has been a stronger drive to hire migrant workers in a wider range of occupations, including sales, retail, information technology and medical work. There has also been a noticeably larger presence of 'wealthy' migrants in banks, financial services and consultancies. In the past decade, the sheer diversity of new migrants in Singapore has been striking, with migrants at all levels from all across Asia and beyond.

As of 2015, almost 30% of the people living in Singapore were 'non-resident' (Singapore Department of Statistics, 2015). Within this category, however, there is evident polarization in how the government welcomes different groups of migrants and which migrants may move out of the category of non-resident and obtain permanent residence permits. A senior government official, speaking of those working in the financial sector, explains that Singapore wants to 'collect top talent in large numbers', offer them 'the full accoutrement of living needs that they want' to encourage 'a fair proportion of them [to] sink roots and enrich our gene pool' (George Yeo, quoted in *The Straits Times*, 5 March 2001, cited in Yeoh 2004a: 2439). Meanwhile, 'foreign workers' as they are called in the state discourse, in contrast to 'highly-skilled foreign talent', at the other end of the spectrum, are in Singapore on temporary

---

4. The POEA (2013) has a stock estimate of 203.243 Filipinos in Singapore.

contracts without a pathway to citizenship, and are thus kept in a position of transience with limited rights. Singapore's immigration policy differentiates the terms on which different types of migrants can enter and live in Singapore. While some migrants are perceived as desirable, others are seen as 'necessary costs' for Singapore's development and hence a polarized discourse and policy on immigration exists to valorize highly skilled 'foreign talent', and to devalue 'foreign workers' (working-class migrants from neighbouring countries).

The politico-legal system controls the mobilities and rights of different migrants by granting work visas according to the migrant worker's occupation, salary and skill level. Figure 2 provides an overview of these visa categories. Sometimes these are categories that are used by my interlocutors when negotiating the boundaries between themselves and others on different visas. This affects what rights they have, as well as their mobility in Singapore's urban space.

At the top end of the hierarchy is the 'Employment Pass' for highly paid professionals (e.g. doctors, bankers, consultants and executives). On this pass, migrants are highly mobile and enjoy many rights and freedoms. One category down is the 'S-Pass' for 'semi-skilled' and 'technical' workers, which include many of the medical workers I knew (e.g. nurses, physiotherapists, technicians). However, if they earn less than $5000 per month (and many do earn less) they are not allowed to bring their families to Singapore unless they apply for permanent residence.[5] The 'work permit' at the bottom of the visa hierarchy is the most restrictive of all. For instance, migrants on this permit are tied to specific employers, are not allowed to bring their families, are not eligible for permanent residence, and moreover, levies and security bonds are payable by employers (which makes them perceive that they own the worker) 'in case the worker goes missing'. Domestic workers are also bound by laws not allowing them to become pregnant while in Singapore, or marry Singapore citizens or permanent residents. There is one clause in the 'work permit' legislation stating that 'the foreign employee shall not be involved in any illegal, immoral or undesirable activities, including breaking up families in Singapore' (Employment of Foreign Manpower

---

5. At the time of my fieldwork (2008–2010), this figure was $2500, which was more than what most of my informants earned at the time. By 2014, the requirement was a monthly salary of more than $5000 to be eligible to bring one's family along.

Figure 2: Singapore's visa categories

Work Visa	Salary Monthly	Job Category	Rights/Conditions
Employment pass (EP)	>$3300	Professionals e.g. doctors, bankers, consultants, executive and managerial staff (usually with a university degree and professional qualifications)	Eligible for permanent residence (PR) No quota or levy payable on EPs Migrants free to change employers Allowed to bring dependents
S-Pass	> $2200	Mid-level skilled staff (with a degree, diploma or technical certificate to demonstrate qualifications) e.g. nurses, medical technicians, IT workers	Eligible for PR Quota to cap the number of S-pass holders. Companies pay a levy to hire S-Pass holders Those earning > $5000 are eligible for a dependent's pass for their spouse or children Those earning < $5000 are not allowed to bring dependents Medical insurance provided by employer Two-year validity, renewable
Work permit	No requirement of min. or max. but generally <$2200	'Unskilled' or 'semi-skilled' labour. E.g. in sectors such as construction, shipbuilding and domestic work, performing artistes, and caregivers	Tied to a specific employer Not allowed to bring dependents Two-year validity, renewable Quota to cap the number of work permit holders. Levy payable by companies to hire WP holders Employers must pay a 'security bond' to the government in case the worker goes missing Employers must provide medical insurance Not eligible for PR The permit is cancelled 7 days after a work contract has been terminated

Source: Adapted from http://www.mom.gov.sg, Singapore Ministry of Manpower website, 2016)

Act, Ministry of Manpower). There is a distinct and discriminatory hierarchy in the ordering of these visas, which is also mirrored in a negative public discourse towards 'foreign workers', reflected in moral panics about migrant behaviour and their uses of public space on weekends. Brenda Yeoh (2004a: 2431) underlines how 'government-inspired and articulated visions of a cosmopolitan future' do not resonate with ground realities given the exclusions and the 'inhuman conditions' that accompany such visions (Cheah, 2006).[6]

Migrants' chances to acquire residency rights in Singapore are based on calculated inclusions and exclusions. While most of my informants are on the S-pass, there are a number of nursing aides in Singapore on a work permit. Their mobilities within Singapore are far more restricted than those who enter on an S-pass, even if they work in the same institution (e.g. a healthcare assistant may be on a work permit and a junior nurse on an S-pass). Those on the S-Pass do have a chance of obtaining Singapore PR (and citizenship eventually), whereas those on work permits have none. This is the legal framework within which migrant medical workers are situated in Singapore.

Migration and Medical Work

States across the world have taken different approaches to the mobility of their medical workers. The Cuban case is particularly striking as it has involved a large-scale movement of medical workers on state-sponsored missions across the developing world for specific healthcare projects.[7] Medical workers are employed by the Cuban state to participate in medical aid projects and diplomatic initiatives that are organized on a government-to-government level and always return to Cuba after missions. According to Kirk and Erisman (2009) health care in Cuba was 'of necessity, to be provided by a new breed of professionals, one

6. The high level of surveillance means that undocumented immigration is not so prevalent; many undocumented workers are criminalized and deported. There are nonetheless some undocumented workers who remain, and often seek support from local NGOs. Some of those who are undocumented (most often those promised jobs in the construction sector or in domestic work) find themselves without work in Singapore as a result of fraudulent recruitment agents, or they might be trafficked.

7. According to Kirk and Erisman (2009: 3), since the 1960s 'approximately 100 other governments (mostly in sub-Saharan Africa and Latin America) have concluded agreements resulting in a sustained presence of Cuban aid delegations involving a grand total of more than 100,000 health professionals'.

for whom the profit motive should never enter into the analysis – and whose essential duty was to serve those in need of medical support'. Humanitarian awareness, rather than a lucrative moneymaking career, was seen as the hallmark of Cuba's medical internationalism. The case of Cuba is similar to Susan Bayly's (2007) account of Vietnamese experts in technical fields who migrated for specific medical missions to other states in the wider socialist world. Bayly (2007: 204–205) recounts that, 'several thousand Vietnamese with training in scientific and technical fields worked in a dozen or more African countries in the 1980s and early 90s ... on the face of it, this "expert" work was in the best tradition of the socialist ecumene unimpeachable as an enactment of nation-to-nation "friendship" and the improving power of state-managed science'. Among these technical experts were, for example, electric acupuncture nurses who went on overseas sojourns as 'acts of care and nurture both for Vietnam and for the countries in which they worked'. They were state-organized sojourns expressing solidarity with other socialist nations, rather than lasting migrations. The Cuban and Vietnamese examples provide a contrast to the Philippine case of medical worker migration taking a fundamentally different form.

The Philippines' labour export strategy is tied to the trends of the global capitalist labour market (here the previous two cases differ), and dire domestic economic conditions.[8] The movement of healthcare workers in search of better professional and personal opportunities has accelerated significantly in recent years (Clark *et al.*, 2006). John Connell (2008: 1–2) suggests that the migration of skilled medical workers 'reflects the growth and accelerated internationalization of the service sector in the last two decades ... such professional services as health care are part of the new internationalization of labour, and migration has largely been demand driven (or at least facilitated), with the growing global integration of health care markets'. From a purely economic and instrumental viewpoint, the demand for medical workers is driven by shortages of medical professionals in some parts of the world and is being matched by large supplies of medical workers from other parts of the world who are willing to be globally mobile.

---

8. The Philippines is only one of many countries seeing the emigration of nurses on a large-scale – India, Burma, Zimbabwe and Kenya are among the others.

Yet the reasons for medical workers' movements cannot be reduced to instrumental factors. Their migration is shaped by many intersecting factors that are institutional and structural, but also driven by personal and familial aspirations, imaginaries, needs and desires. The migration of medical workers from the Philippines is driven by a desire for a better life elsewhere in social, cultural and economic terms, particularly given the socioeconomic precarity in the Philippines that makes it challenging to find opportunities and sustain livelihoods that many aspire towards. As this book argues, medical work has become intrinsically bound up with a desire for a lucrative salary overseas. Their movements abroad are therefore not perceived as temporary. The Alliance for Health Workers and the University of Philippines College of Public Health suggest that the exodus of nurses is underpinned by three structural factors: the government's labour exportation policy which includes health workers and professionals, the 'aggressive' strategies of labour recruitment agencies and the historically-rooted 'Western orientation of nursing education which makes Filipino graduates marketable to foreign countries' (cited in Ortin, 1994: 126). Meanwhile, the Department of Health recognizes this exodus as a symptom of low salaries and the undervaluation of the nursing profession in the Philippines, excessive workloads due to nursing shortages in some areas and the lack of security and opportunities for career development (Ortin, 1994: 126).

The Philippines is the country with the largest number of migrant nurses (Lorenzo, 2002: 46; Ball, 2008: 31). Since the late 1970s, the numbers and geographical distribution of Filipino nurses increased significantly, as nurse migration became embedded within a wider institutional framework of state-endorsed overseas labour migration, the international demand for medical labour and the fact that more and more nurses were going overseas on temporary work contracts (Ball, 2008: 30). Since this time, there have been concerns about this large-scale migration of medical workers and the impacts of this on public health outcomes and the quality of health services at home, as nurses trained in the Philippines became prepared for work in international labour markets and the turnover in medical institutions was high (Ball, 2008: 33–36). In recent years, this has been partially addressed through the signing of Memoranda of Understanding (MOU) between the Philippine government and the countries receiving its healthcare workers. For instance, the Philippine Department of Labour and Employment (DOLE) signed agreements with Saskatchewan and Manitoba states in Canada agreeing on the 'ethical and effective recruitment' of health care workers, while also agreeing to mutually support and sustain the development of human resources in the Philippines through financial means, training and exchanges.[9] These bilateral agreements that stipulate two-way exchanges offer a channel for implementing the World Health Organization's Global Code of Practice on the International Recruitment of Health Personnel, adopted at the 2010 World Health Assembly (Dimaya et al., 2012).

However, alongside these initial efforts to address questions of ethical recruitment, the migration of nurses continues through active recruitment practices by employers and agencies, migrants' personal networks of family and friends in other countries, and the Philippine government-to-government bilateral arrangements, which match the skills of potential migrant workers with the needs in receiving countries' labour markets and seek to ensure the protection and fair treatment of migrants abroad (Lorenzo, 2002: 47; Rodriguez, 2008a). The 'migration-industrial complex [involves] diverse agents: recruitment, travel and remittance agents and agencies' as well as 'state regulatory and promotional authorities', NGOs concerned with migrants' rights, and migrants' own networks (Yeates, 2009b: 178). The 'migration-industrial complex' is constituted by and constitutive of an increasingly transnational field of care, within which migrants from the Philippines (and other countries) find work as professional nurses, caregivers or domestic workers.

Transnational Care

The changing global configurations of care have influenced a great deal of the large-scale movements of care labour. In Asia, this coincided with a rising number of female Asian migrants in occupations such as domestic, service, entertainment and sex work. One significant factor in this was the rapidly increasing participation of middle-class women in white-collar employment in a number of relatively affluent countries, which has required an increasing dependence upon migrant domestic workers to take care of and sustain their households (Hochschild, 2000;

---

9. Government of Manitoba Immigration Department (2010) and Government of Saskatchewan Advanced Education, Employment and Immigration, (2006).

Parreñas, 2001; Yeates, 2009a; 2009b; Ehrenreich and Hochschild, 2003). Neoliberal social policies across the world that cut back social and care services provided by the state accentuates this demand for migrant care labour. These processes have been discussed in much of the sociological literature in terms of 'global care chains'. Arlie Hochschild (2000: 357) explains a global care chain as 'a series of personal links between people across the globe based on the paid or unpaid work of caring ... each kind of chain expresses an invisible human *ecology of care*, one care worker depending on another'.

The care chains analysis highlights the transnational dimensions of care and has been important in feminist analyses of social reproductive labour in the world investigating the political, economic and social inequalities which configure migrant care labour flows and the accompanying forms of exploitation that are often a part of this mobility. Nicola Yeates (2009a: 4) has written about how these 'relations and practices of care' need to be situated 'in the context of the formation and reproduction of global social hierarchies'. Care is global and spans borders, she argues; it is governed by economic, political and social structures and institutions and it concerns mobile labour, paid or unpaid, in a variety of contexts – voluntary, corporate, state and domestic (Yeates, 2009a: 4–6; 2009b: 176). 'Care-chains' emerge from a global economy of care, its commodification in different forms and the interdependencies of care arrangements around the world (Misra, Woodring and Merz, 2006).

However, any model of migration is likely to occlude a lot of the ambiguities that are, as my ethnographic research has revealed, part of migrant experience. Among the limitations of a 'care-chain' approach is its linear focus. Tracing how care moves from one place to another unidirectionally overlooks movements which do not take this form; not all movements involve poor women serving wealthy women (normally assumed to be in the 'West'); in this case many nurses are of middle-class backgrounds in the Philippines and caring for working-class elderly patients in nursing homes in Singapore (even if it is in a higher-income country). Some migrant journeys involve multiple stops and circular movements back and forth. Furthermore, the focus in the feminist care chain analyses is primarily on the exploitation of migrant women. While flagging up abusive and poor conditions of work, this perspective also, perhaps inadvertently, risks victimizing these women. Many of these migrations also have the potential to provide opportunities for empowerment. Care chains, moreover, are not just constituted by 'nannies', but a wide range of caregivers and professional medical workers, most of whom are women but also include an increasing number of men. Martin Manalansan's (2008) critique of care chains is that they reinforce normative ideals of care and love, as female, 'authentic' and heterosexual. He calls for alternative ways to analyse the mobility of care workers who do not see their absence from their home countries and families as a 'global heart transplant' and the displacement of 'authentic' caring emotions and maternal instincts. Not all migrants perceive their journeys in such terms as they are often driven by other kinds of aspirations. Moreover, we see a great range of migrant carers who embody a number of intersectional identities (gay, heterosexual, single, married, male, female, transgendered). Also crucial is a closer understanding of what care means in specific local contexts, and how it might be 'differentially embedded in cultural, political and economic formations such as the family, the market, the state and the community sector in different ways' (Raghuram, 2012: 156). As such, this book is attentive to migrants' own understandings of what care means, and how it is practiced, valued and transformed in and through their experiences of mobility.

The transnational field of care also comprises medical travel. Medical travel as a growing social and economic phenomenon underscores the changing demands of healthcare consumers and is an important factor in the international migration of medical workers (Chee and Whittaker, 2010; Whittaker, 2008). The industry in medical travel has grown significantly in the past decade and its growth is related to the opening up of the health sector under the General Agreement on Trade in Services (GATS) (enabling the mobility of health services, consumption, investment and personnel) and the privatization of medical care in Asian medical institutions (Whittaker, 2008: 271). The rise in medical travel and the demand for highly technologized medical services and expertise is also related to increasing life expectancies, an increase in the prevalence of chronic and lifestyle diseases and a growing affluent middle class. Much of this expansion is fuelled by foreign investment (Whittaker, 2008: 274–276). This medical travel industry has taken on particular salience in Malaysia and Singapore (Chee, 2010: 336). It is a significant factor in the development of these countries as 'medical hubs' in the region. Health, since the late 1990s, has been understood as a driver of economic growth in these countries, with states investing in the expansion of medical services to foreign patients (Chee, 2010: 337). There is greater demand for medical professionals to work in this elite sector of medical care. The growth of medical travel is likely to see medical workers being attracted to lucrative job opportunities at destinations for medical tourists; moreover, alongside the movement of health workers across borders, is the movement of patients, something that is becoming a significant item on the research agendas of global public health institutions (Helble, 2011).

The final point to make about the transnational field of medical care is that it is not purely socioeconomic factors that generate such mobilities, but also demographic factors. The demand for migrant workers is taking place at a particular demographic moment of rapidly ageing populations – in Singapore, as well as in Japan and many European and North American countries (Teo *et al.*, 2006). As Mehta (2002: 150) suggests, 'while it is well known that Singapore has one of the fastest ageing populations in the Asia-Pacific region, the speed of the demographic ageing process has been less emphasized. What developed countries experienced over a period of eighty to one hundred or more years is being experienced in less than half the time in a number of countries such as Japan, Hong Kong and Singapore'. This ageing population has required an expansion of the healthcare system with a greater emphasis on long-term care. The rapid ageing of Singapore's population can be attributed to two demographic events: increased longevity as a result of good public health infrastructure and policies and a general increased standard of living, and a dramatic fall in the birth rate. (Teo *et al.*, 2006: 19) According to a report by the National Population Secretariat of Singapore, 'our total fertility rate, which has remained below replacement level since 1976, has resulted in a smaller resident population aged below 35 compared with the older generations'. The proportion of residents aged 65 and above increased from 6.8% in 1998 to 13.1% in 2015 (NPS, 2009: 5; SDS, 2015).

The Singapore government has had to rethink its medical infrastructure to respond to the ageing of its population. In his National Day Rally

Speech in 2009, the Singapore Prime Minister Lee Hsien Loong spoke of the greater need in Singapore to integrate acute hospitals with 'step-down' care, by which he means nursing homes, community hospitals and home care. Larger hospitals, smaller community hospitals, voluntary welfare organizations, together with nurses and live-in domestic workers (mostly migrants) provide this new integration of healthcare provision. Many of my informants in Singapore were taking care of older patients. Yet it appears this process of integration is also tied to a neoliberal turn towards the concentration of transnational and state capital investments into prestigious acute hospitals, with their profit-making models of healthcare provision serving those who can afford to pay.

As a point of comparison within Asia, Japan's ageing society and 'elderly care crisis' has led to debates on the extent to which Japan ought to depend on migrant nurses and caregivers in elderly care (Ohno, 2012: 541). Between 2008 and 2011, over a thousand Indonesian and Filipino candidates arrived in Japan as registered nurses and certified care workers under Economic Partnership Agreements (EPA) that Japan had signed bilaterally with the Philippines and Indonesia. However, as both Ohno (2012) and Ogawa (2012) argue, these agreements were not so much to address the shortages in Japan's healthcare sector, but more to recognize the country's commitments within the framework of the WTO's GATS agreement that includes the trade in health services.[10] It was therefore not explicitly formulated as a social or migration policy (Ogawa, 2012: 571). While there are provisions for decent working conditions under this programme, it also has very high requirements for migrant nurses and caregivers as they remain 'candidates' gaining practical experience until they pass the Japanese nursing examinations in the Japanese language. The long-term viability of this programme is thus in question given the strict requirements, the deskilling that foreign nurses encounter, and the fact that after 2010, more Japanese candidates entered these medical and care professions (Ohno, 2012; Ogawa, 2012).[11]

---

10. Under Mode 4, Movement of Natural Persons (MNP).

11. There was a similar government-to-government (G to G) agreement signed between the Philippine and German governments in 2013 in response to nursing shortages in Germany which will likely be intensified as a consequence of demographic changes. The 'Triple Win Project' between the POEA and the German Federal Employment Agency, will see Filipino nurses move to Germany through an institutionalized programme with support given for German language skills,

Beyond the formalized movement of migrant care workers under this programme, other care arrangements exist alongside. Faier's (2009a; 2009b) work on Filipina migrant women's marriages to rural Japanese men illuminates how care in the context of ageing populations may also take the form of international marriages. Her ethnographic fieldwork in the central Kiso region of Japan highlighted that households needed people to 'care for the elderly, bear and raise children, and work in local businesses and fields'. Moreover, 'a number of local men were lonely and wanted companions, caretakers and families' and Filipina women have offered this companionship and intimate and practical support (Faier, 2009b: 139). This case demonstrates that broader notions of care – such as companionship and the security of having someone to care for oneself in old age – are important to ageing societies, in addition to professional nursing or domestic labour. Moreover, as some of the Filipina women who married Japanese men in Faier's study were formerly working as 'entertainers' in Japan, it can be seen that migrant women shift from one identity or role to another, or hold multiple roles simultaneously, some paid and others unpaid (Faier, 2009a; 2009b; Ogawa, 2012: 589). The boundaries between care, companionship and intimate labour are not clearly discernable. Ageing societies will therefore witness a proliferation of diverse care arrangements. Migrants will no doubt play a role in these care arrangements, though there are specific debates taking place in different countries which will shape the extent of migrants' roles. In Japan, for example, elder care is not yet seen as a niche occupied by migrants.

The focus of this chapter has been on the structural factors which govern the migration of medical workers: the forms that this migration takes, the restrictions and opportunities migrants have for citizenship and the role of states and institutions in governing different forms of migration, as well as the healthcare sector. Fundamental political and economic inequalities together with macro-level transformations in the global and regional landscape of care drive these movements and arrangements. This, alongside state policies that encourage overseas migration, new investments in health institutions in the societies that re-ceive migrant medical workers, and demographic changes are demand-

---

training and placements (http://www.manila.diplo.de/Vertretung/manila/en/06/filipino_20nurses_20to_20germany.html).

ing new solutions and arrangements in this sector. However, they do not determine the way that migrants make decisions or live their lives. The following chapters will reveal the personal narratives and experiences of Filipino migrant medical workers as they negotiate and question these broader political, economic and legal structures. Boundaries are not set in stone and individual and familial aspirations engage dynamically with these structures through everyday life encounters. Migrants develop their subjectivities as mobile people with their own hopes, desires and expectations.

CHAPTER THREE

Migrant Imaginaries and the Act of Leaving

A place does not merely exist ... it has to be invented in one's imagination

– Amitav Ghosh (1988)

'A re you from India? Which part?' Melody, a clinical nursing instructor, asks as we sit at a rest stop in the town of Pagsanjan in the Philippines for breakfast. I am on my way to a village in Laguna province with Melody and a bus full of nursing students from Manila. They are going there to implement a community health education programme. When I answer, 'Chennai', Melody exclaims 'Oh Chennai!' in a way that sounds as if she has known the city intimately for years. 'You know, I was in Saudi for 20 years and so many of my friends there are also Indian – from Chennai, Hyderabad, Bombay, Kerala, so I have heard of all these places! I came back a year ago', she explains with some regret in her voice. 'How come?' I ask her. 'Well', she says, 'my friends there were leaving me one by one, going to the UK or the US. I was scared I was going to be left alone! So that's why I decided to come back and then I found this job here. But you know I miss them so much. We were together there for 20 years! When I see you I think of Shabnam, you look the same. I am always thinking about them. Sometimes I get a phone card and call them up and we talk'. For the remainder of our breakfast stop, Melody continues to talk – animatedly but with a sense of nostalgia – about her Indian friends in 'Saudi', telling me about the Hindi that she knows, the Bollywood and Kollywood actors that she likes, and the Indian dishes she has learned to cook (explaining simultaneously what these dishes are made of to her Filipina colleague next to us, who is not familiar with them). Before we continue our journey to the village, Melody hesitates momentarily before saying, 'it was difficult to be away from my family for 20 years, but I gave them a good life'.

My encounter with Melody, and the stories she told about working in Saudi Arabia for 20 years, revealed how a sense of adventure, the forging of new relationships and developing a wider knowledge about the world, co-exist with uncertainties and hardships in the lives of migrant medical workers. Melody's story is fairly typical of the new worlds of experience and knowledge that my informants often exude, as migrants and aspiring migrants. Their imagined and actual connections to places around the world is an enduring feature of their inherently multi-sited lives, regardless of where I, as an anthropologist, might choose to draw the boundaries of my field site (Marcus, 1995). In this chapter, I lay out the contours of this imaginary. I will look particularly at the ambivalent process of leaving the Philippines for a life overseas in light of the now inevitable associations of nursing with overseas migration. The process of leaving entails overlapping yet often messy entanglements between individual aspirations, familial and community expectations and the contradictory discourses of the Philippine state in its attempt to govern the emigration of medical workers. All of these voices claim to have a stake in these departures; and the claims are affectively imbued with notions such as care, sacrifice and duty.

This chapter draws primarily on ethnographic fieldwork conducted in Manila, presenting the voices of nursing students and nurses, recruitment agencies and public officials. Firstly, it traces what I call a 'cartography of care', which encompasses the imaginative maps of migrants; the journeys they undertake alongside the journeys they wish to one day embark on as medical workers. It also conveys the spatial dimensions that care takes in its multiple forms and the ways in which it simultaneously comes up against and crosses boundaries. Migrants leave the Philippines to care for others in private homes and in institutionalized care settings, developing new relations of care in the countries to which they migrate, while simultaneously caring, emotionally and practically, for their families in the Philippines and for their future life-projects in places further afield. Meanwhile, migrants often explain their departures in terms of a lack of care shown to them by the Philippine state towards its citizens. The spatial imagination of Filipinos today is not by any means constrained within the boundaries of the Philippine state. The possibility of going overseas for work is a real and tangible possibility for those from urban areas, as well as those from smaller *barrios* (villages). Numerous villages across the Philippines are connected to wide transnational networks.

Yet alongside this imaginary that extends far beyond the Philippine nation-state, which the first part of the chapter addresses, I also consider the difficulties that often complicate the expansive dreams that migrants hold. These difficulties are expressed in debates concerning the migration of medical workers and its impacts on public health in the Philippines, said to be in 'crisis' and fuelled by the brain drain, to draw upon the popular terms to describe the situation. I argue that the discussions surrounding the migration of medical workers and the personal dilemmas that potential migrants face in their decisions to go overseas are essentially debates about citizenship. This chapter explores the claims that the state and its citizens make on each other, and the shades of grey which occupy these claims; the tensions and contradictions, for instance, between freedom and responsibility, the individual and the collective, the family and the nation, aspirations and realities (Werbner, 1998: 4). I will examine how such debates – which preoccupy nation-states across the world – take on specificity as they crystallize around the figure of the mobile medical worker in the Philippines. This is because medical workers are seen as particular kinds of citizens with a unique status. Indeed, they are the ones who are responsible for keeping citizens healthy and deal intimately with questions of life and death in their work. However, this expectation of medical workers to serve and care for fellow citizens is contradicting the state's other vision of its citizens which revolves around going overseas to work and serving one's family, *barrio* and nation through remittances. It is an ideal that is ingrained in the fabric of everyday life and in the plans and aspirations of many medical workers. The contradictions between service and duty, alongside freedom and entitlement, converge in affectively charged idioms of guilt and blame, pride and shame. What citizenship means in the contemporary Philippines and how different people attempt to define it is at the heart of this chapter.

The Ubiquity of Nursing

In the basement of the University of the Philippines library, I sit with books about nursing in the Philippines in order to better understand the

Figure 3: Nurses in their white uniforms are visible in public spaces across Manila (author's photo)

Philippines' history of nursing education. I take a few relevant articles to the photocopying counter. Tita Marly, the lady in charge of photocopying, starts quietly to photocopy the articles in one corner of the reading room, until she realizes that I am reading articles about nursing. Suddenly her face lights up. 'Are you studying nursing?' she inquires. Before I can answer, she says 'my son is a nurse. He has been working in California as a nurse for nine years. Nine years! Now he is a nursing manager there! I have been there to California two times to see him'. It did not take many words, but what she said was enough to convey the pride she had in her son being a successful nurse in California. I encountered many such conversations during my stay in the Philippines with taxi drivers, shop assistants, informants and their friends, about people taking up nursing. Radio shows play jingles advertising recruitment drives for nurses and caregivers to countries abroad. Billboards and posters along Manila's main thoroughfare *Epifanio de los Santos Avenue* (EDSA), and every-

Figure 4: A scene in a nursing college in Manila (author's photo)

where along the Recto University Belt, advertise nursing courses, nurs-ing exam centres and nursing recruitment agencies. The white uniforms of nurses are frequently seen in shopping malls, fast-food restaurants, and on different modes of public transportation such as jeepneys and the metro. The white uniforms stand not only for 'nurse', but they stand also for 'migrant'. Outside of the Philippines, people are also talking about nursing. I remember once chatting with a Filipina beautician in Singapore's Lucky Plaza. She had previously worked in beauty salons in Abu Dhabi, dedicating her working life to earn money abroad in order to put her daughter through nursing college in Manila. The nurse (*ang nars*) is everywhere in the Philippines and among Filipinos abroad.

This nursing craze is part of the wider culture of migration that is so deeply embedded in contemporary Filipino society. One can see this in the conversations that people have, in the material culture of urban Manila and of provincial towns and in the way that people imagine their futures. In Manila, the road next to the Philippine Overseas Employment Agency (POEA) is busy with people handing out flyers from recruitment agencies that advertise overseas opportunities and sell passport covers and other materials associated with overseas work and travel. The POEA itself is filled with almost- or repeat-migrants getting their papers signed, stamped, certified, accepted and rejected in a bureaucratic maze. With the sheer number of people going overseas, village life is now inherently translocal, as a recent ethnography of Barangay Paraiso, a small village community in the Philippine province of Batangas demonstrates (Aguilar et al., 2009). Overseas migration is seen as legitimate among those in the village, and their normal lives are marked by transnational communications between family members in the village and those abroad, as well as by numerous comings and goings. There are also flexible care arrangements in migrant families, which see the extended family (as well as paid domestic workers) playing a role in caring for children whose parents are working overseas (Aguilar et al., 2009). When I speak about the family in this chapter, it refers both to the immediate nuclear family, but also to the wider extended family of cousins, aunts and uncles, since they too play an important role in migration decisions. With migration now a norm among Filipino families, there are nonetheless specific dilemmas which migrants face before they begin their overseas journeys. I will outline the typical stories of migrant nurses wanting to go overseas, as well as pointing out the concerns about leaving that specifically relate to nurses and medical workers.

The Process of Migration

In order to meet the high demand for nursing courses in the Philippines, the number of nursing colleges in the country went up from 175 in the 1990s to over 460 in 2008 (WHO, 2011; Divinagracia, 2005). One recruitment agent to whom I spoke in Manila said that nursing has become so popular that new dubious nursing colleges are sprouting up, along with scandals about cheating in the Nursing Board Exams and increasing fears of deteriorating standards (Matsuno, 2011). 'Everybody is a second courser', she tells me, and 'even doctors retrain as nurses'. With approximately 80,000 nurses per year graduating with a Bachelors of Science in Nursing degree, a steep increase in the numbers of graduates has taken place during the 2000s (WHO, 2011). Many then go on to take the Nursing Licensure Exams, the professional exams, which enable graduates to qualify as practising nurses (Lorenzo *et. al*, 2007). However, typically less than 50% of the people who take this exam pass it (PNA, 2008). This high rate of failure means that many aspiring nurses are left unemployed. Those who pass it often start off working as unpaid volunteers in a hospital – a common practice because there are not enough jobs available – while others who find paid work in hospitals simultaneously start their search for jobs overseas. [1] In 2014, almost 20,000 professional nurses left the Philippines, along with more than 12,000 caregivers and caretakers (POEA, 2014).

A large range of recruitment agencies operate in the Metro Manila area and indeed across the Philippines, offering different routes out of the country for nurses in a variety of nursing or care positions. Some of these agencies are unlicensed and involved in irregular channels of migration, advertising jobs for caregivers but leading recruits into other kinds of jobs instead. The POEA monitors the presence of such agencies but it is not possible to fully regulate the black market. Nonetheless, arranging work overseas through an agency is common. Many nurses sign temporary contracts for overseas work, in what has become a key characteristic of overseas nurse migration from the Philippines in the past two decades (Ball, 2004). On my visits to Manila's top hospitals, there were often people handing out flyers advertising their agencies to nurses after their shifts, offering opportunities abroad. Recruitment agencies discursively promote Filipinos as honest and hard-working labour commodities to other countries, just as the Philippine govern-

---

1. Project 'NARS' (Nurses Assigned to Rural Service) was set up in 2009 as a 'Training cum Deployment Project, jointly implemented by the Department of Labor and Employment (DOLE), the Department of Health (DOH) and the Professional Regulation Commission, Board of Nursing (PRC-BON), designed to mobilize unemployed registered nurses to the 1,000 poorest municipalities of the country to improve the delivery of health care services' (http://www.dole.gov.ph/projects/view/3). According to Dimaya *et al.* (2012), it was seen as a 'stop-gap solution to unemployment through deployment of nurses to rural, underserved areas for a six-month commitment'. Yet their qualitative study demonstrated that while nurses were well received in these communities and that they became exposed to key public health challenges in the country, the six-month period was 'inadequate to maintain sustainability'.

ment does (Tyner, 2004). One particular agency that I interviewed told me that they prefer not to approach nurses in hospitals because, 'it is unethical - we cannot just pirate nurses from the hospitals here'. Debates about how to ethically hire nurses are thus also central to the practices of recruitment. The procedures that nurses have to follow to migrate to various countries and the types of fees they pay vary widely.[2] According to the agency I visited, it takes approximately three years for an application to the USA to be processed. This includes the time needed for exam preparation, taking the actual NCLEX[3] examination (sometimes involving several attempts), and allowing the nurse to develop sufficient work experience. Some nurses choose to migrate first to cities like Singapore, believing that gaining work experience there will speed up the process of moving onwards to the USA. Some are willing to 'downgrade', for instance, by working as nursing assistants instead of registered nurses as a faster route out. Even when business among these agencies slowed down during the 2008-9 global recession, nurses continued to be hired directly by hospitals abroad or they moved with the assistance of networks of family and friends.

I now turn to look at the typical stories of aspiring nurse migrants in the contemporary Philippines.

On my trip to Laguna province with the nursing students, I encountered Christian, a nineteen-year old nursing student. He told me that 'some people say nursing is like a vocation or a service for others. But honestly, no, it's not really true when they say that. We don't really enjoy community work. Well, it's okay. Of course we like to meet people and help them, but that's not why we took nursing. It's for the money'. Not all nurses are as frank as Christian; others are more defensive, and do not explicitly admit to not seeing nursing as a vocation or a calling. Christian continued by saying, 'everyone in my batch wants to go overseas. I think if I go overseas, it would be the US. I have an aunt working there. I'm not

---

2. Based on discussions with nurses, agency fees and conditions also vary widely; some agencies have contracts with hospitals abroad, reducing the fees for nurses. Others charge high fees or deduct proportions of nurses' salaries when they go abroad as agency fees.

3. NCLEX (National Council Licensure Examination) is an examination for the professional licensing of nurses in the United States.

sure exactly what she does but she can help me to go there. The salary is really good compared to here. How is it like to work in Singapore?' he asked with great interest. Curiosity among students and nurses about life overseas often put me in the position of the one being interviewed.

Another nurse I met in Manila, Liza, has a fairly typical story. Liza is the cousin of a domestic worker I met in Singapore. When I first met Liza in a shopping mall in Cubao, Manila, she had been working for two years as a nurse in a private hospital before deciding to take up a job at the Philippine Heart Centre. Her application to the Heart Centre, a highly regarded public hospital, was accepted after a two-year wait. Liza is the only nurse in her family and one of the few in her village. Her village in Laguna province is classed as a 'fourth-class municipality'[4]; most of its economy is based on agriculture. According to Liza, there is still a lot of poverty there. Many young people do not finish school and instead help their families on the farms. The village also has a history of overseas migration, with many women going abroad as domestic workers and men as seafarers or manual labourers. Liza's aunts are currently working, or had previously worked, as domestic workers in Singapore, Hong Kong and parts of Canada. Her sisters now work as domestic workers overseas. All of them have completed college education, which Liza's mother insisted on, even though it was a great financial struggle. Liza's sister, who graduated with a degree in Accountancy would earn less as an office worker in Manila than she does as a domestic worker in Singapore ('*sayang*' [it's a shame], said Liza, 'because she's very smart'). Liza, however, stumbled upon nursing and only later realized what an opportunity she had provided for herself and her family. Liza's *barangay*[5] has a small health centre for midwives and is visited by a doctor and a few nurses once a week. Nursing students also come from Manila along with nursing instructors for community health education programmes every few months. Professional medics in the village are therefore not in abundant supply and Liza, being a nurse, is looked up to by many in the *barangay*. Much is expected of her as someone with a high income, an

---

4. Municipalities in the Philippines are local government units. There are six classes of municipality in the Philippines which are divided by levels of income, 'first-class' being the highest-income municipalities and 'sixth-class' being the lowest-income municipalities.

5. *Barangay* is the smallest administrative division in the Philippines, usually a district within a town or city.

income that will grow significantly if she goes overseas. Liza explained, 'my parents are so *masipag* (industrious) ... I really have to show them my gratitude for what they have done for us with our education [her eyes glistening with tears]'. Even during our first meeting, Liza adamantly stated, 'I don't want to stay here [in the Philippines]'. Her dream is to travel the world as a single woman and build her career. The waiting time for applications to the US is too long, so Singapore and the Middle East are possibilities for her. Liza continued to speak with enthusiasm about other places: 'I have one friend in Dortmund, she tells me, it is so beautiful in Germany. I also have friends in Singapore, they paid 100.000–300.000 pesos to the agency to go there. So I asked my mother if she can help me, but she said no, she has to sell the house to pay that much. It is too much!'

On my next visit to Manila I met with Liza again, this time at her new work place, the Philippine Heart Centre. She came down after her night shift to meet me in the lobby, dressed in a long white skirt, white shirt and white suit jacket on which her name was pinned. 'Look, my uniform is so conservative!' she giggled. We sat down over a coffee in the lobby. 'It's exhausting', said Liza, 'I still have to go to a meeting after this, even after night duty'. She continued to explain, 'it's good, but very tiring, some of my colleagues are so bossy! I know one other girl here, my batchmate in nursing college. We are the only two who made it in the Heart Centre as staff nurses. But because I'm new, they ask me to do so many favours for them and I can't complain because I'm new'. In spite of the challenges of her new job, Liza seemed happy about her decision to take up this post; the compensation is also better than her previous job. 'But', she jumped in with annoyance, 'I have one batchmate in the US, who told me "your salary is my tip!"'.[6] The prestige of training in a highly specialized public service job at the Philippine Heart Centre, is not seen as prestigious enough in this competitive environment where any overseas job is positioned higher up in the hierarchy of desirability. '"*Ubos*

---

6. The monthly salary for an entry-level nurse in the Philippines is between 13,000 pesos (in the private sector) and 19,000 pesos (in the public sector). Entry-level nurses in the public sector will soon earn by law a minimum of 28,000 pesos according to the Philippine government's Department of Budget and Management and the Salary Standardization Law of 2015 (SSL 2015, http://www.dbm.gov. ph/?p=14234). The bill was passed in the senate at the end of 2015.

mo" [you are so boastful], I told her! She is only a caregiver in Houston now, not even a nurse. But her salary is good'. Meanwhile, Liza was arranging to submit papers to an agency that would send her to the USA. The agency would sponsor her qualification examinations, although this process may take up to three years. Half of her salary in the USA would be deducted each month by the agency until she pays the agency fees back in full. The job is expected to be in Houston or California. Liza hopes it is California because apparently 'the facilities in Texas are not so good if you look at the website. I told that to my friend in Texas, that the facilities there are not good, not updated. She said, "no, we have the number one cardio-vascular unit in Texas". Then I said, "oh really [Liza smiled knowingly], that's not what the website said, I told my friend"'. Liza claims that her friends overseas boast about the hospitals, but her theory is that they just want to make people in the Philippines jealous by telling them false stories about life overseas; 'I just don't know what is true', she sighed. Liza spoke about the pressures she gets from others when they ask, 'what are you still doing here? Why are you wasting your time in the Philippines?' These constant remarks put much pressure on nurses to leave, and certainly hasten the process among those who are already thinking about going abroad.

Liza's story illuminates a number of characteristics of a typical story. Firstly, it highlights what a nursing degree can achieve for a family aspiring to change their social and economic standing. The nursing profession is linked to social mobility and is increasingly an economic strategy among those of modest socio-economic backgrounds to reach a middle-class status. Liza explains how her family's 'industriousness' enabled her to go to college. Nursing college is costly, but lower-income families might still attempt to put at least one child through nursing college.[7] As a nursing manager in a hospital in Manila told me, 'people

---

7. Based on tuition costs for 2014–2015 outlined by the University of Santo Tomas for example, which is home to one of the renowned nursing colleges in Manila, it costs approximately 275,000 to 300,000 pesos for a nursing degree. The fees for nursing colleges can vary, and could certainly cost more in other private universities or less in public universities. The College of Nursing in the University of the Philippines, Manila is one of the most prestigious in the country, with many more applications than places available. One reason for opting for a more expensive pri-

really value education in the Philippines. Even if you're from a poor family, they will sell their land to educate their children. They know, if their children finish nursing, there will be a return on investment'. This idea of a return on investment refers to the expected wealth that a nurse would accrue overseas, which is why nurses who do not go overseas are seen to be 'wasting time', and not working in favour of self and familial advancement. It is a discourse that mirrors a view that citizenship, in this age of neoliberal globalization, is increasingly articulated in terms of the responsibilities of individuals, families and communities to shape their own futures and life outcomes (Rose, 1996). Nursing is not a purely instrumental choice though, as it is also clear how deteriorating political-economic structural conditions in the Philippines, and explicit state policies that encourage these processes, have influenced the form that these decisions take. Aside from these factors, it is also important to note the cosmopolitan aspirations of many nurses (as well as the cosmopolitan performances of those abroad inciting envy). The desire for adventure, travel, new relationships and new forms of consumption together form an imaginary around the lifestyle of a nurse abroad.

The Migrant Imagination

A central feature in migrants' discussions of the ever-present elsewhere, is the media; in particular, new communications technologies, or polyme-dia, a 'proliferation of ... increasingly converged communication tech-nologies', such as mobile phones, instant messaging, Skype and social media, which are 'radically transforming interpersonal communication at a distance' (Madianou and Miller, 2012: 170). In Liza's case, it was her own research on Internet websites and looking at friends' photos on social networking websites, which played a role in shaping her imaginary towards other places. Anthropologists have studied how the media and migration have a 'joint effect on the work of the imagination as a con-stitutive feature of modern subjectivity', the digital media offering 'new resources and new disciplines for the construction of imagined selves and imagined worlds' (Appadurai, 1996: 3). The imagination, however,

vate college is the difficulty in getting a place in a public university. Some private universities are well respected (e.g. the University of Santo Tomas), others are unknown (Sources: University of Santo Tomas, 2014, https://myuste.ust.edu.ph/forms/files/myuste/SCHEDULEOFFEESAY1stSem2014-2015.pdf,Guardian, 2011 and personal conversations).

has never been confined historically to bounded political territories (Tadiar, 2004); globalization and its constitutive features did not just suddenly arrive – people have always had far-reaching imaginaries and the circulation of people, ideas, stories and material and visual culture have long and global histories (McKeown, 1999; Cooper, 2005, Said, 2000). Nonetheless, the Internet has represented a change in both the *operation* of this imagination and its reach. In my own fieldwork, poly-media was a very real part of migrants' daily lives; their online worlds are just as pertinent as those offline (Miller and Slater, 2000). Filipinos, I observed, share stories (*kuwentuhan*) on web forums and blogs, and display their lives on social networking websites. These online practices exist alongside other media and cultural engagements featuring soap operas, American popular culture, beauty pageants and Filipino films with a migration-related theme (Cannell, 1999; Tolentino, 2001). One such film, for example, is *Dubai* which depicts how Filipino migrants go through a process of self-transformation, discover love, a life with material comforts, adventure and glamour, as the characters of the film drive through sand dunes and hold barbeques on the beach with the *Burj Al-Arab* as a backdrop.

The migrant nurses I met engage frequently with information that circulates on the Internet about migration conditions and possibilities. Friendster and Facebook, social networking websites, were two of the most widely used platforms for migrant nurses at the time of fieldwork to communicate with friends and relatives based all over the world, as were Yahoo Messenger and Skype. These platforms are important for nurses in the Philippines before they embark on overseas journeys and are equally important in Singapore, from where nurses plan onward journeys. They use such networks to obtain and interpret information about opportunities abroad. This was of particular interest when the global economic crisis in 2008–9 created uncertainties with regard to job openings in healthcare professions around the world. More signifi-cant than the *actual* impact of the crisis on these nurses' lives – most of my informants still had their jobs and were able to find new ones during this period – was the way in which gossip, stories and rumours about the impact of the crisis circulated through informal online communi-cation networks. That a nurse in the Philippines may listen to stories from friends about retrenchments or hiring freezes in the USA and then hesitate to approach a recruitment agency was a common story during the crisis. Sources of information to which my informants give a lot of weight are Web forums specifically for Filipino nurses that circulate personalized stories such as, 'this is what happened to my brother's girlfriend', or 'this is what happened to a former classmate'. Questions are often posed and advice sought on job openings, on life in particular countries and on practical concerns such as family reunification and visas. Even recruitment agencies utilize these platforms to reach a bigger group of people. This online information is widely distributed and difficult to record. It is no longer letters, or even e-mails, that migrants use as means of communication, but it is rather polymedia that constitute an archive of today's migrant experiences. This 'archive' is a transient, chaotic domain of elusive, diffuse words, ideas and images, filled with migrants 'writing their own stories and their own histories' (Amrith, 2011: 16).

To illustrate the workings of these online social networks, I recall Flor's story and her uses of online social media. Flor was the head nurse of a cardiovascular unit in a private hospital in Manila. Her cosmopolitan aspirations were immediately apparent when she heard that I was an anthropologist based in the UK. She started telling me about her travels to Bristol to visit her fiancée and their trips around Europe. It appeared that Flor was from a comfortable economic background, able to afford regular travel, attend parties and live an urban lifestyle with material comforts. Nevertheless, Flor was still yearning for something more both personally and professionally that she felt was not available to her in the Philippines. A purely rational, economic explanation does not capture this sense of longing. Through her posts on Facebook, the nature of this yearning became more apparent. Flor had recently landed a job in Saudi Arabia and she used Facebook to document each moment of her move there. 'I choose. I wait. Bring it on', she stated on her personal biographical section. Subsequent updates then included: 'starting to prep my things. The journey will begin SOON', and 'today determines the rest of my LIFE'. In response to those, she received many sentimental good luck messages: 'I'm so excited for you Flor', 'Godspeed Flor', tributes to her nursing skills, messages asking for updates on her new life, and 'see you at the Pyramids of Gaza'. Flor responded to these comments by saying how much she will miss the hospital in Manila but that she needs to start the next stage of her life. Once Flor moved to Saudi Arabia, she was still very active updating the details of her new life on Facebook; 'feeling the dry heat, wearing the *abaya*, not as bad as I thought it would be'. She wrote about nursing etiquette during Ramadan; she also uploaded photographs going on weekend trips, of herself with other Filipina nurses with whom she shared a dorm and a photograph of her first salary in cash laid out on her bed with the caption 'in a few weeks time I'm going to gain weight because of these fancy papers on my bed'. The photos received plenty of comments from friends at home, particularly nursing juniors: 'wow Ma'am!' '*daming pera ah* [a lot of money]'! Flor responded to one comment saying, 'it is nothing compared to what you are earning in the US'. Migrants construct narratives about their journeys and display it to their friends, both for support and to demonstrate success, resilience and new cultural experiences. Rarely does one see or hear the stories of hardship displayed on social networking websites. On forums, when stories documenting hardship do appear, they are often followed with a comment on how 'we Filipinos' endure hardships, but that it is worth it, or they attribute it to sheer 'bad luck' (Osella and Osella, 2006). Moreover, when nurses and nursing students in the Philippines speak of relatives abroad, and when I ask what these relatives do or how they find life overseas, they respond with fairly vague answers such as 'I'm not exactly sure', or 'I think they are happy there'. In spite of a strong engagement with polymedia to find out about and share the lives of friends abroad, there is still a sense of the unknown surrounding the overseas adventures of others.

Departing Nurses: Duty and Care

The migration of nurses, however, is far from seamless and I will now turn to investigate the dilemmas, which accompany these expansive imaginations and aspirations. The 'brain-drain' phenomenon, which entails the emigration of large numbers of skilled professionals from a country, has been well documented and debated across disciplines (see Asperilla, 1971; Ozden and Schiff, 2006; Bach 2006; Ball, 2004; Galvez-Tan *et al.*, 2004). The primary consequence of medical workers going abroad, one could argue, is the draining of a state's public health facilities of highly educated, trained medical personnel. In 1968, Carlos Romulo (cited in Asperilla, 1971: 46–48) spoke about the 'nursing crisis' facing the government and private hospitals in the country. He said:

> The Philippines cannot leave to chance the task of remaking the rewards and opportunities for growth of the nursing profession … I feel that it is incumbent upon the administration to try to bring about an end to the conditions which have made the exodus possible and sometimes necessary from the point of view of the nurse … . Something must be done and done quickly if adequate and quality nursing service even in our country alone is to keep pace with the growth of the population.

The departure of nurses from the Philippines, as well as the very ingrained *idea* of departure, has created significant concerns about public health provision in the country. These concerns have persisted since the 1960s. Over the years, scholars and policy makers have come up with more optimistic alternatives, conceptualizing 'brain drain', in terms, for example, of 'brain gain' or 'brain circulation'.[8] Others are more pessimistic as they speak of this phenomenon as a 'brain haemorrhage', the graphic medical metaphor conveying a sense of urgency and crisis (Bulatlat, 2004). I interviewed a POEA official who explained that the root of the problem is not that there is a shortage of nurses, something I was surprised to learn. On the contrary, he went on, there are too many nurses but the *rural areas* suffer from a shortage with high rates of infant and maternal mortality, while nurses are concentrated in places like Manila and Cebu. He said, 'the government envisages that medical services in provinces with poorer regions would collapse because only mediocre nurses stay'. Taking on a more emotional tone, the official explains, 'every goddamn year 22,000 per year graduate. But where will they go? We have an army of unemployed. Do they get work after six months? Do they go to the US? Do they go to the countryside to serve the poor?' In fact, it is no longer just nursing that these dilemmas apply to, but also physiotherapy, medical-technician posts and other allied health professions. Moreover, with so many graduates and not enough jobs many nurses end up working in call centres. In hospitals, highly skilled medical workers are the ones who leave, making this a question also about the quality of medical

---

8. 'Brain gain' refers to the potential skills and knowledge that migrants bring back to the country after working overseas, while ideas of 'brain circulation' attempt to consider initiatives which see exchanges of medical expertise across the world as beneficial (Kingma, 2007).

care (Lorenzo *et al.*, 2005). Such are the debates that frame the departures of many Filipino medical workers when they go to work in other countries.

The existing work on migrants leaving the Philippines has focused largely on the departures of 'lesser-skilled' migrants, in particular domestic workers. Here discourses on the one hand blame migrant women for being 'bad', 'absent' mothers; on the other, they celebrate migrants' heroic sacrifices for the family and for the country (Parreñas, 2001; 2005; Aguilar, 2002, 2009; Tadiar, 2004; Gibson, Law, McKay, 2001). However, the migration of medical workers entails a series of ethical debates related to the health of a nation, and the medical profession's duty to serve the people of the nation. Some might accuse a nurse of leaving his or her nation behind when needed in order to care for citizens of another country. The accusation is that they are failing as citizens, particularly as the rest of the citizenry depends on them. Health is regarded as a duty of the state and a right of its citizens. The Philippine constitution (Article II, Section 15, 1987) indicates that 'the state shall protect and promote the right to health of the people and instil health consciousness among them'. Indeed, the state depends on medical workers to carry this out and expects them to feel a duty to care for one's 'own people'. It projects on medical workers and nurses nationalistic expectations on many different levels. It is not simply the state that has an interest in them; their families too have certain expectations of them as nurses to go abroad and earn, and they themselves – as I have documented – have personal and professional aspirations of their own. In other words, medical workers have multiple loyalties and hold their own dynamic interpretations and engagements with prescriptive state pronouncements and policies (Silvey, 2006: 27). In this case, it is also pertinent that the state discourse itself is not consistent. The notion of service and duty to the nation is at odds with the state's other vision that has become so ingrained in daily life in the Philippines: to go abroad, represent the nation, earn a decent living and send money back home in the form of remittances. Migrants suggest that to go overseas means to care for their futures and this has very much become a part of what it means to be a Filipino citizen today.

The macro-level debates about the migration of health professionals do not pay attention to the nuanced processes that accompany nurses' decisions to leave. The 'brain drain' discourse that focuses on highly skilled professionals leaving the Philippines has not captured the layered narratives put forward by the nurses that I met. Leaving is not a straightforward act, and frequently, the focus on where migrants go (the destination) overlooks the often difficult process of uprooting oneself from home and the subjective dilemmas that accompany this process of uprooting (Mahler, 1995: 31). Obscured by the word 'leaving' is, in this Philippine case, a complex series of negotiations among and between nurses, families and the state. Divergent ideas about what it means to be a good citizen, or a good son or daughter, produce internal conflicts among migrants. Hence, I shall also look at exceptions to the typical story: those who voluntarily choose to stay in the Philippines in spite of pressures from family and friends to leave.

Exceptions

The narratives of two nurses amongst those I interviewed in Manila hospitals about choosing to stay in the Philippines stood out in particular. One interview was with Carlo, a young 25-year-old clinical supervisor. For someone his age, he is in a fairly senior position in a prestigious private hospital in Manila. 'My choice of career', Carlo explained, 'was *parang magulo* [confused, haphazard]. My mom just suggested to me why not take nursing'. Carlo admitted that he really did not like nursing to start with. But he later started to see that:

It's a noble job … you have to get away from your comfort zone, to give something of yourself, to give something beneficial. If I'm changing a diaper, it is a responsibility. If you show what you're doing is degrading, the patient will not open up, will not trust you. If you make your environment free, open from negative thoughts, the patient will open up, express what they want to you. So there is a pride in the work, you empower the patient, you give them the resources to decide.

Giving his opinion on the vast numbers of people taking up nursing in the Philippines, Carlo said, 'you cannot blame students for taking it for monetary gain – it is not a fair remark for the nursing profession when you hear people say that. If you really don't like it, it will reflect in your performance. You have to give yourself to the patient. To feel it and love it'.

The fees for Carlo's nursing education were covered by a company which stipulated that upon graduation he must work partly in the

Philippines and partly in the United States; after that he could apply for a US Immigrant Visa. His departure to the US, however, was delayed; 'the US is closed, lucky for me. The hiring of nurses has stopped because of the recession, the economic crisis'. Carlo's preference to stay in the Philippines is a reminder that while many leave, a number of nurses do stay. He explained, 'I am enjoying my career in the Philippines. I am doing well in the Philippines even if the salary is not as high as overseas. As I said, nursing is not just a job'. If he wanted so much to go overseas, Carlo said he would have found a way to leave sooner. His mother's dream is for him (and subsequently her) to live abroad. Carlo admitted that sometimes he is tempted to just pay the company one million pesos to get out of it: 'I have been having long talks with my mom about this – whether to pursue the contract or not, to pay back the company or not …'. He searched for more words, but then stopped. On his friends living overseas, he added: 'Of course they have more bling blings, cars, condo units already! But these are material things I can get later if I want. I'm just working on what I have, I am not spending on unnecessary things'. And then once again he returned to the debate about staying or leaving, arguing that: 'I do have a motivation to contribute to nursing, to take care of Filipinos. I want to stay, be a nurse in the Philippines. Even if I go overseas, I will still go back here as a Filipino nurse. And make my contribution to the people here'.

Only one other nurse during my visit to Manila shared Carlo's sentiments. 'Sir Jasper', the Director of Nursing in the same private hospital, said with honesty that he had absolutely no desire to go overseas: 'I have participated in the board of directors for nursing. I am thinking of the country. For some it is about supporting the family, for financial reasons'. However, for Jasper, a single person coming from a well-to-do family he does not need to bring in the dollars by working overseas. He said: 'One colleague of mine went to Canada as a caregiver – she tells me, "oh come on go there, the pay is good, you can learn a lot". She encourages me. But she hasn't convinced me. I am happy and fulfilled in the Philippines'. Both Carlo and Jasper progressed in their careers in Manila very quickly; both speak, at least rhetorically, about serving the country. Jasper's case illuminates that his family background is a reason why he does not need to go, and it reaffirms the potential a nursing education holds for social mobility, particularly for those from lower-income families.

The Politics of Leaving

The sentiments of Carlo and Jasper were exceptions in the chorus of voices I heard. There are concerted attempts among public health officials to challenge the taken-for-granted trajectory of leaving, asking people to *stay*. While carrying out fieldwork in Manila, I had the chance to interview a powerful public figure – a medical doctor, who was a faculty member in the university and has held prominent government positions in the public health sector and in the private sector. I met him one Saturday morning at the studio of a radio station where he was recording his weekly radio programme. He sat down with me to explain some of the initiatives that exist to deal with the problem of health professionals leaving in the Philippines. One issue he raised was about contracts. It is necessary, the doctor asserted, to develop contracts, which require nursing graduates to serve Filipino hospitals for a minimum amount of time before they pursue opportunities overseas. This is being implemented in the form of a 'Return Service Agreement' for those enrolling in health-related courses at the University of the Philippines in Manila, stipulating a minimum of five years of public service in the Philippines following graduation.[9] He was also enthusiastic about the potential of a different model – a social contract – which he believes will be even more effective in keeping people in the country. There are attempts to structure the nursing curriculum so that classroom learning is integrated with community service. He explained, 'here there is no written contract but a social contract. They have to take a pledge to their community that they will stay, that they will serve the community. And it works - they stay!' The main obstacle ahead in implementing the curriculum widely, however, is a conflictual landscape in the politics of health policy.

But staying, he said, is more than just contracts; to him, it is above all about passion and patriotism. He told me:

> We cannot be silent role models. We have to be affirmative. Graduates, they waiver, they waiver and they waiver. They start to question themselves. Why am I here? The graduating class looks to us for affirmative encouragement. The graduating class told us that; that they need us to say this when they waiver. I want you to stay, I *need* you to stay. Your country needs you.

---

9. UP-Manila: Return Service Agreement: http://www.upm.edu.ph/node/56

The idea of waivering is a testament to the ambivalence, the dilemmas and the anxieties about leaving. No doubt, migrants are constantly wondering and hoping that they have made the right decision, as we have seen from Flor's Facebook page and with Carlo's inclination to stay in the Philippines. This doctor's talk was fiercely patriotic, appealing also to a romanticized idea of social contracts. He spoke about a module that he plans to teach, entitled 'Affirmative Patriotic Health'. He continued to say, 'we are the patriots. The forty per cent [of doctors] who stayed. The remaining sixty are in the US. We know, they know, that we are the patriots'. The health module teaches students to service their country and love their country through healthcare and serving the marginalized and disenfranchised. Public health, migration, development and patriotism are thus all infused into one module, in a desperate attempt to hold onto those leaving.

Medical work is frequently linked to a notion of national service and patriotic sentiment, and is often central to state-sponsored humanitarian projects abroad or as a part of wartime service and duty (Bayly, 2007; Kirk and Erisman, 2009; Weiss, 1997). But in the case of the Philippines, there is a tension between this notion of national service, and the pull of a wider transnational economic form of citizenship. The Philippines has always been oriented to places beyond the physical nation state, and even more so since the 1970s when the Philippine state developed its explicit policy of labour migration. Contrary to claims about the demise of the nation state, social theorists have demonstrated that the national and the global exist in a commensurable relation (Cooper, 2005; Sassen, 2000; Trouillot, 2001; Ferguson and Gupta, 2002). Through migration policies and institutions, states remain powerful actors in the governance of transnational migration and in discursively shaping citizens' loyalties to the home nation while abroad (Rodriguez, 2008a, 2008b; Guevarra, 2009). These arguments are deeply relevant for an understanding of the contemporary Philippines today. Yet the specific case of medical workers reiterates the moments of tension when the state struggles to balance the national and the transnational. Medical workers are told to be a part of the transnational labour market; this is the explicit policy of labour migration as a means for economic development in the Philippines, encouraging people to look abroad for work. At the same time, they are expected to hold back, and be rooted physically in the Philippines; this is the direction of health policy. There is a clear contradiction between these two policies.

A POEA official illustrates this further by explaining that 'there is a sense of nationalism. Public service is still around. But you cannot eat. So we cannot stop people from leaving. We talk about service to the country, but then only 10 in 100,000 opt for the provinces because wages are so low'. This comment captures the dilemma precisely, revealing how states and its citizens are in a deeply entangled mutual relationship. Citizens too expect the state to deliver (in this instance, providing acceptable wages to nurses). His comment also highlights that the state itself is not an anonymous machine, but one that uses a 'language of kin, family and body to lend immediacy to its pronouncements' (Herzfeld, 1997: 2); it is made up of people like migrants themselves who understand why going abroad to improve their life prospects is also a marker of being a 'good' citizen.

Nurses in a private hospital in Manila also expressed mixed feelings about leaving. This emerged in a group discussion I had with them:

Nico: Philippine nurses are in demand abroad. Everyone around the world knows that we are good, caring, God-fearing nurses. We like to excel, we are flexible, we value culture and religion in other countries. In Saudi, the culture is so different but they know Filipinos respect the culture of the Arabians, their attitudes. We are not biased.

Anna: But there is also a negative image of nursing – people see it as the way to migrate. It is global. So the care, helping others is covered up, it is not given emphasis. They are just dollar earners.

Kat: We have good intentions, we have a good heart and passion. Even if we want to go abroad, you cannot blame us. We have to earn money because of our economy. We cannot blame people if they have these intentions. If we have the opportunity, why not? Of all the professionals, we nurses are the most underpaid. If the government pays us more, we won't go. We face hardships in the Philippines, so we go. We need to change our economic status.

They went on to talk about their friends' experiences of other countries and pondered on how not to lose one's Filipino values abroad. When we were having this discussion, the nurses were animated, excited and curious, as they collectively planned futures overseas. When I asked them if anyone encouraged them to stay in the Philippines, they responded in unison with a 'no!' Rather, 'they encourage the opposite. They say just go abroad *now*. They are just waiting for us to say yes. Waiting for us to go overseas and bring them dollars'. Expectations weigh heavily on the conscience of many nurses.

Echoing Kat's comment in particular, I heard throughout my field-work in the Philippines and in Singapore numerous voices that were quick to defend nurses' desires to leave the Philippines. 'You cannot blame us', they all say defensively, but repeatedly with conviction. These feelings of guilt and blame recall the tension between the notion of na-tional public service, and the desire to pursue their own aspirations and also meet their family's social and economic needs while abroad. They illuminate the different levels of affinity that people hold. Thus, many still believe that they nobly serve the family, neighbourhood, village and future, and that this is a part of what it means to be a good Filipino citizen (the nurses, for example, were keen to express their desires to hold on to their 'Filipino values'). In 1950, T. H. Marshall wrote that the 'national community is too large and remote to command this kind of loyalty' (Marshall, 1950: 80), and perhaps this is why the more tangible and immediate commitments and loyalties are more compelling to nurses.

To reiterate a point I made earlier with regard to the typical stories: nursing is not seen any longer as a calling with religious underpinnings. Nursing education is an economic decision and a family project. For those with a choice, the abstract and intangible notion of the nation is hard to grasp when one sees friends' success in a tangible way such as a better education for the children, a house with a garden in American suburbia, a car and other material signifiers of wealth. The socio-economic conditions of the contemporary Philippines, urban and rural inequalities, a ruling political class, which has left many disillusioned, are a part of the backdrop. This debate is also fundamentally about care; that 'the government doesn't care about us' is a widely shared sentiment among my informants. When the state does not care for its citizens, migrants argue, how can they expect us to stay? Even if they *want* to take care of the nation, financial incentives and employment opportunities are not sufficient. The notion of citizenship has an aspirational politics, as Werbner (1998: 5) argues, for it 'raises its eyes towards the future, to common destinies' and 'constitute[s] horizons of possibility'. The reason for many nurses leaving is the idea that the Philippines does not provide that image of a stable and secure future.

Status and money are central to people's contemporary understand-ings of citizenship and increasing inequalities lead to feelings of disem-powerment. Citizenship is not just about formal rights and duties, but also in a more substantive sense, about feeling a sense of belonging and participation (Holston and Appadurai, 1996). Many medical workers – who, like the state, see themselves as particular kinds of citizens – do not feel that they are being accorded due recognition. Some health workers advocate for their rights and make claims for recognition as health professionals within the Philippines. The Alliance for Health Workers (AHW), for example, is one such civil society organization that campaigns for higher salaries and better working conditions, claiming in 2008 that a nurse in the Philippines may earn less than 10,000 pesos per month (AHW, 2008). [10] A further issue that is often raised is the fact that nurses must work as volunteers in hospitals for a long period of time be-fore they are paid. In comparison, nurses tell me that overseas monthly salaries can range from the equivalent of 40,000 pesos in Saudi Arabia to 400,000 pesos in the USA. [11] Rather than advocating for rights at home and better conditions at home, many nurses attempt to determine their own futures abroad as transnational citizens, in line with the state policy.

With the rise of the middle-classes in Asia, aspirations and practices of consumption are increasingly taking varied and transnational forms. Even if a nurse working in a private hospital is earning a decent salary in the Philippines, there is often the sense that there is something better and more secure elsewhere, something that peer and family pressure ac-centuates. The images and discussions of the potential material benefits of a 'respectable' life abroad are often related to consumption. It involves cultivating subjectivities that are linked to that of an upwardly mobile middle-class professional in the neoliberal world (even if it is, ironically, neoliberal forces which in part contribute to conditions that give nurses a feeling of disenfranchisement in the Philippines). The 'same image of the good life' is being projected all over the world as a part of 'the global production of desire', even as this image is localized in particular

10. Organizations such as the Alliance for Health Workers and the Philippine Nursing Association have long stated that nurses' salaries are inadequate, and that working conditions are poor.

11. These are the ideas that potential migrants have about salaries abroad. Other sources suggest 250,000 pesos are more common for a nurses' salary in the US (Matsuno 2011; Galvez-Tan et. al, 2004).

and place-specific ways (Trouillot, 2001: 129). Nurses and their families believe that if they work hard, they deserve material rewards and will honourably share them with those at home. All of these ideas are underlined in the film *Caregiver*, released at the very beginning of my fieldwork period in 2008. It depicted one woman's journey from being a schoolteacher in the Philippines, to working as a caregiver in the UK, outlining the trials she faced in her family life, the indignities of her work and the arduous living conditions of overseas life. But it nonetheless conveyed an overall message that in spite of such challenges, a journey abroad and hard work is still one that is empowering and that holds the promise, for the future, of big hopes and dreams. The film moved many of my informants.

Routes

Migrants' lives are characterized by a sense of movement even before the journey overseas begins. The manner in which Filipino migrant nurses are always talking about other places is something they carry with them to Singapore. Singapore – and a number of cities in the Middle East – are seen primarily as stepping stones for migrants on their way to North America, Europe or Australia where they hope to join friends and family who they believe have found success. Map 3 (opposite) shows these typical routes of migrants that include transit stops en route to more desirable destinations. There are of course exceptions to these routes outlined (such as direct moves from the Philippines to Japan or to Germany under bilateral programmes or those who found direct routes to the US), but I found these multi-stop journeys to be common among the people I spoke with during my fieldwork period.

As a point of comparison, my encounters with Burmese and Chinese nurses (who constitute the other main groups of migrant nurses in Singapore) revealed their aspirations to be very different to those of Filipino nurses. Singapore is for them, a place to work and live. A few Burmese nurses revealed to me that they intend to stay in Singapore for the duration of their working lives. They would then return home to Burma to retire and later send their children to work in Singapore. Among Chinese nurses, Singapore also appears more of a place to settle. There is some curiosity about other countries, but also hesitation about

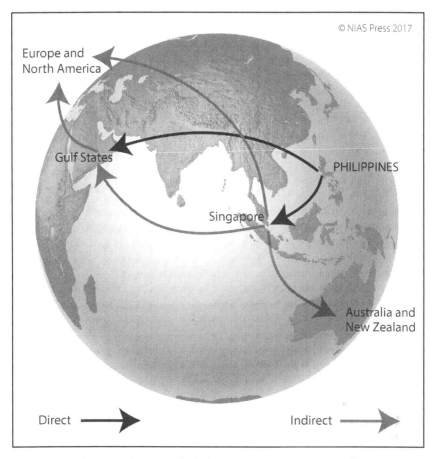

Map 3: Typical routes of migrants (relief map © Mountain High Maps)

working in the 'West'. Singapore, they believe, is a good place to be with its proximity to China, where language is also easier to navigate.

The spatial and temporal role of Singapore is established from the outset for Filipino medical workers; it is not perceived as a place to put down roots. The lives they lead are still very much linked to other places through their desires, personal contacts, and media engagement. Migrants live their Singapore lives 'in waiting'. The majority of my informants continue the discussions they started in the Philippines, about the UK, Canada and Australia. Yet rising recruitment costs, the long waiting times for visa processing, high examination fees for mandatory nursing exams in other countries, temporary bans on deployment, and immigration restrictions are factors which create a sense of insecurity among migrants. It also means that migrant journeys are often delayed and transit cities become a part of migrants' lives for longer than they expect.

I have suggested how debates about what it means to be a good Filipino citizen are significant to the lives of medical workers before they leave the Philippines for a life abroad. The state's contradictory ideas about citizenship entangle with migrants own mixed feelings about leaving combining excitement and curiosity about their futures, pressure from family and peers, and anxiety and guilt. In the following chapters I shall explore the kinds of relationships and the forms of sociality which migrants experience as they wait in Singapore, where the temporal condition of waiting becomes integrated into their daily routines. I start off following the migrants to Singapore, where they begin their overseas journeys and wait for what they hope to achieve.

CHAPTER FOUR

'Just Carers?' Understandings of Medical Labour

Sa aki'y katutubo ang maging mapagmahal
Ako ay Pilipino, ako ay Pilipino
[It's in my nature to be loving
I am a Filipino, I am a Filipino]

Popular Filipino song by Kuh Ledesma (1983)

The year of my fieldwork saw two public outcries that made headlines in the Philippines. Both concerned statements made about Filipino migrants in the world. The first outcry followed an episode of the American television show *Desperate Housewives* where one character questioned her doctor's credentials by saying, 'Can I check those diplomas ... because I want to make sure they're not from some med school in the Philippines'. Filipinos at home and abroad were upset by the comment that questioned the credibility of the country's medical institutions and its medical workers around the world; the President's office released a statement calling it a 'racial slur' while other Filipino politicians demanded a public apology from the show's producers. In the second incident, Hong Kong journalist Chip Tsao wrote a column in which he called the Philippines 'a nation of servants', triggering protests by Filipino workers in Hong Kong and a series of debates in Philippine newspapers. Both episodes did much to illuminate the often trying relationship between Filipinos and their migrant labour around the world. This chapter follows the working lives and professional concerns of Filipino medical workers in Singapore. It looks particularly at the insecurities, which arise in relation to the notion of care, as they are intimately tied to the concerns about the image of Philippine labour around the world and of how medical workers negotiate it.

As we have seen, medical work, particularly nursing, in the Philippines carries with it an elevated status given its associations with overseas work. Nurses imagine their lives abroad as respectable and empowered migrants who build a future of their choosing for themselves and their families. Singapore is often the first stop for many nurses and their first taste of overseas work. Confident that Filipinos are 'caring professionals' and that going overseas will fulfil aspirations, which they believe cannot be fulfilled in the Philippines, migrants' expectations of their overseas lives are very high when they leave the Philippines. This chapter reveals how these expectations are often not fulfilled when they arrive at their Singapore workspaces, as the daily textures, rhythms and encounters at work displace their sense of profession and status. Migrants encounter different cultural understandings and practices of labour and profession, with contestations emerging frequently over what care labour is in their worlds of work.

In the first section of the chapter, I examine the various institutions and spaces of care in which migrant nurses are embedded. Migrants occupy a range of ranked positions in large government and private hospitals, in charitable nursing homes and community hospitals, and even in private homes. The landscape of care in Singapore is layered. I focus specifically on two very different spaces: firstly, the modern, highly technologized space of a large government hospital and secondly, the bleak and bare spaces of a charitable Buddhist nursing home. A focus on these two institutions sheds light on the commodification of care, as well as the biopolitical centrality of migrant nurses to Singapore's landscape of care. Through the lens of these institutions, we see not only the aspirations and insecurities of the Singapore state, but also those of the people who provide care labour. Contestations about what care is, who provides it and how it should be provided are primary questions in these spaces of care.

In the second part of the chapter, I look more closely at these contests over the meaning of care labour. They are influenced by discourses on the image and status of nursing and on the placing of certain nationalities in a hierarchy of workers. Medical workers from the Philippines find their self-identification as a respectable class of 'caring professional labour' destabilized in Singapore. Not only do they perform a range of tasks that they do not associate with their profession – highlighting a difference in how nursing is regarded and practised– in Singapore they also simultaneously confront widespread associations of Filipinos with domestic workers or 'unskilled' care labour. The tension between nursing as a profession and nursing as a 'low-status', domesticated form of care work has always been present in historical and contemporary understandings of nursing around the world (Marks, 1994; McDowell, 2009; George, 2000; England, 2005; Bashford, 1997). However, this tension between the professional and the domestic is further accentuated by the low-status of nursing in Singapore's economy, and the typecasting of the Philippine national as synonymous with subservient domestic care labour. Care, a trope which features prominently in migrants' initial narratives about the Filipino nurse (as 'inherently caring'), then becomes a trope evoking shame. Migrants distance themselves from ideas of care when it comes to their labour, attempting to shed the long-standing associations of Filipinos with care work, as 'global servants of global capitalism' (Parreñas, 2001: 3).

It becomes increasingly apparent that the category of care labour is deeply ambiguous. Care labour captures a range of occupations – including registered nurse, nursing aide, healthcare assistant, medical technician and domestic caregiver. In Singapore, the lines between medical semi-professional and 'unskilled' caregiver are blurred and intersect with the racialization of those who do this work (primarily migrants), while illuminating divergent valorizations of care labour. These experiences unsettle migrants who were once assured of their sense of professional distinction in the Philippines. While care labour has traditional normative associations with love and nurture, the tensions evident within this category of labour that relate to profession, gender and nationality also highlight the sense of 'disaffection' and the politics that accompanies the labour of care (Manalansan, 2008).

Care Labour and Biopolitics in Singapore

The contemporary migration of medical workers occurs as a part of broader shifts in global labour and capitalism, whereby the care for others is increasingly commodified in the global service economy. Linda McDowell (2009: 13) argues, however, that this kind of commodified labour is unlike other commodities because 'men and women enter their place of work as a set of living beings, opinionated, awkward, obstinate, deferential, embedded in sets of social relationships of kin and friendship'. Medical labour, moreover, is 'embodied knowledge', that is, 'knowledge sensed through and with the body' (Cassell, 1998: 31–32). It is also spoken of as 'emotional labour' and 'affective labour' to refer to the commodification of care and affect in the capitalist world order, and where feelings and emotions associated with care are 'sold for a wage' (Hochschild, 1983: 7–8; Hardt and Negri, 2000; Hardt, 1999). The shift towards an economy dominated by services has thus seen the growing role of internationalized care labour. The wide circulation of migrant medical workers around the world demonstrates this (Kingma, 2005).

The global circulation of medical workers must also be understood as a part of biopolitics, or what Nikolas Rose (2007: 3) calls 'the politics of life itself'. This is accompanied by 'somatic expertise ... and the rise of multiple subprofessions that claim expertise and exercise their divisive powers in the management of particular aspects of our somatic experi- ence' (Rose, 2007: 6). Such biopolitical questions can be seen across the world, and most certainly in the field of medical work, which is concerned with questions over life and death. Medical workers receive training in procedures, conduct, routines and practices in the particular healthcare institutions they enter, public and private, as they move around the world to provide care for the lives of others.

Singapore positions itself as a hypermodern city-state in the world and a 'cutting-edge' hub for biomedical services and research. Healthcare, which increasingly has become corporatized, is regarded as an integral part of Singapore's economic power. Tony Tan, the current President of Singapore, in a speech to mark the opening of Singapore's new biomedical research hub Biopolis in 2003, said:

> The R&D [research and development] work at Biopolis represents the apex of our biomedical efforts, where new discoveries and knowledge will be created. These knowledge generators at Biopolis will energise other downstream activities in healthcare delivery and in the produc- tion of pharmaceutical products and medical devices for the global market. These will provide skilled jobs and generate high-value eco- nomic activity for Singapore. This evening's audience ... is a snapshot of the diversity of talent that will be integrated and synergised to make Singapore a vibrant global player in the biomedical sciences arena.

Nurses and auxiliary medical workers – local and migrant – are bound up with this bigger picture and play a role in key aspects of 'healthcare delivery'. The role of nurses in Singapore's health system and economy is most evident in two hospital orientation programmes that I attended in a large government hospital in Singapore. The first orientation, known as the 'corporate orientation', explicitly addresses the service culture of the hospital and how best to satisfy patients and customers. The second orientation is a foundational course that introduces new nurses to the nursing practices of the hospital. These orientations powerfully highlight how Singapore perceives itself as embodying a different medical standard, its system far more complex, sophisticated and 'First World', compared to those of the 'Third World' countries from which many migrant nurses have come. The orientations highlight some of the Filipino nurses' first encounters with a new labour regime, as they arrive in Singapore eager to fulfil cosmopolitan and professional aspirations.

On a Wednesday morning at 8:30am, new nurses and technicians from the Philippines, India and Singapore gather for their first day at their new workplace – a large government hospital – for a corporate orientation. Held every month by the Human Resources department of the hospital, this orientation introduces new medical workers to the corporate culture of the hospital, where providing the best customer service to its patients is a cornerstone of its ethos. The orientation aligns itself with other campaigns in Singapore – 'Go the Extra Mile in Service (GEMS)' for example, a public nation-wide campaign to promote good service in Singapore – which seek to enhance customer satisfaction.[1] The orientation is like a management training class, drawing heavily on corporate motivational language. The leader tells the group: 'Alright everybody, welcome to care class! Are you all feeling good? Today we are going to learn about how to put customer first through "sunny-side up" service and "CARE" (Confidence, Attentiveness, Respect, Empathy)'. The new

---

1. Campaigns to mould public social behaviour are very common in Singapore. They take the form of public announcements, posters and television advertisements that promote a particular issue, and are sponsored by the relevant government agency. With these campaigns, the government aims to correct the 'undesirable' behaviour of Singapore citizens in a paternalistic manner. Examples include the National Courtesy Campaign and the Keep Singapore Clean Campaign.

staff members then embark on two days of team-building activities: leading each other through hospital corridors blindfolded to develop qualities of trust; practicing how to smile and how to make eye-contact with customers/patients ('look at the T zone, don't glare into the eyes, have a gentle gaze, not hawking eyes') while volunteers are called up to demonstrate bad body language (arms folded, rolling eyes). They also watch two videos. The first video is about 'Johnny the bagger', a supermarket bagger in the United States who staples 'thoughts of the day' onto shoppers' supermarket plastic bags as an example of excellent service. The second video is Randy Pausch's 'Last Lecture', a lecture delivered by a professor diagnosed with terminal cancer on how to live one's life – this made the new nurses sitting next to me cry. In his concluding comments, Pausch says, 'show gratitude, don't complain, work harder, find the best in everybody and be prepared … if you lead your life the right way, the karma will take care of itself, the dreams will come to you'; this made the nurses next to me nod in agreement and clap. Throughout the session, the leader of the orientation says, 'give yourselves a pat on the back … give your neighbour a pat on the back … give yourselves a round of applause'. The purpose of the orientation session is to cultivate the manner of a customer service professional into new medical workers: even government healthcare institutions are run like private corporations with branding and service at the core.

The following week, nurses embark on their own foundational orientation course. In the auditorium of the hospital's education centre, about 150 nurses gather – more than half are from the Philippines, while the rest are from India and Singapore. They will join the two thousand nurses currently working in the hospital. The orientation highlights first and foremost, that nurses are important to Singapore. The course begins by outlining the hospital's goal of adding years of healthy life to the people of Singapore. They are told by the one of the senior nursing directors:

> Our concern is how to keep you so that you don't use us as just a stepping-stone. I hope you don't do that. We welcome foreign talent, you can settle down here, apply for PR [permanent residence] – but we must like you, you must have a good attitude … . You need qualifications to progress … for those that settle here, there are plenty of opportunities.

You must continue upgrading yourself. If you reach Level 3, you can earn $6,000 onwards [the group of new nurses gasp, whispering to each other, $6,000!],[2] but first you have to settle and see whether you can adjust to us.

A number of speakers then come in to speak about the 'Singapore standard' – one that is presented as occupying a different league from standards in the countries of migrant nurses. As the head Singaporean nurse says, 'especially for our foreign staff, our operating system is very different from your country … we have a lot of firsts in Singapore, a lot of research breakthroughs'. The infection control nurse then comes along to talk about the biohazardous material of medical work and the hospital's colour-coded waste system. She tells them a story about Pulau Semakau, an offshore island where waste is deposited, describing it as:

> Singapore's excellent effort. You can't see the garbage anywhere. I know in other countries, you see people living next to garbage heaps. You don't see that in Singapore. The garbage is buried in layers, then the trees change colour when the water is contaminated, so we know that it is contaminated. The efficiency is really excellent I tell you. Some Singaporeans don't even know how much their government does to ensure their safety.

The migrant nurses are evidently impressed by what they hear, as their constant expressions of surprise, wows and claps reveal. Next, the hospital porter gives a presentation about a new electronic system aiming to reduce patient turnover in the hospital – to improve communication, efficiency and accountability. Next, they learn about Singapore's multiculturalism, its different 'races' and 'religions' through a series of videos presented in lecture form with step-by-step rules on how to touch and care for the people in these different, discrete communities.

---

2. In practice, it is not so easy for foreign nurses to reach this level. One nursing manager in the same hospital explained that 70% of nurses in positions of 'registered nurse', 'enrolled nurse' and 'healthcare assistant' are migrant nurses. Local nurses predominantly fill the more senior positions (clinical supervisor, nurse manager). It is possible for a migrant nurse to reach a higher position if they have a strong nursing degree, have worked in Singapore a long time and have taken up advanced nursing courses. However, among my informants in government hospitals, I heard of a number who upgraded from enrolled nurse to registered nurse, but not far beyond that (see Appendix B).

The presentation of Singapore to others and to the outside world as a high-tech, efficient and cutting-edge place for medicine is the orientation's primary message. What is of further interest is how these state visions of biomedical advancement are intertwined with its regime of immigration. Those who come to do 'research and development' in Singapore are highly paid scientists from overseas who can enter Singapore with myriad privileges. Nurses and medical workers meanwhile enter on different kinds of work visas according to the roles they play – nursing aides or healthcare assistants enter on the lowest type of work visa (often the same visa accorded to domestic workers and manual labourers), while staff nurses come in one step higher. The rights accorded to migrants vary according to the visa. Nurses, although not as prized as the highly paid biomedical scientists, are still regarded as 'desirable' migrants and are seen as valuable, or in fact fundamental, to the Singapore state in their provision of medical care to the population. Migrant nurses' primary function is care for the lives of Singaporeans. The nurses are agents – and targets – of 'governmentality' (Foucault, [1978] 1991), as they care for the health of the Singaporean population: ensuring the welfare of all through the welfare of each. Yet this is a governmentality that depends on outsiders who are not a part of the state and as a result, foreign medical workers become actors in the biopolitics of health and well-being. The case, however, is different for migrant domestic workers (many of whom are also involved in the labour of care, working as caregivers for the elderly in private homes) in Singapore, who enter the country on a work permit, which restricts them as a temporary pool of contract labour. Pheng Cheah (2006: 202) insightfully argues that:

> ... such bodies do not need to be cultivated and augmented in the same way as those belonging to the permanent labor force. They do not need to be subjectified as members of the population because their presence is only temporary ... this is, therefore, a form of labor whose constitution involves discipline and regulation but *without either increasing/enhancing workers' bodily forces through concerted training or any subjectification.*

Domestic workers, therefore, are not treated by the Singapore state as valuable in the way that nurses are. Migrant nurses in hospital and care institutions undergo constant training on how to care for Singaporeans and how to use Singapore's high-technology hospital apparatus and medical recording systems. Those who do not adjust cannot remain, while others who become accustomed to 'the Singapore system' continue to train, upgrade and stay on as permanent residents (if they opt to). Much of the training is focused on developing a nursing habitus, techniques of the self that work not simply on nurses' knowledge but also on their bodily manners, their gestures and competencies; and not only as nurses but as customer service representatives. Meanwhile, mastering such practices simultaneously furthers their own migratory projects to be successful overseas migrants providing well for their families (Foucault, [1982] 1997; Bourdieu, 1986; Cassell, 1998; Rabinow and Rose, 2006).

The commodification of care, as seen in the corporate orientation which teaches nurses how to smile, is reminiscent of Arlie Hochschild's (1983: 4–5) example of flight attendants who are required to smile in their jobs, where the smile is an 'asset', a performance which in fact estranges workers from their own smiles. However, seeing the amazement of the newly-inducted Filipino nurses about to embark on their overseas adventure, the corporate face of the orientation clearly gives them a sense of pride; pride to be in a modern setting epitomizing what life abroad can provide. They are told that they are 'foreign talent' and they see themselves as professionals at the forefront of biomedicine. It is glamorous medicine, at first glance, for these nurses. Yet the reality of mundane working life undermines this sense of glamour. The expectations of glamour are further thwarted when they see the other face of medical care in Singapore: the nursing homes and community hospitals.

The celebratory picture of Singapore as a fast-paced hub for advanced biomedical research however, is qualified by the Prime Minister of Singapore Lee Hsien Loong in a recent speech in which he points towards the overall medical scene in Singapore. In the speech, he mentions the other side of medical care: the residues, as it were, of Singapore's hyper development. Speaking of the increasingly important role of community hospitals in the care for the elderly, Lee Hsien Loong said in August 2009:

> This is not sexy, glamorous medicine but this is how we can help Singaporeans look after their elderly, look after ourselves when we are elderly, look after our healthcare costs. We have to think about the whole system, provide the right treatment at the right place to patients

with different needs ... please do not insist on being in the high acute hospital, getting high-tech fast medicine. If the doctor advises you that you would be ok, go to the community hospital. It is more suitable; you get better and more appropriate treatment.

Contrasting the 'fast medicine' of the acute hospital – which is how Singapore presents itself to the world – with the 'slow medicine' of community hospitals, greater attention has recently been granted to this typically overshadowed underside of Singapore's medical scene. In Singapore's nursing homes and community hospitals, one enters a very different world. Elderly and chronically ill Singaporeans, who stay or live in these homes, are primarily cared for by migrant nurses. The 'quasi-familial setting' of these homes sees migrant nurses providing long-term and intimate medical and affective support that involves 'the knowledge of anticipating [the] needs and desires' of those who nurses care for; nurses and residents are co-present in the space of the nursing home (McDowell, 2009: 164; Diamond, 1992: 144). In these nursing homes, there is on the one hand, a sense of loneliness and neglect among the residents, at the same time as care workers fill this absence, negotiating their professional roles in this setting, alongside intimate, interpersonal relationships that develop with residents and patients. Nursing homes are also places where negative sentiments emerge in the forms of resentment, alienation and abuse, driven often by the poor and precarious conditions of work (Diamond, 1992; The Straits Times, 2011; Today, 2011).

My fieldwork in a Buddhist nursing home is a case in point: it is a place where one starkly can see those who have been left out of Singapore's economic prosperity. These nursing homes exist mostly for Singapore's 'dialect-speaking' working classes.[3] One nurse I spoke to was convinced

---

3. One central dimension of Chinese language politics in Singapore has been the tension between speaking in Mandarin and speaking in dialect. The Speak Mandarin Campaign was launched by the state: 'The Speak Mandarin Campaign (SMC) was launched by Prime Minister Mr Lee Kuan Yew in 1979 to transform a deeply entrenched social-linguistic habit of Chinese Singaporeans who were long used to the speaking of dialects. The objectives were to simplify the language environment and understanding amongst Chinese Singaporeans; to improve communication and understanding amongst Chinese Singaporeans and create a Mandarin-speaking environment conducive to the successful implementation of the bilingual education programme in Singapore' (National Library Board, Singapore, 2004). To speak in 'dialect', therefore, was to go against the grain of state prescriptions, and seen as backward and a hindrance to 'progress'.

that many of her patients were 'former gang members'. For the majority of the elderly and chronically ill patients there, family members have gone overseas or are unable to care for them at home.[4] The role of charity here is vital, because in Singapore it is normally Voluntary Welfare Organizations (VWOs) that take care of social concerns such as 'the elderly, the youth and the disabled'. The Singapore state has typically dismissed the idea of the welfare state. Lee Kuan Yew, Singapore's first Prime Minister, said it was a system which 'undermined self-reliance. People did not have to work for their families' well-being' (Barr, 1998: 33; Lee, 2000: 104). Instead of universal health coverage provided by the state, a system was set up so that a portion of each person's wages each month would be set aside for future personal and familial medical expenses. Lower-income families contribute to the scheme at special rates and may additionally be eligible for other schemes oriented to supporting elderly and lower-income patients. However, in spite of these programmes, many still have to pay a portion of their medical expenses. Charitable medical organizations step in to fill the large gaps left by the state, at a time now where longer-term institutional care plays a significant role in care arrangements. What these charitable institutions for the elderly also bring to light are debates about the decline of 'filial piety' in Singapore, which has long been a point of anxiety for the state. In recent years, many of these charitable institutions have been involved in corruption scandals concerning misused funds from donors, which have tainted the image of these institutions, situating them further on the margins of society.

As I shall outline in the next section, the rhythms of work in this nursing home differ greatly from the rhythms of the acute government hospital. Migrant nurses are integral to both, though their proportion in relation to local nurses varies according to the kind of institution. The government hospital has a mix of migrant nurses (from the Philippines, India, Malaysia and China) and local nurses, while in the nursing home

---

4. While there is a sense of abandonment, it is not so simple a notion. Diamond (1992: 72–73) reveals that while many medical workers see their patients as being 'abandoned' by family members, this is not always how residents themselves see it. Moreover, abandonment is not solely linked to the family, but also to restrictive social policies. Sarah Pinto (2009) writes of the ambiguities in distinguishing between spaces of confinement and spaces of care, as well as between cure, abuse and freedom. The nursing home could hold multiple meanings for its residents.

staff is almost entirely from overseas (from Burma, the Philippines, China and India).

Everyday Life in the Hospital

Joan Cassell's (1998) ethnography of the life of female surgeons is a rich exploration of the embodied practice and art of surgery, a study detailing the bodily dispositions of surgeons at work. Speaking of doing fieldwork in hospitals amongst surgeons, Cassell (1998: 2, 31) recounts that 'as a medical speciality, surgery is uniquely physical, distinctively embodied'. She continues:

> in a medical setting, one's position [as an anthropologist] is in some ways [like] … that of an inexperienced medical student … In acquiring the language, one assimilates words, grammar *and* choreography: one masters the appropriate behavior associated with various terms and phrases.

Certainly, my experiences as an observer in Singapore's medical institutions provided insights into the embodied practice of nursing and other kinds of medical-related work, such as the work of physiotherapists and healthcare assistants. The daily rhythms of the hospital and the nursing home were revelatory of the different dimensions of the healthcare system, the different kinds of care that migrants negotiate, as well as the relationships nurses have with other medics at different levels. It becomes evident that care does not only involve the professionals, but also the machines, medicines, bodies, technologies and procedures (Mol, 2008: 19). Moreover, these institutional spaces are also spaces of sociability (McDowell, 2009; Bangko, 2011; Carsten, 2013).

A typical day in the big government hospital, where I conducted a part of my fieldwork, sees a very fast pace. I was accorded the role of a volunteer in the hospital which allowed me access to the subsidized wards, specializing in geriatric, cardiac, orthopaedic, respiratory and gastroenterology care. In these wards, I observed the daily routines, interactions and movements of the nurses, but was instructed at the beginning of my stint that I was not to disturb the hospital staff during my observations. The nature of the arrangement itself was revealing of the hospital's work-ethic, for it became evident that most nurses working in the wards were too busy to even talk to each other, let alone take a proper lunch break. It was only in the corridors between wards and in the lifts where I saw healthcare assistants (the lowest level of staff, doing largely janitorial work) gossip with each other and where I felt most free to chat with them. On a typical day in the wards, nurses are moving in and out of patients' wards to perform routine medical care tasks, filling in forms, entering information into laptops sitting on mobile trolleys, moving to and from other departments, transferring patients, making phone calls and attending to emergency cases. It is a highly-strung, fast-paced and stressful environment. The nurses wear different uniforms according to their level of seniority: a darker trouser and shirt uniform for senior staff nurses, a white and flowery shirt and trouser uniform for staff nurses, a white dress for junior nurses and a grey-white shirt and trouser uniform for healthcare assistants. Doctors do not wear a uniform. The patients that staff cares for are from all ethnic and linguistic backgrounds in Singapore and they stay in different wards according to their level of income. Patients also include migrant workers and medical tourists from across the region and beyond.

Alyssa is one of the nurses I met at the hospital orientation. A few weeks later, I met her at the McDonalds below her flat when she finished her morning shift at the hospital. Alyssa had recently arrived from Pampanga in the Philippines, where she worked as a registered nurse in a private hospital. It was the first time I had seen her since the orientation where she had been very energetic and sociable, introducing herself to all the new people around her, asking many questions, eager to embark on a new adventure. This time, however, she looked exhausted and spent most of our time together explaining how tired she was, and how tired all her fellow Filipina nurse flatmates were. 'Meg', she would say repeatedly, 'I am so busy, I have so much stress, I lost some weight [here in Singapore] ... in the Philippines, it is not like this. Here it looks like all the people might die from stress, so I'm also stressed', and 'sometimes we just come home and cry, then pray, then sleep, then wake up and go again'. The initial positive first impressions, which new nurses had when they attended the hospital orientation, quickly dissipated. One of Alyssa's flatmates had already handed in her resignation and was getting ready to go back to her job in Baguio, in the northern Philippines. The model of Singaporean perfection presented at the orientation was, one month later, a cold, stressful and hierarchical model.

The scene is rather different on the opposite end of the island in the Buddhist nursing home where I also conducted fieldwork. It is located in a peripheral part of Singapore, not far from a residential neighbourhood and in an area with a surprising amount of open space, given how built up much of Singapore is. This is also the location of several other nursing homes and charitable institutions. In this nursing home, the corridors are noticeably darker than those of the acute hospital: a single light over the nurses' station is on, while the rest of the ward remains shaded. The corridors are also dramatically emptier. Walking down the corridor, one hears, amidst the silences, cries of pain, wailing, moaning and people talking to themselves. A smell of dirty diapers lingers in the corridors. Chinese soap operas play silently on the televisions. Early in the morning, patients are bathed and diapers changed; some of the patients then move to a common area for physiotherapy exercises. During the rest of the day, the staff attends to administering medicine, feeding patients, making beds, taking vitals, and constantly monitoring patients. The pace of work is significantly slower than that I observed in the acute hospital. There is more time for the staff to chat, banter, tease and gossip; doctors and janitors are included in conversations among nurses and while giving medicines to chronically-ill patients, the Filipinos in Ward D shout out to each other about their weekend plans. Things are far more relaxed, there seems to be more camaraderie among the medical workers, though also a sense of boredom. In this home, relationships with patients are longer-term and intimate. For some nurses, care involves communicating with chronically ill and rather passive patients; for others, it is about maintaining relationships with elderly residents in the nursing home whose moods regularly change. There is still a regimented set of tasks that nurses must do each day, working according to the orders given from senior nurses, while balancing the 'unplanned, contingent nature of everyday tending' (Diamond, 1992: 143). In the nursing home where I did fieldwork, nurses wear a blue uniform, their rank indicated by the position of the prints on the uniform. The patients who nurses care for are typically lower-income Chinese, the majority Hokkien-speaking (though other 'dialects' are also represented), and a few Malay and Indian patients.

The two institutional settings are worlds apart, each demonstrating distinctive material as well as physical and affective realities. These distinct textures have a bearing on how nurses feel and understand the work that they do. They may hear of working conditions abroad from others before they leave the Philippines, but it is only by *doing* the work that they truly experience it. Concerns about the meaning of care labour come to occupy the minds of many Filipino medical workers, and notions of pride and shame emerge about the nature of the care work they perform on a daily basis.

Understandings of Nursing

For migrant medical workers, the understandings of their labour that they encounter in Singapore are at odds with the professional identifications they cultivate in the Philippines. The image of nurses' professionalism is firm in the Filipino imagination today and to a great extent it is this image that fuels the current hype surrounding nursing. Nurses see themselves, and are seen by others, as occupying a respectable class of their own, a respectability that emerges more from the professional and international – rather than ethical or vocational – associations with nursing. In the process of crossing borders, however, this sense of professional security is shaken and gives way to feelings of professional anxiety instead. Divergent understandings of care are at the core of these anxieties. Where professionalism is taken-for-granted in the Philippines, in Singapore it is undermined by people at various levels (patients, doctors, technicians). This puts nurses and other auxiliary medical workers in an ambiguous position as 'semi-professionals' or 'paraprofessionals' (Benedicto, 2009; Manalansan, 2008; Marshall, 1950). They sit uncomfortably in between the doctors and biomedical scientists who are valorized in Singapore as the true professionals, and the subservient care labour that is stereotypically associated with Filipinos.

Care labour is often imagined in the Philippines and across the world as the domain of Filipinos. The idea that 'Filipinos are inherently caring' is widely uttered by Filipinos (my informants included) and by others around the world (e.g. those who hire Filipinos). That said, the stories of Filipino nurses revealed a far more fraught relationship with the notion of care. Initially presented with pride as an intrinsically Filipino quality, nurses later distance themselves from care when regarded by Singaporeans as 'just carers'. The value – or devaluation– of their labour becomes a prominent insecurity as evident in recurrent discussions that I had with informants on this issue. The first point of contention has to do with the image and perception of their nursing labour, which highlights, firstly, a difference in how nursing is viewed in Singapore and in the Philippines; and, secondly, how Filipinos are viewed in Singapore. Over the period of fieldwork, I met a range of Filipino nurses who reiterated comments such as: 'they [patients] think we are just caregivers, not professionals with skills', 'they think that we are just maids, that all Filipinas are just maids'. One nurse, MeAnn, working in the oncology ward of a large government hospital, told me with much bitterness, 'to them we are just maids, here to clean them, wipe their asses. They don't respect us. We are professionals, we have degrees. The Singaporeans don't even have degrees, only diplomas'. These kinds of comments came from nurses working in hospitals who do not associate this treatment with a hospital context. In one story, Aida, a qualified doctor in the Philippines, spoke to me of her experience of working as a medical trainee in the wards of a Singapore government hospital, before becoming a medical auditor. She spoke of a moment during her traineeship in the wards where a patient refused her touch saying 'you are the same kind [orang] like my maid, that stupid woman'. The rankings of medical labour, with roles delineated according to rank, collapse at that moment. The consistency with which such sentiments were expressed by my informants illuminates the shame and resentment that care evokes and suggests a desire among the medical workers to distance themselves from the lesser-skilled 'underclass' of Filipino care labourers (domestic workers and caregivers). It is clear that nurses' initial positive impressions of the hospital – where they are portrayed as biomedical pioneers in a glamorous hospital at the orientation meeting – quickly dissipate upon encountering the everyday realities of hospital life where they are seen as maids.

To counter the idea that they are 'just carers', nurses are quick to assert their professionalism. As MeAnn and other nurses told me, they are degree-holders. Several times I am reminded that nurses in white uniforms are looked up to in the Philippines. As Nelia, a nurse in another government hospital relates, 'in the Philippines, they [people] look up to us, as professionals with degrees, we are something. We have something they don't have. When you wear the white uniform there, people will stare at you, they will bow to you, some will even salute you'. This was echoed by a group of nurses working in a private hospital who said that 'in the Philippines the image of nursing is very high'. One nurse in this group, Rose, who worked as an operating theatre nurse, said, 'our work is not just care like compassion ... it is about life. We have so much responsibility ... [and] we have the skills'. To reiterate this point, nurses emphasize their medical expertise and their own self-perception as partners in healthcare with the doctors, rather than as orderlies. Another operating theatre nurse, Juliet, spoke with pride of her 'surgical skills', emphasizing that her 'secret' in performing these skills was a calm, steady comportment, unlike many of the other nurses who 'are so stressed'. My conversations with Ella, a key informant in Singapore, were most revealing in this regard. Ella is a nursing graduate from a college in Ilocos province in the Northern Philippines. Soon after graduation, she moved to Singapore in a nursing aide position and has over ten years worked her way up to a position of senior staff nurse, in the same government hospital. In that period, she got married to a man from her Philippine village, Joel, and they both live in Singapore with their three children. For Ella, being a nurse is fundamentally about being a professional with medical knowledge. Ella spoke at length about her role as a senior staff nurse in the high-dependency unit of a government hospital dealing with the daily challenges of managing lower-level nurses of different backgrounds with different 'work habits', and about her role advising general surgeons and doctors on medical decisions. It is the nurse, she argued, who knows the patient best. She explained how once a doctor was required to give the first dose of antibiotics to a patient, but did not know how. In the end, it was Ella herself who had to instruct him how to go about it. She also told me the following story illuminating the often tense relationship between senior nurses and doctors:

> There was one ortho case we had ... I used my own discretion because the patient is about to go to surgery, so my own thinking is that we cannot give the dosage of the medicine because the patient will be at risk of bleeding. Then the doctor came and he said, 'you never gave the dosage? Why not?' I explained to him, but still he said, 'why did you never give the dosage?' I told him, you give the medicine yourself. I am not going to give it. I told him like that. Then later the other people assessing the patient, they say it was correct to omit that dose. And he still has the guts to argue. I am doing it for patient safety, but you get some doctors like this, they act like they know everything.

In Ella's stories, she is as a nurse the central player in medical decision-making. Ella positions herself quite differently from a caregiver sitting at the bedside of an elderly patient, watching over him or her in a hospital ward. Nonetheless, in spite of the medical expertise characterizing her work Ella often found her professionalism challenged at different stages of her working life in the hospital. The second – and related – point of disquiet among nurses was the fact that nursing in Singapore is 'dirty work'. This was not simply a question of image, but a question of performing tasks that migrant nurses do not associate with their jobs. It reveals very different cultural understandings of the nursing profession in Singapore and in the Philippines. In Singapore, it is the 'high-tech' dimension of its healthcare sector that is valorized (the biomedical scientists, doctors and experts) while 'high-touch' jobs such as nursing involve bodily care and are seen as 'low-status' (McDowell, 2009).[5] Nurses are fundamental to Singapore's health system yet they still occupy the lower-end of the healthcare system in terms of prestige and respectability. Nurses' roles are seen as more physical than biomedical, as they deal with bodily fluids and the bedside care of patients. Certainly, the nursing home settings are regarded as even more 'dirty' and less professional being further removed from the fast-paced and high-technology medical environment of an acute hospital and even more proximate to direct contact with bodily fluids and smells; involving tasks such as lifting, bathing and changing diapers. Nurses in hospitals said that Singapore is more advanced than the Philippines. For example, one male healthcare assistant I met working in a famous private hospital, said with some pride, 'you can see there is a lot of innovation here. It is a 5-star hospital'. However, this is not enough to compensate for the shock that nurses feel when they find themselves performing tasks in Singapore that they do not associate with their profession in the Philippines; tasks which *are* generally associated with a nursing job among Singaporean nurses.[6] Confronting these different understandings

5. Marks (1994) comments on the case of South Africa and the intersections of race and bodily care: 'the fact that highly paid doctors remained for the most part white, regardless of the skin colour of their patients seems not to have been noticed by the racial ideologues (maleness – or medical qualifications – apparently provided protection against pollution by racial contact)'.

6. In other countries, for instance, in Singapore and in India, nursing is still regarded widely as 'dirty work'; see Sheba George's (2000) work on nurses from Kerala. According to Magnus Marsden (2005: 99), in Chitral, Pakistan, nursing is a dubious profession for young women, and many who choose it have to do so 'in the

of nursing labour in Singapore is a common experience for all nurses, even those in the more prestigious hospitals. Some sub-specialties of nursing are regarded as more professional than others (ICU nursing, for instance, is more desirable than geriatric nursing). Nonetheless, nursing in Singapore involves a great deal of bedside care at all levels. Tasks such as sponging and bathing patients are not those which Filipino nurses associate with their job description in the Philippines.

The idea that nurses are just carers or maids is therefore not just a perception, but has to do with the very work that they do. As Nelia related, 'here we are professional maids, and if you see the work we do, it's true … we do the dirty job … I worked for so many years, paid so much for my education and I end up doing this? It is degrading'. This is a matter capturing the very ambiguity of medical work at the semi-professional level because the distinction between a nurse and a domestic caregiver is not always so clear-cut in practice. Nurses protest that they have to do everything for the patient and the patients' relatives – getting a glass of water, wiping saliva from the patient's mouth, pressing a button to alter the position of a bed. Importantly, as many nurses told me, it is the relatives who perform these tasks in the Philippines, not nurses. Nurses there deal with the medical side of care (the administering of medicine, the insertion of tubes, the taking of blood), while bedside care (cleaning, feeding) is the domain of the family. Care of the elderly in the Philippines is still largely unpaid family care within the household. One could say that there is a moral expectation in the Philippines that relatives care for their ill family members at the bedside.

Nurses moreover, allude to a more economistic understanding of care prevalent in Singapore as they recount how Singaporean relatives expect nurses to do everything because they are paying for it. As a group of ward nurses in a private hospital said, 'in the Philippines, they see us and they say, "please can you help me nurse, my mother is sick". Here they say, "hey, we pay you for what?"'. The commodification of care manifests itself in the kinds of relationships nurses develop with patients and their relatives – even as the nurses themselves, as migrant dollar-earners, are a part of this commodification process. In the Philippines,

---

face of considerable criticism from other villagers and family members'. In the Philippines, nursing is neither regarded as 'dirty work' nor as a dubious profession for young women.

the purchase of care for the elderly is not regarded as appropriate, nurses suggest (Zelizer, 2005). There is thus a palpable sense of shock among nurses that they are paid to do such bedside tasks. The greater shock for the Philippine nurses is that Singaporean relatives not only refuse to do this work, but they do not know how.

It is worth noting here that, in contrast with Filipino nurses, Singaporean nurses' professional expectations are not as high. In my conversations with some Singaporean nurses, nursing is not seen as a highly-professional job but a safe and acceptable career choice for women, particularly working-class women, on par with working in the police force as an older Malay nurse told me. Nursing, she suggested, is often a choice among those unsure whether to join the workforce or to stay at home. The gendered associations of nursing as women's work seem far more relevant in the accounts of Singaporean nurses' reasons for choosing nursing than for Filipinos.[7] The sentimental images of nursing as a selfless community or public service, or as a calling are precisely what appeal to Singaporean women who choose a nursing career. A very senior nurse in Singapore told me quite frankly that she would never want her daughter to be a nurse for it is not associated with prestige or professionalism (although there are now efforts to change the image of nursing in Singapore).[8] She would rather her daughter becomes a doctor. In the Philippines, however, nurses are often seen differently, their sense of professional respectability comes, above all, from their lucrative economic potential.

In the nursing home, this association with degrading care is heightened. The very atmosphere in the home, the darkness of the spaces and its smells, gives it a feeling of desolation; one can *feel* that such homes exist at the margins of Singapore. I remember a Singaporean-Chinese physiotherapist once saying to me, 'our PAP [People's Action Party] abbreviation for Pay and Pay, it's bullshit, BS. Look at these ministers; they just want to show the world how rich they are. But here - nothing'. In a group discussion with nurses from China, the Philippines and Burma,

---

7. See Tan (2004) on Singaporean nurses' reflections on their careers, many of which reinforce the idea of nursing as a vocation for women.

8. There are growing attempts to professionalize the image of nursing in Singapore; these efforts have led to the creation of a new degree programme in nursing which started in 2008 (previously, one could only get a Diploma in nursing). There are similar debates about nursing all over the world.

they all agreed when an older Burmese nurse said, 'in our countries, we have so much responsibility, procedure wise, patient wise. But here, our position is so low but hard working. Everybody say our country, no sweat. Here, we work, a lot of sweat'. A Singaporean nurse in the nursing home told me that the few local nurses who worked there were promoted quickly in order to keep them in the job. Others moved away to hospitals, which pay better.[9] This particular nurse said that she was only in the job because her income was supplemented with income from a family business. Hence, lower-rung positions were therefore all occupied by migrants who carry out tasks such as sponging and bathing patients, changing their diapers, spoon feeding them and recording details of their bodily functions on forms. Catherine Choy (2003: 192) quotes a Filipina nurse activist in the 1960s who asked, 'do we bring our nursing skills to the USA as professionals and to fill a need in a medical health care crisis ... or are we brought to the USA as their little brown-skinned sisters to empty bedpans and work in nursing homes?'

As I shall explore in the next chapter, my informants do develop close relationships with those they care for long-term; it is not entirely a negative and disempowering picture. Yet the low-status of working in a nursing home is brought out further in the uneasy relation between charitable nursing homes and the commodification of care. Quasi-religious charitable nursing homes evoke a particular history of nursing, whereby 'care for the sick' was 'constructed as an act of charity and compassion'. (McDowell, 2009: 163). Women's 'innate' abilities to care constructed nursing as a vocation, an act of self-sacrifice and devotion which consequently allowed this work to be highly-regarded and respected, but also poorly valued and compensated.[10] My informants who see their work and Catholic faith as mutually reinforcing still nonetheless have primary aspirations that remain professional. Being closer to the scientific aspect of nursing and away from the care aspect, allows them to preserve this sense of professional respectability. Yet working in a nursing home makes this challenging. Moreover, charitable nursing homes are often

---

9. Hospitals pay staff or registered nurses approximately $2,500 per month. Nursing aides in nursing homes can earn as little as $500–$600 per month, after some of their salary is deducted by nursing homes for accommodation costs.

10. Nursing was often associated with religious sisterhoods, where 'the emphasis was as much on the moral and spiritual demands of nursing as on its practical effect' (Marks, 1994: 6, 19; also Dingwall, Rafferty and Webster, 1998).

associated with care for the poor and destitute. Similarly, most of the patients in the Buddhist nursing home are from poorer, working-class backgrounds in Singapore. Among nurses, this is less prestigious than caring for wealthier patients in the acute hospitals. Even as they might critique the commodification of care, nurses desire to work in the wards where patients pay the most, especially the private wards where the wealthy medical tourists are.

Marie, a Filipina staff nurse working in the HIV/AIDS wards of Singapore's 'Communicable Diseases Centre' (CDC), raised further questions about the varying desirability of Singapore's different institutions of care. The CDC is a complex of older one-storey non air-conditioned wards, spread out over a green area, each ward isolated from another. The pace was slow, just like in the nursing homes. Marie sat down with me one afternoon to recount her experiences. She explained, 'they told me I would be in ward 76, on my first day here … then I said, ward 76? Where is it? Then they told me it is the CDC. Then they told me it was HIV/AIDS patients. I was so scared'. But over the years, Marie changed her outlook on working in this ward, as she learned of the stigmatization that her patients had been through. Many had been rejected by their families. They did not get much financial support from the state and only a few charitable organizations provided assistance. Dealing with families, social workers, counsellors, nurses and doctors, Marie said, 'being here has taught me a *lot*. I am now confident to manage these patients and I really love to work here, Megha, really'. Often, she said, that her husband asked her:

> 'Don't you want to change to the hospital? Why do you want to stay with these kinds of patients?' … but by now I feel very close to these patients and really enjoy this holistic care. So many of my friends tell me to join them in the big hospital, they say CDC must be so lousy, so lonely; there is nothing to learn. But for me it is a passion to care for the sick, just like Florence Nightingale.

Marie is one of the few nurses I met who spoke with conviction about nursing as a vocation. Her narrative also highlighted the hierarchy of desirable care institutions in Singapore, where the HIV/AIDS ward was linked with backwardness; its undesirability was also linked to a wider rejection of these particular patients who were stigmatized. People in Singapore speak with some fear about the 'CDC', just as they speak negatively about the Institute of Mental Health (IMH).

I recall Marks (1994: 73) quoting a South African nurse matron in the 1950s who said, 'no task in nursing was degrading no matter how menial. Nursing was the most selfless of all callings'. But for the majority of migrant nurses I met, apart from Marie, this was not the reality. I remember once asking a Filipino male nursing aide to explain to me the task he was doing one morning in the nursing home. He responded with hesitation, 'why do you want to know? You ask the staff nurse'. When I explained my research to him, he then said with some embarrassment, 'okay I will tell you. I am doing the chart for patient bowel motion'. A few minutes later, I happened to overhear him speaking to another colleague, 'I want to go home. If I knew the work here is like that, I wouldn't want it'. There is a powerful sense of shame performing tasks which do not fit in with the nurses' sense of professional belonging – which calls for a dignity of labour through high pay, good working conditions and the performance of tasks related to the more medicalized and technical aspects of nursing. Many nurses, however, will take a downgrade from 'staff nurse' to 'nursing aide' simply because it is the fastest way out of the Philippines. Some nurses find it difficult to move out of this position if their supervisors in Singapore do not sponsor the training and exams they need for promotions. Some nurses do find a way out: over the course of my fieldwork period, one of my key informants, Grace – whose stories I shall return to in more detail later – transferred from working in the Buddhist nursing home to working as a phlebotomist, a blood technician in Biopolis alongside scientists. She was quick to tell her friends about her more prestigious nursing job[11] and a few of her friends then followed suit.

The domestication of nursing is at the crux of the nurses' anxieties. It means that there is a blurring of boundaries between domestic work (with which bedside care is associated) and the more medicalized aspects of professional nursing. The blurring of this specific boundary also brings to light the relationship between Filipino nurses and the significant population of Filipina domestic workers in Singapore, and the

---

11. Jacob Copeman (2009: 21) has spoken of the 'cosmopolitan, professional sensibilities of blood service staff', which reflects Grace's own characterization of her work. Moreover, Copeman argues that to be an advocate for blood donation is to be 'modern' in a number of locales around the world, where 'the refusal to donate blood ... is thus equated with a refusal to be modern'. Blood donation is seen as 'a measure or indicator of civility'.

immediate associations that are made between Filipinos – particularly women – and certain types of work.

The Intrusion of the 'Domestic'

The history of nursing and its professionalization has often been accompanied by the need to assert professional boundaries and control over caregivers and midwives (Marks, 1994: 4). This is because of a fundamental sense of ambiguity in the field of nursing, much of which stems from the 'stigma of domestic labour' which has been in conflict with the image of nursing as a respectable occupation for refined middle-class women (Marks, 1994: 9). The lines between the medical, the physical and the menial tasks are not so clearly demarcated. Marks captures the centrality of these tensions in colonial medical environments in South Africa 'where noble aspirations and polluting domestic labour constantly rubbed shoulders'. In order to deal with the ambiguities and shifting boundaries within the profession, there are constant efforts to preserve hierarchies and delineate roles and statuses through 'uniform, badge and insignia' (Marks, 1997: 31). Yet these symbols themselves do not prevent overlaps in roles and statuses in practice.

Alongside this history of nursing which sees the uncomfortable relation between professionalizing aspirations and the domestic, I have suggested that the performance, by nurses, of tasks associated with domesticity is something which Filipino nurses in Singapore, in particular, find disorienting. For these female nurses, the dissolution of the boundary they seek to maintain between themselves and other Filipina women is the cause for anxiety; they fear that Filipina women are synonymous with being maids, leading to a sense of 'transnational shame' (Aguilar, 1996).[12] The impact of these stereotypes linked to Filipino migrants has been highlighted in other studies, for instance, explaining how Filipino professionals distance themselves from Filipina domestic workers in Singapore (Aguilar, 1996; Cabañes, 2009). In the case of nurses, the desire to establish a distance from their domestic worker *kababayans* (fellow country people) is stronger given the proximity of the work

---

12. The racialization of Filipino migrant women occurs not just in Singapore; in Hong Kong, for example, which also has a very large population of Filipina domestic workers, 'the term *banmui* ("Philippine girl") was used interchangeably with "maid" or "servant"' (Constable 1997: 42).

they do. Some domestic workers in Singapore also engage in care work. Private care workers for elderly individuals who work in peoples' homes are often classified in Singapore's immigration scheme as domestic workers. This proximity leads nurses to differentiate themselves from domestic workers. In Chapter 6, I continue to look at how the boundaries between these two groups of Filipinos are negotiated in their forms and practices of sociality. I also show how domestic workers themselves seek to professionalize their own image through skills courses, making the boundary even more porous. This relation between nurses, caregivers and domestic workers reveals tensions among Filipino migrants in care labour in Singapore where questions of social differentiation and status are salient.

Male Nurses

The fear or scorn of the domestic, however, also concerns Filipino male nurses. Although the majority of my informants were female, I shall now turn to the experiences of a few male nurses that I encountered. Nursing homes in Singapore generally employ a higher proportion of migrant nursing staff. Nursing homes are also the location in which a lot of male nurses work. In the government hospital orientation, there was not a single male nurse present. In the nursing home where I did my research, however, there was a significantly larger presence of male nurses. I heard from some informants that this is because 'men are stronger and can help carry the patients and bathe them'. The male nurses in the nursing home settings, moreover, were primarily those in nursing aide positions. Meanwhile, female nurses occupied more senior positions – as staff nurses – in government acute hospitals, reinforcing the normative ideals of nursing in Singapore as feminine work. As a representative of one of Singapore's healthcare groups told me, 'it looks better' to have female nurses in the big, prestigious hospitals.

Curious to hear more from male nurses, I arranged to meet a few of them after their morning shift one Saturday afternoon. After their shift, Jose and Roy changed into their casual, off duty clothes and took a couple of their male patients by wheelchair to the nearby shopping mall where the men could buy groceries and cigarettes. At about 5pm, once the nurses had dropped their patients and friends back in the nursing home, we sat down for a chat at KFC. They invited another friend,

Rommel, a male nurse from Singapore's mental health hospital, to join us. 'We don't do this all the time, even if we want to, we can't take them [our patients] out every time after our shift because we are tired, but we feel for them. We are like their brothers', said Roy. Roy, the eldest among the three, recounted that he worked for ten years as a staff nurse in a private hospital in Dagupan city in the Philippines. Previously, he had worked for one year in Saudi Arabia, but did not like it and returned to the Philippines before trying his luck in Singapore. Jose and Rommel, however, were fresh graduates from Baguio, with only a little voluntary nursing experience in the Philippines after graduation. Singapore was one of their first experiences of a nursing job. In Roy's case, being a nurse was what he always wanted. Seeing three of his aunts working as nurses, he said, 'they are working in the US … you can see how if you work in the US as a nurse, you can have so many savings … so since my childhood I aspired to be a nurse'. Among his five siblings, four are nurses. Roy declared, 'it's nothing like male cannot be nurses. If you are female or male, you can be a nurse'. Rommel admitted that, 'at the beginning, nursing is not my first choice, but I have one auntie who is a nurse, she influenced me to take up nursing, because it is so in demand. Then I realized it's also very professional. In the Philippines, many men are nurses'. All three men expressed shock upon coming to Singapore, as they related their experiences to me:

> **Rommel:** I have some regrets, because in the Philippines, if you are a nurse, you are really respected. People will see you are a nurse and they will say WOW. But here, I only realize when I come here, if you are a nurse, they don't respect you.

> **Roy:** I was working as a staff nurse in the medical surgical ward in Dagupan. Then for Singapore, I thought why not, it's an opportunity to access other countries. Even if you are a nursing aide, you can still get the Singapore stamp in your passport. But if you are a staff nurse, you are limited to take care of your patients only - you don't do other jobs. Before, we are the one to make the decisions in the wards, but now we cannot make any decisions at all. It's a big adjustment for me to be a nursing aide - [shakes his head and clenches his fist at his heart] this is the biggest difficulty for me.

> **Jose:** Yeah, for me, in my mind, I thought the nursing is the same as in the Philippines. But when I come here, I'm so surprised. We have to

change the diaper of the patient - this is our work. What, I say? I am shock that I have to do this kind of work.

Roy: In the Philippines, the relatives do this ...

Jose: The most challenging part is being a helper – *katulong* – to someone who is not related to me. I feel so bad that I am not there to even help my own family, my grandparents, I am not washing their, you know, *pangsai* [Hokkien: shit]. But I will do it for them, these people who are not my own relatives.

Roy: In the Philippines, nursing is a lighter job. The work is lighter, mostly paperwork, we do the i.v., give medicine – it's more professional. Here we also clear the garbage, mop the floor, we do the dishes ... [Resigned, he laughs]. This is what we have to do as nursing aides. And for me, it's that -when you are so tired, you work such a long day - still, even then your patients will spit in your face. Even you are talking, your mouth is open, they will spit. Sometimes I am thinking: this is my profession? What am I doing? Even in the Middle East, they would never do this.

Rommel: I don't want my younger brothers to do nursing; I don't want them to go through what I have to go through now. It's really difficult. It's like we're dogs here. Here it's not about keeping the money, but keeping the dignity.

My conversation with Roy, Jose and Rommel demonstrates how the boundaries of gender, nursing and migration uncomfortably intersect with each other. While some male nurses from the Philippines are pressured into it, many others see it as entirely natural because of the professional associations that nursing has in the Philippines. It is not necessarily labelled as work that is inherently for women, as it is in many other countries. Rather, nursing is regarded as a category of labour that is linked to progress and success, regardless of gender. The impression I got from Roy, in particular, is that nursing itself is not what challenged his dignity and masculinity, but it was performing domestic tasks as nurses. To them, this fitted neither with their sensibilities as nurses nor their masculinities. Nursing may confer social distinction but the melding of the domestic – and hence the overtly feminine – with nursing (which in the Philippines, is becoming decreasingly feminized as an occupation) disrupts sexual divisions of labour and produces visceral reactions among these male nurses. Drawing on Pierre Bourdieu

(1986: 474–475) these visceral reactions come from the overturning of the 'social order' and the need for 'distinction', which 'demands that certain things be brought together and others kept apart'. Many nurses are aware that when they leave the Philippines they will be working as nursing aides, but they do not necessarily realize what this work feels like until they get to Singapore. The men's stories also highlight that caring relations are not inherently harmonious, but also marked with resentment and disgust. Their comments illuminate the uncomfortable history of Filipinos in service labour around the world that involved not only women, but also men who worked as low-level service staff in the US Navy, and as domestic servants in the colonial Philippines (Espiritu, 1995; Rafael, 2000; Parreñas, 2008).[13] Historical experiences of emasculation and subservience among Filipino men have left enduring legacies. Dress and uniform similarly recall these legacies. While in the Philippines, the all-white uniform is something which nurses display publically – it is something which, to a certain extent, transcends one's class background and one's gender – in Singapore, the uniform is something to hide. During my chat with the three men, Jose explained the different uniforms to me. He pulled his own uniform out of his bag, 'this is the one for nursing aides. Doesn't it look like I work in a hotel, like a waiter? It has so many flowers, this is not a nurse's uniform'. This explanation reminded me of another time when Glenda, a nurse in the same nursing home, recounted how when she and her friends leave work in their blue uniform and go to the adjacent shopping mall after work, they are sometimes approached by toilet cleaning staff who see the blue uniform and ask, 'do you work here too?' The history of Filipinos working as servers around the world is thus again alluded to with discomfort (Espiritu, 1995, 2002; Tadiar, 2004; Tolentino, 2001; Parreñas, 2001; 2008).

---

13. Rafael (2000: 69–70) writes about male servants in colonial households. He says that, 'it is useful to point out the heterogeneous composition of domestic workers in the Philippines at the turn of the century. Colonial households employed predominantly male servants, both Chinese and Filipino ... . Unlike the United States at this time, where the majority of domestics were females. In the Philippine colony over three-fourth of the live-in servants were males, with a smaller number of females working as day laborers, usually doing laundry. Hired as wage laborers, rather than indentured servants, those who lived in the house were referred to by the infantilizing and desexualized Spanish term *muchachos* or "boys" in English, regardless of their age'.

The Embodied Practice of Labour

Filipino migrant medical workers are fundamental to Singapore's land-scape of care being a part of Singapore's drive to become a world-class centre for biomedical sciences and health, as well as a crucial support for an ageing population and Singapore's poor. Within the various institutional and private spaces of care in which migrants embed themselves, discussions about professionalism and about the nature of care labour manifest themselves in the everyday encounters and experiences of migrant workers. Not only is there a different perception of the nursing profession in Singapore, compared to the Philippines, but, there is also a regular embodied *practice* of labour powerfully highlighting the differences for migrants. Filipino migrant nurses challenge both their own initial self-descriptions as innately caring workers, while confronting the 'stigma of the domestic': a stigma which has always existed within the nursing profession, and which is accentuated as OFWs are stereotyped in demeaning ways as unskilled and 'subservient' care workers. The high expectations that migrants have upon leaving the Philippines, and the weight of expectations attached to them as particular kinds of citizens with great potential for social mobility, are shaken in Singapore.

Feelings of shame circulate alongside migrants' attempts to differentiate themselves as professionals, distancing themselves from unskilled care labour. Boundaries are prominent in the lives of nurses, not simply in terms of cultural boundaries (as I will discuss further in the next chapter), but the powerful boundaries of their labour identities. While they maintain that nursing in the Philippines is a respectable, lucrative profession, *within* the community of medical workers, in Singapore, one encounters distinctions and divisions related to one's nursing sub-specialty, one's rank, one's institutional setting; divisions and distinctions which are accentuated through the migration process and which threaten to challenge the public face of the Filipino nurse's labour. Boundaries of care, gender, nationality and profession are continually broken down and reasserted. Yet the desire for something better persists. Ironically, many nurses – frustrated as they are with the deprofessionalization of their labour in Singapore – still aspire to move to other countries, even as caregivers.

This chapter has also highlighted the notion of service as contradictory. On the one hand, service is linked to the profit-making, customer-oriented service sector, in which healthcare is increasingly playing a key role. Service in this context is highly skilled and highly valued. On the other hand, and equally central, is the subservient care labour that services the global economy – this is especially linked to the history of Philippine labour migration. The religious inflections of service make the picture more layered. Service in this sense is associated with care for the poor and the sick, but this interpretation detracts from the professionalized image of nursing. Filipino migrants do use the term service in the religious sense at times to add moral legitimization to their service jobs, which often are degrading (I remember one male nursing aide saying with resignation and not much conviction, 'oh well, whenever I feel frustrated I just have to tell myself, nursing is about sacrifice, serving God'). Care and service take on multiple and indeterminate inflections in the contemporary global economy.

What I suggest, however, is that migrants' experiences of shame are not simply a consequence of a politics of exclusion by Singaporeans towards migrant care workers, or the victimization of Filipinos in the world. It is more a story of differentially articulated understandings and expectations of medical and care labour, and also domestic work, in the Philippines, in Singapore and in the world. In the next chapter, I shall explore the mutual negotiations of difference and the boundaries of inclusion and exclusion among and between Filipinos, different groups of migrants and diverse Singaporeans. This is a story of a wide range of people interpreting and understanding caring relations differently. The supposed universalisms relating to medicine and care are challenged by questions of race, nationality and morality.

CHAPTER FIVE

Caring for Others

Cultural Encounters in Asia

'In nursing, you always have in your mind the idea of the other'. This simple statement from a male nurse to whom I spoke in a Manila hospital powerfully captured the notion that in medical work one must intimately know the other for whom one cares.[1] I ask what it means for migrants to care for and work alongside people of different nationalities, religions and 'races' in the intra-Asian context of migration. Thus, I investigate the relations of care in which migrants engage, and their understandings of such relations in a landscape of immense cultural diversity.

The previous chapter explored how the Singaporean public often stereotypes Filipinos as 'low-status' domestic workers, particularly given that nursing is not valued as a profession in the same way as it is in the Philippines. Filipino medical workers attempt to challenge the view of the low-status Filipino migrant worker through the assertion of their professional identities. In this chapter, I look specifically at how migrants articulate these professional identifications and a sense of belonging through their cultural encounters with the diverse others they care for and work with. Within the specific field of care work, it is important to consider the nature, depth and significance of the relations that Filipino medical workers develop with the 'others' that they meet and care for in a multicultural Asian city. Does the physical and emotional intimacy of medical workers' interactions with those they encounter create empowering intimacies, or tensions, fears and ambivalences? Migrant nurses leave the Philippines with a confidence in their ability to care for people of different ethnic, religious, linguistic and national backgrounds. My

---

1. He also referred to the word *kapwa* when speaking about the 'other', explaining how in Filipino the notion of *pakikipagkapwa* refers to how one relates to other fellow human beings.

informants frequently used self-descriptions such as 'we respect others' and 'we have compassion', implying that a certain cosmopolitan 'openness to the world' (Werbner, 1999) is taken for granted as part of their identities as Filipino nurses.

The ethnographic context of Singapore is fitting for an exploration of Asian pluralisms, given its heterogeneous and mixed population with people of different backgrounds, as well its own history of migration. Timothy Harper (1997: 262) has pointed out how:

> ... nation-building has been an experience fraught with tensions. Singapore's history has also been shaped by other seams of political thought: the complementary rhetoric of regionalism; the lure of transnational ethnoscapes; the advocacy of wider civilizational values; a tradition of cultural hybridity; competing meanings of 'multi-racialism'.

These seams of political thought that have been central to Singapore's history occupy its contemporary landscape, with its new arrivals of migrants, with a similar vigour.

The cultural politics of care takes on specific dynamics in this intra-Asian context. My informants find comfort and familiarity in caring for other Asians, while also opening themselves up to new friendships and cultural exchanges with the people they care for. However, this sense of comfort was often limited, even fleeting, given the prominence of mutual cultural stereotypes and prejudice that I repeatedly encountered. Divisions based on nationality, I found, were more salient than I expected and indeed more than my informants might have expected. I observed a number of narrowly held affiliations and practices based on stereotypes about race, language and one's 'place' in a hierarchy within Asia and the world. Competition for distinction is rife among diverse Asians and notions of 'First World' and 'Third World', 'modern' and 'backward', 'caring' and 'uncaring' are prevalent in their seemingly ordinary judgements of others. The ambiguities of the care profession and the intimacies of the workplace offer distinct ways of charting and understanding these dynamics. These encounters frequently raise morally charged questions about how one ought to care for a family, about the hesitance of being touched by someone perceived as different, and about the role of profession and of faith. Filipino migrants develop social critiques of the types of caring relationships they encounter, assert their global aspirations and their moral reflections on how to live and care for others, while simultaneously creating distance from those who, they believe, do not share such aspirations and moral views.

This chapter is an exploration of how citizens of different Asian nation-states regard one another in the context of regional inequality. It examines the aspirations, expectations and identifications of Filipino migrants, and of other migrant groups that they encounter in Singapore. Thus, this study gives us a chance to observe Asia through the eyes of migrants who cross borders within the region and who see their encounters with other Asians as culturally familiar, yet alien. In these journeys, migrants often perceive the others that they care for and work with as 'fellow Asians'. Yet, through the process of migration and their encounters with others, migrants begin to think critically about the tensions and complexities within their own region and find that their understandings of the region and its 'values' are far from self-evident. These understandings are not based on state pro-nouncements about Asian values; rather, the very notion of Asian values is contested through the views that citizens of different Asian nations have of each other. It is notable that my informants, through their narratives and comments, place Asia as a distinct cultural entity apart from the 'West'. The 'West', however, remains a dominant imaginary and point of reference for them. It represents the 'elsewhere' that they seek and wish to reach, a glamorous and desired destination, at the same time as they see it as an entity holding morally inferior values. As with the construction of Asia as a singular entity, the West too is spoken of as a monolithic cultural bloc; it goes without saying that this too is an artificial construction with ambiguous boundaries. Rather, Asia (and the West) are complex and diverse assemblages of nations, peoples, languages and identities. This is therefore a story about the fashioning (self and collective) of Asians and their ambivalent relationships to each other and to the West.

This chapter is about the transformations in migrant subjectivities as they experience and evaluate a range of intimate cultural encounters during their journeys as medical carers in the region. It gives space to the narratives of migrants themselves on the shifting representations and understandings of their national and regional identifications.

'We are all Asian'

Generally, nursing, and medical work, have often been associated with a cosmopolitan ideal embodying an inherent openness to the other. One

Filipina nursing assistant, Angie, working in a Buddhist nursing home in Singapore, explained the intrinsic universality of her work: 'To me nursing is universal. It's not you're from this country, the nursing care is different from that country. It's all the same. Caring, showing your compassion regardless of race. It's a patient, a human'. From this point of view, nursing is perceived as a universal profession, a medical mission, and a humanitarian calling. Nursing is celebrated as a 'medico-social service' as one book on nursing in the Philippines describes it, high-lighting the contributions of figures all over the world to the nursing profession (Giron-Tupas, 1961). Filipino nurses self-identify as people with cosmopolitan inclinations, open to a wide range of others. In such self-descriptions, there is a suggestion that a part of what it means to be Filipino is to be cosmopolitan, echoing the notion of a 'rooted cosmopolitan' (which moves away from an association of cosmopolitanism with an elitist and universalizing definition) (Appiah, 1997; Pollock *et al.*, 2000; Falzon, 2005). Migrants confidently anticipate cultivating new relationships across cultural boundaries in their journeys as globally mobile professionals in medical care. Yet, as I shall demonstrate, their sense of openness and the perceptions they hold of self and other take on specific forms in this context of migration within the Asian region. Filipino medical workers work alongside migrants from Burma, China and India, take care of Singaporeans of different backgrounds (who may for instance, speak Tamil, Malay, Hokkien, Cantonese) medical tourists and other migrants from the Asian region. Thus, more relevant to this ethnography than an open-ended and abstract cosmopolitanism, is how cultural encounters in the sphere of medical work foster a sense of pan-Asian belonging across ethnic or national differences within the region; or whether migrants encounter a reinforcement or tightening of such boundaries and differences.

The notion of 'Asian values' has been called upon frequently in Singapore's post-independence history, and more recently in pan-Asian gatherings, such as Association of Southeast Asian Nations (ASEAN) meetings (Almonte, 2004). That Asians have values, which are some-how unique and different to those in the West, is a belief present in much government rhetoric in Asia, as well as in everyday interactions. This idea has been a cornerstone to the Singapore government's brand of capitalism; aligned with the West economically but self-defined as distinctively Asian in the cultural configuration of its capitalist society, with Asia holding 'morally superior' social values (Chua, 1995; Chua and Kuo, 1995; Hill and Lian, 1995). This 'us' and 'them' rhetoric, referring to Asia and the West respectively, is mirrored by many Filipino migrants that I met. But at the same time as they espouse this sense of Asianness, they also point to the complexities within this vast notion. The majority of the migrants whom I encountered acknowledge that their journeys to Singapore are journeys within Asia. There is a grounded familiarity with its spaces, its people, its forms of sociability and modernity. For many Filipino medical workers, an openness to others in Singapore is made easier by this feeling of shared Asianness. Most informants recall that they did not have any problems when they first arrived in Singapore 'because it is also an Asian country; there are many different nationalities here but because we are all Asian we can get along easily'. The geographical and perceived cultural proximity of another Asian country provided a sense of comfort to the medical workers I spoke with while they made their decisions to move to Singapore; it made the move seem less daunting. Asia here is understood as a unifying category that is different from the West. Arlene, a Filipina nurse in a government hospital in Singapore, explained that, 'it's easy to get along with Asian patients rather than Western patients. I am a bit scared of this group of people because I always think of the discrimination. So I am more comfortable in Singapore because it is still Asia and the people are Asians'. Another nurse, Mary, said 'adapting to Singapore was easy. I didn't have any problem because it is also an Asian country'. It was reiterated again when I spoke to a group of two Filipino nurses, a Chinese and Burmese nurse. When I asked, 'why Singapore?' there was consensus among them that it was 'because it's an Asian country'. The two Filipinos added that they perceived it to be a good starting point to get used to overseas life before continuing journeys further afield. As an anthropologist with origins in the region myself, I felt that when my informants made these comments in a very taken-for-granted manner, that they expected I immediately would be able to relate to their sentiments.

There are connections felt by medical workers threading together the different histories, religions and people in this geographical region. They imply that the borders within Asia are more porous than those outside of it. It is worth asking whether, for some Filipinos, this feeling of belonging to a community of Asians is something they discover through their migrant journeys to Singapore. Despite the geographical proximity of the Philippines to other Southeast Asian countries, the Philippines has often been thought of as different from the rest of Southeast Asia, more 'Western' and its affinity to an imagined community of Asians relatively new and even contested (Anderson, 1991,1998; Zialcita, 2005). Many people that I met in the Philippines, in fact, would speak of their own nationality story as a mixed one, a crossroads of East and West, often calling upon their Malay, Chinese, Spanish and American heritages (a point I return to later). It is therefore notable that many nurses start off their narratives by suggesting that moving to Singapore was easy because it was also Asian.

Angie, a nursing assistant I met working in a nursing home, suggested that she became a 'better person', through her work as a migrant nurse. She said, '[Singapore] is a multiracial country with many races … so if you work with Chinese you have to deal with them in one way, with Moslem a different way, Indians. So you become flexible in dealing with different types of people and then you are able to adjust to the working environment, with different people around you. I have become a better person, I have a broader mind'. In Singapore hospitals, one witnesses plenty of moments of cultural exchange and translation: nurses learning terms of endearment in Hokkien, communicating in sign-language, joking with colleagues, code-switching between different languages and Filipina nurses helping Malay patients improve their English. These exchanges can enrich migrants' experiences as they open up to new relationships and worlds of knowledge within the category of Asianness.

The stories I heard from another nurse and one of my key informants, Grace, were revealing of the kind of relationships she had with the people she cared for in the Buddhist Nursing Home. Grace, a nurse from Panay Island in the Philippines, was working as a registered nurse in a private hospital in Manila before joining the Buddhist nursing home in Singapore as a junior nurse. She left her son in the Philippines with her sister (as her husband is a seafarer), and worked in the nursing home for four years. She cared mostly for Chinese female patients in one ward, apart from two Malay women and one Tamil woman, and the care she provided to them was all of a long-term nature. A daily routine for Grace was to bathe and clean the patients, feed them, give them medicines, take them to physiotherapy sessions and simply to chat and sit with them.

Grace however, due to the relatively low compensation of this work, changed her job to work as a phlebotomist. In spite of the sudden professionalization of her nursing position in Singapore, Grace felt that she still had obligations to fulfil with the patients she left behind at the nursing home such as meaningful friendships emerging from regular and frequent co-presence. She wanted to spend time with these patients whenever she had the time to go and visit. The following story is about the time when she returned to the nursing home to take one of her former patients – who she calls Auntie – to a Vegetarian Food Fiesta that was organized as a fundraiser in the hospital. Auntie was a Hokkien-speaking lady in her late sixties who had been living in the nursing home for the past five years. A single woman all her life, Auntie worked with her sister to run a small convenience shop in one of Singapore's residential estates.

'Auntie does not have family, she only has me', says Grace, as we walk along to the hospital that day. When we approach, Grace points towards Auntie, 'there she is, she is already waiting for us outside! You see, she's there already!' Grace goes and gives her a big hug. 'Auntie, how are you?' she says gently while holding her. 'Glaaay, Glaaay', Auntie says with her own pronunciation of Grace's name, 'we go *makan* [eat]'. Auntie shows us several coupon books excitedly which she will use to buy things at the food fiesta. Before we leave, Grace waves at another patient, 'that is the Indian man I told you about', she tells me. 'He is so funny, so funny', she laughs as they joke with each other at a distance through sign language. 'His son is coming later I think, that's why he is dressed up. He makes me laugh so much'.

We set off for the food fair, Grace pushing Auntie on the wheelchair. When we arrive at the plaza, it is bustling with people wandering around the numerous food stalls. Auntie chats away in Mandarin and Hokkien with everyone she meets along the way. 'She's so popular', says Grace. They move slowly through the crowds as Auntie buys many different varieties of green tea, coffee, local food and snacks like *nasi lemak*, barley drinks, as well as mobile phone accessories and balloons. Grace tears her coupons off and puts her purchases, in plastic bags, on the hooks of her wheelchair until they can hold no more bags. As Auntie eats *laksa* (noodles), Grace sits with her, helps her, wipes her face and mouth and holds on to her to give her support. After eating, we walk around more and Grace stops to admire a t-shirt. 'Glaaay, Glaaay I buy for you'; Auntie buys her this t-shirt as well as popcorn and several other goodies. 'She's like my mother', says Grace smiling at Auntie. 'She is single, never married, no kids. She has nieces and nephews though. Before when I am so tired during duty, I will tell her, Auntie I have headache, then she will say, 'you sit' and she gives me a head massage. She called me so many times yesterday, she said, "Grace, you coming tomorrow?" She wants to make sure I am coming today to bring her here'. We are at the food fair for a few hours and eventually, it is time to drop Auntie back off at the nursing home. We walk into the ward and we pass patients who are looking listless, curled up and lying down. Grace sees one patient in a funny position and wonders, 'Why is she like that?' checking on her. Grace sees her other patients, hugging them one by one and saying quiet words to them. She pokes one of them saying 'chubby' in Hokkien, continuing a long-running joke between them. 'I miss you', she tells her patient. Moving onto the male ward, Grace laughs with them as they all ask where she had been. Another patient is in a daze, eyes half closed, leaning to one side. Grace holds onto him and tells us (myself and another male nurse) about the time when he would not wake up, 'we threw water on him, he's not waking up, I got so scared', she says, 'I thought he died already. But this one is hard to wake up'.

Grace's constant presence with Auntie (and other patients) is revelatory of the new intimacies and forms of empathy that accompany the 'care for strangers' taking on an increasingly global character. The caregiver and the cared for develop affinities to each other through this daily co-presence, as well as through the sharing of practical knowledge such as language (e.g. Hokkien) and through nurses picking up certain joking mannerisms and intimate knowledge about their patients' bodily and emotional needs – so that they are no longer strangers. It is also notable that class is a point of implicit connection between Grace and some of her patients. They have proximate experiences of socio-economic marginalization (as migrant workers and as low-income Singaporeans) and shared understandings of everyday consumption decisions, as seen, for example, in discussions over which food stall sells the tastiest noodles at the lowest price, the prices of cigarettes and the increasing unafford-

Figure 5: Food fair run by the charitable nursing home (author's photo)

ability of Singapore.[2] The relationship between Grace and Auntie is one that conveys a sense of pan-Asian relatedness which, within the familiar yet delimited category of 'Asianness', allows each to learn from the other, at the same time as it momentarily transcends ethnic, national, religious and linguistic boundaries between self and other. Their connection highlights how the idea of 'caring and being cared for', is at the heart of their relationship (Borneman, 1997: 573)

However, alongside these bonds of trust – as seen between Grace and Auntie – are simultaneous misunderstandings, where relations of care are tinged with prejudice. In the next section, I explore in greater depth how these caring relations are often tentatively formed as the tensions within this notion of 'Asianness' become starkly apparent.

Fragile Affinities

My encounters with nurses revealed that the intimate relationships and affinities with patients are also fragile and ambivalent. The close rapport

2. I am reminded of Pnina Werbner's (1999: 23) notion of 'working class cosmopolitanism' – 'a knowledge of and openness to other cultures'; in this case, in the intimate context of the care home, there are 'close encounters between people from different nationalities [which] results in an esprit de corps, a collective sentiment of interdependency' (Werbner, 1999: 23).

that Grace has with Aunty, for instance, is also at times marked by resentment and accompanied by an acknowledgement of the precarious conditions of commodified care labour. Grace and her colleagues often spoke about how difficult their patients could be in their complaining and bullying, though, this was often a symptom of their isolation and low self-esteem as residents in the nursing home.

While this care for 'other Asians' provides a feeling of immediate familiarity to Filipino migrants in Singapore, it is far from coherent or stable. The moments of familiarity give way to moments of profound disorientation and shock, revealing the ruptures – based on labour, status, race and language – within this community of Asians. In addition, the tangential position of the Philippines in Southeast Asia and the articulation of regional economic inequalities – notions of 'First' and 'Third World' – enter into the picture. The West – as much as it is critiqued for being different from Asia – is still a central point of reference in the self-definitions of many Asian migrants who fashion themselves in its likeness. Postcolonial theory has of course critiqued the binary dichotomy between the 'West' and the 'rest', and between 'First World' and 'Third World' yet these are the very categories that migrants frequently use in their observations. Migrants' experiences and their terms of speech demonstrate how 'postcolonialism is neither western nor non-western, but a dialectical product of interaction between the two' – in other words, whether self-definition is developed through a critique of the West or whether it encompasses a desire to be a part of it, the West as an other is a part of how my informants define themselves and their aspirations (Young, 2001: 68; Spivak, 1999). The West, as I shall demonstrate, may be associated positively with fluency in English, material wealth, a glamorous and mobile lifestyle or it may be associated negatively with a lack of 'family values' and 'community morals'.

Firstly I shall discuss tensions in relation to race and nationality in the construction of the other. The centrality of stereotypes based on these markers in institutional spaces of care was made very clear to me when a senior Singaporean-Chinese nurse shared what she thought were the cultural characteristics of the different groups of migrant nurses:

> Myanmar nurses are placid, they have no strong ambition, they are not risk takers, but they are compliant. They are good middle strata people. They won't be drivers. Indians, we have management problems with

them, they are too submissive and cannot assert themselves in front of dominant male patients; the Chinese from China, they are okay at work, they are happy because the culture is similar to theirs, but they create so many social problems outside; the Filipinos have charm, they are good entertainers. They are drivers, but sometimes they are too passionate, you see how they beat each other up.

The blatant ascription of essential characteristics that this nurse gives to each national group is revelatory of how recent migrants to Singapore are viewed, and more consequentially, how labour is managed accordingly. Racial stereotyping is, and has always been, omnipresent in Singapore.[3] Along with the 'CMIO' (abbreviation which categorizes Singaporeans into discrete racial groups) are ideological constructs about the qualities of each different race, which have endured over the decades (Li, 1989). There has long been talk of a 'Malay dilemma' in Singapore with a number of pejorative comments by politicians or ordinary citizens labelling Malays as a 'backward race', and blaming them for being 'lazy, unmotivated and failing' (Mahathir, 1970; Li, 1989; Rahim, 1998; Long, 2009).[4] Singaporeans see Filipinos in a number of ways. Some perceive them as 'backward' people from a 'Third World' country who work in Singapore as maids – perhaps the most common view. At other times, they are conflated with Malays, or they are seen as a 'novelty', people who resemble Malays but who come to Singapore with different skills, English and a sense of professionalism.

The slippages over race were evident from hushed comments I heard a few times at the nursing home where I did my research. As I sat down to watch the physiotherapy exercises one morning at the Buddhist nursing home, a Singaporean-Chinese nurse came to sit next to me. As we watched the physiotherapy session, she told me:

3. A look at the newspaper archives of Singapore's *Straits Times* (1933, 1950, 1951, 1952) reveals how the issue of race has been prominent in nursing historically. With initial tensions surfacing between European nurses and 'Asiatic' nurses, nursing later grappled with the tensions involving the inclusion of Malay nurses into a Chinese-dominated profession. What is different now with migrant nurses, is that race becomes more deeply entangled with debates concerning nationality and citizenship.

4. Mahathir Mohamad, former Prime Minister of Malaysia, famously wrote in *The Malay Dilemma* (1970) in strongly racialized terms of 'innate' qualities of the 'Malay race', arguing in this text that the value systems and codes of ethics of Malays hindered them from 'progressing'.

Some of the patients can be rehabilitated. Some of them after some time can walk, talk, buy food for friends and other patients. They feel useful. But I won't lie that these patients are difficult. They are intelligent, but difficult … they complain about this nurse, about that nurse. If you work here, you have to be strong; you have to be able to take it. China nurses, no the patients don't complain about them because same skin [she points to her skin]. But yes they will complain about other nurses, because different skin. Darker skin *lah*, they don't want. Especially Malays, the other foreign staff, Filipinos … . But even working with these foreign nurses, I tell you it is difficult; they all want to help only each other because they are same skin.

Similarly, the physiotherapist who I encountered there on a different occasion told me about the challenges of dealing with elderly and chronically ill patients. He said, 'you cannot hit the patient, even if you are a foreigner, I tell the foreign staff. Some of those foreign nurses, I see they slap the patients because they have no patience – I'm just letting you know'. In these cases the role of rumour and blame about and between foreign medical workers, local medical workers and patients underline quite starkly the visibility of nationality and race. The interactions here also involve the very sensitive issue of touch, and who can legitimately touch the other. These comments also reiterate a blurring of Malay and Filipino nurses in some Chinese patients' aversion to being touched by someone of 'different' or 'darker skin'. Nurses too have their own racial theories, demonstrating how such perceptions occur from many directions and not only from the 'host society' towards migrants. One Filipino nurse, Juliet, who works in the surgical operating theatre of a government hospital in Singapore, spoke of her observations on which cultures make better nurses. She related that:

The way of caring for the patients is different back home. Here of course you watch your colleagues when they are working, and you can see that when they speak to the patients they do not even look at them, or touch them or spend time with them, they are only looking at their paper and filling in the forms. And I can see the differences in the cultures. We can say that the Chinese are very fast-paced in their work, and they are always doing their paperwork. The Indians – well they don't care! And the Malays, they want to care, but they overdo it, it's too much. There is no subtlety. We are different, in the Philippines. We touch the patient, we listen, we spend time listening to them. And patients, they appreciate when we do. They like us ... in the ward for private [paying] patients, foreigners ... 70% or more working there are Pinoys because these patients like us.

Juliet's comments reaffirm the existence of mutual prejudices in these plural spaces of work and of care. I remember MeAnn, a nurse who was generally very bitter about Singapore life said, 'I don't like how the Chinese people eat their food, so noisy. I also don't like how some of the people smell here'. Her comment adds to others that I heard about how the Filipino nurse is 'in-demand' because 'we are clean' (*malinis tayo*). Hygiene becomes a racialized quality and the aversion to those deemed to be less hygienic becomes an issue when one's work requires close bodily proximity to racialized others. These comments I heard, and undercurrents I felt, demonstrate striking continuities with earlier descriptions of the links between race, nursing and intimacy in different cultural and historical contexts – from the relationships between the Dutch in colonial Java who instructed their Javanese nursemaids, 'to hold their charges away from their bodies so that the infants would not "smell of their sweat"' (Stoler, 2002: 6); to the explicit entanglements between race and nursing in South Africa under Apartheid and the profound anxieties triggered by the contact of bodies marked as racially different (Marks, 1994: 164). While the racial prescriptions in this ethnographic context may not be as explicit as these historical examples, racialized tensions and aversions are nonetheless palpable in these institutions of care in Singapore. Two years after my period of fieldwork, nursing homes in Singapore were in the headlines with reports documenting the abuse of the elderly by their carers. In both cases, the reports were based on undercover exposés of these abuses, taken through concealed video cameras in wards. The cases of abuse signalled an important need to re-evaluate the system of care. In Singapore, however, the public response which followed was – on news websites and online discussion forums – almost singularly focussed on the fact that most carers in nursing homes are 'foreign', adopting a xenophobic tone as people spoke of the abusive hands of 'foreign others' on Singaporean bodies.

First World, Third World

The tensions also take on an economic dimension. A typical attitude in Singapore is that migrants are 'Third World' people coming to work in 'our First World country'. 'They ought to be grateful' is the tone adopted in many newspaper articles and letters to the editor. Filipinos are regarded as doing low-status service jobs, and along with contract labourers from Bangladesh, India and Thailand, they are lumped into the category of 'Third World' migrant workers.[5] Singapore puts itself in an almost quasi-colonial relation to migrants' home countries. However, migrants do not see themselves as belonging to a singular, homogeneous category. I remember the time during fieldwork when I had planned to meet with Alyssa when she cancelled at the last minute because of a mass casualty case she had to attend to in the emergency department. The case involved a truck full of Bangladeshi construction workers crashing into a tree. Migrant construction workers in Singapore – those who come on the most restrictive work permits – are transported to and from their work places on open-back cargo trucks without any seatbelts. A few of the workers died and many had injuries. Meeting Alyssa a few days after the case, she appeared quite shaken. Telling her flatmate, Cecille and I about it, she said, 'I felt so much pity [*awa*], they are only construction workers, all of them, forty-five of them. I felt so sad. I am helping them but I felt so bad, some of them are in ICU, *grabe talaga* [it's really serious]'. 'Meg', she then asked, 'where is Bangladesh? Is it a civilised place? Because so many of them are only construction workers. Why they are all here like construction workers? *Nakakaawa* [it makes me sad, it makes me feel pity]'. Alyssa's encounters with these Bangladeshi workers, caring for them after a serious accident, opened her up to feeling pity for fellow migrants at the same time as she expressed, with some horror, the stark differences between herself (and Filipinos more generally) and these Bangladeshi men who in her eyes are fundamentally 'other'. To her, they are from an unknown country, doing menial jobs that do not correspond with her view of 'civilization' and moreover, they are mostly Muslim (while Alyssa is Catholic).[6] There is a clear hierarchy within the category of migrant workers, with each group making judge-

---

5. This discourse is echoed in some economic and policy oriented works (e.g. Severino and Salazar's (2007) 'Whither the Philippines in the 21st Century?'), portraying the Philippines as a country in social and economic crisis compared to neighbouring Asian countries, or in statements made by politicians and the media about the Philippines being the 'sick man of Asia'.

6. Bangladeshi construction workers in Singapore come from a range of socio-economic backgrounds, some previously working as dentists or accountants in Dhaka.

ments on who is 'humane' and who is 'backward'. Alyssa's reaction to the incident also highlights the limits of the category of Asianness. Clearly, the geographical and cultural imagining of Asia has its exclusions; in this case, Alyssa is not sure where to place the Bangladeshis.[7] They are not 'like us' in her view, nor are they 'Western', and it is thus worth drawing attention to the other markers such as race, labour and religion which come into play in migrants' perceptions and divisions of the world.

Money is often used as a marker of social status among Filipino nurses. As Juliet (quoted earlier) suggested, Filipino nurses are often chosen to work in the wards for private and international patients; these patients include medical tourists who come to Singapore for treatment. The way she boasts about Filipinos working in these wards and how they are well liked reveals that caring for 'private' or 'international' patients (those with money) is more desirable and prestigious. That said, none of my informants worked directly on a daily basis with these wealthier, international patients (who in any case, are a minority). It is also worth noting that, in spite of early claims of being at home with the Asianness of Singapore, Singapore is not perceived as a desirable location to settle down in and what my informants really want is to move on to the West which they associate also with higher earnings, greater material wealth and a dignified future. Their elevated status as nurses overseas and the promise of social mobility which this holds, in the eyes of those at home in the Philippines, depends in part on making it to the West, especially 'America', perhaps even more so than their domestic worker compatriots.

The pride in caring for international patients and the appeal of moving on to the West is also related to their English language skills. One of the ways through which Filipino nurses counter the 'First World' attitudes of Singaporeans, is to assert their own superiority by speaking better English than Singaporeans and migrant nurses from other countries. While there are four official languages in Singapore – Mandarin, Malay, Tamil and English – English has long been the first language in national education, adopted at independence for the 'fashioning of a new productive work-force' and 'retained as the language of the new

---

7. As we will see in Chapter 6, domestic workers, unlike Alyssa and other nurses, are far more open to migrants from other countries in their social lives and are far more likely know about Bangladeshi migrants in Singapore and about Bangladesh.

government, law and commerce' (Chua and Kuo, 1995: 110–113). This usage of English existed alongside the promotion of bilingualism and the retention of 'mother tongue' classes in school curriculums. As a result of a multi-lingual environment, most Singaporeans communicate in Singlish, a hybridized version of English that incorporates words and expressions from Malay, Chinese 'dialects' and Tamil. Singlish is therefore a particularly Singaporean version of English and is often a strong marker of Singaporean identity.[8] In the Philippines, while Filipino (based largely on Tagalog but inclusive of the contributions of other languages and hybrid expressions) is the national language, English too is widely spoken. Indeed, 'speaking good English' is a quality that many Filipinos pride themselves on and is often used discursively by migrant agencies to promote Filipino workers (Tyner, 2004). Filipino medics in Singapore emphasize that good English is one of the key qualities that sets them apart from their Burmese and Chinese colleagues. However, Singlish, for Filipinos, is a source of amusement, as well as irritation, particularly when they have to speak it themselves to be understood. Ana, a senior staff nurse who has worked in Singapore for six years and who has clearly picked up traces of Singlish herself, complained that 'sometimes my patients will tell me they cannot understand me, even if we both speak English. I feel like telling them that I speak English based on the English dictionary, what about you?' On another occasion, MeAnn complained saying, 'I think the English here is very bad. I don't like to speak like them, but sometimes I have to so that they understand me. Sometimes I read the dictionary at night to make sure my English is not as bad as theirs'. In these instances, Filipino medical workers assert their superiority over Singaporeans' Singlish, underlining their unwillingness to speak it and exposing their fears that this much sought after 'skill' of theirs is being degraded in the Singapore context. Parallels can also be drawn with studies of Filipina domestic workers in Singapore and Taiwan who similarly critique their employers for their 'bad English' (Lorente, 2007; Lan, 2003); in the latter case, the domestic workers

8. Singlish is a marker of Singaporean identity in everyday life in Singapore. The Singapore state, however, worries about Singlish being so widely spoken. 'Speak Good English' for instance, is a government campaign that sponsors columns in the newspaper on 'how to speak good English'. Economic motivations, Singapore's relations with other countries, and tourist impressions of Singapore, are some of the key factors behind this campaign.

suggested that 'they [the employers] have more money but we speak better English!' thus challenging and reconfiguring the unequal worker-employer relationship (Lan, 2003).

I observed that speaking good English is seen among Filipino nurses as a most desirable trait. The cosmopolitanism one demonstrates with English fluency and with a 'good accent' (and by this, they mean American accent) incites envy. Many nurses for instance, told me how much they like Kris Aquino, the television personality and daughter of the late former President Corazon Aquino, because 'she speaks English so well ... like an American'. On another occasion, when I spent the afternoon at my informant Ella's house watching *YouTube* videos with her, her sister and three kids, Ella remarked with surprise that the Korean girl group the *Wondergirls* speak English so well. 'Wow', she kept saying, 'they are Korean and they speak so good English'. This ideal of 'good English' among my informants spurs them to imagine and plan further journeys towards the West.

Speaking about these distinctions created among Asians, the observations made by Jeff, an occupational therapist, were particularly memorable. Formerly, Jeff worked to rehabilitate soldiers in the Philippines through occupational therapy. He always dreamt about going to the US, but first followed his girlfriend to Singapore and found a job. Working with elderly patients in Singapore, he says he finds fulfilment in his job, but is not satisfied with his Singapore life. Discrimination, he says, is a key part of that:

> Every place you go there is discrimination. I can feel it ... for the patients, if you are foreigner, they will make you prove yourself, they will test you, are you good enough? Then also [he says with a softer voice], sometimes they do not want to be touched by us. So there is discrimination if you are a Filipino or foreigner here. And then, the colleagues, the Singaporeans, I am aware that Philippines is a Third World country and Singapore is a First World country, but really they act so much more superior to us, like really looking down, they think they know more than us, that's how I feel with the Singaporeans.
>
> I can see also that they are not equal. The Chinese – maybe it's because of Lee Kuan Yew, or I don't know what – but the way they act it's really like they are so hard-working, they act like they are smarter than the other races. Don't you think so? Definitely it's not equal here for Singaporeans. I know because they all come to me – the Chinese will

come to me and say something about 'this Indian didn't do this thing properly, or that one is lazy'. Because the Chinese cannot complain to the Indian, but they can come to me because I'm foreigner, so I get it from all sides. Just the other day I was talking with my colleagues, most of them are Singaporean. We are talking about Australia, some of them are thinking of migrating to Australia but then they are saying if we go to Australia, we will face this discrimination; they are scared to go there because of that. Then they asked me what do I think? I just told them 'to be honest, it exists here also. There is discrimination here also'. Then they were silent, they didn't say anything. They don't realise there is discrimination here also. But if we go to those Western countries, we will all be Asian – they won't see us as Chinese, Filipino, Singaporean, to them we are all just Asians. But here I don't know why, even we are all Asian; they like to make so many categories [he gestures boundaries and boxes]. Don't you think so? If we go to the West we are all the same, we are all Asian. I don't understand how they don't see that.

Jeff's comments here expose the multiple and contradictory layers of discrimination. The category 'Asian' and all the competition to make distinctions and hierarchies in relation to other Asians is pointless in his eyes, for such distinctions collapse on another level, when they may all be seen as homogenous in other countries, no matter which 'type' of Asian they might be.

Care and Morality

The debates about other Asians ultimately lead to bigger questions about morality, the arena of care lending itself to a number of moral observations and reflections. Through this lens we see how nurses may develop connections with patients based on religious affinities (often transcending ethnic lines), where patients' ideas about how to live and how to care for the self and others resonate with migrants' own. In other instances, Filipino nurses encounter an alien sense of morality among Singaporeans when observing relations of care within the family and society, and attribute this to different national cultures of caring.

In the last month of fieldwork, Grace got involved in a cycling accident while on an outing on her day off. With a broken collarbone, she herself was in the role as a patient, experiencing much pain and was forced to take medical leave from work. She was given painkillers by the doctor but did not want to take the painkillers. It was at this point that she alluded to her own beliefs in healing; healing that is not based on taking pills. She complained that Singaporeans just take pills and more pills and that they have no idea what damage they are doing to their body. The next time I accompanied her to the hospital for her doctor's appointment, she told me how in the Philippines, she would first go to a *hilot* – a faith healer – before going to a doctor in the hospital. As soon as she began talking about the *hilot*, Grace could not seem to stop. She continued with one anecdote after another:

> I remember one time my *até* (older sister), Ruth, she have so many pimples on her face. Then we go to the dermatologist, she gets so many creams, this kind and that kind, so expensive. It never worked. Then my mother says to her, you just go visit the *hilot*. So I went with her. Then I cannot believe what I saw with my own eyes. The *hilot* put the ginger, rub it on my sister's face, then it's like real sand is coming out of her face, then the pimples are gone. I got goose bumps, you know? I cannot believe it; it's like a magic. From that time I believed it. Then when I am pregnant, I am in labour for 16 hours already, the baby is not coming out. I am bleeding so much; I am so scared. Then my mother called the *hilot* to the hospital. She put the leaf on my stomach, just placed it there and then I'm shocked, just a few minutes after she placed it there, I am already giving birth. So even I'm a nurse, I believe this.

Grace said that her mother would always encourage her daughters to see a *hilot* before anyone else. As we sat in the waiting room of the hospital clinic, both Grace and I were immersed in the stories she told of *hilots* in the Philippines. She was still fascinated herself by the miracles they perform. Grace was apprehensive about how the doctor was going to treat her. In spite of working in a biomedical setting every day, it is not one in which she is comfortable as a patient. Previously, I had only heard discussions among Filipino nurses related to the nursing and care in biomedical settings. When meeting Ella on a different occasion, I asked if she too goes to a *hilot* in the Philippines. Ella told me:

> Of course scientifically, if you go to the doctor, they will maybe ask you to go for a surgical operation or something, but I believe you can also be healed if you go to the *hilot*. If you have faith, miracles can happen. We call them faith healers … you will not be healed if you don't believe. They will say their own prayer … their own Catholic prayer,

then the oil that they use is blessed oil. Even me, even [though] I am a nurse; I am hesitant to go to the doctor. You know they say that this society is a modern scientific society, but I still believe in our elders … Maybe some people will say it is old-fashioned but I really believe that if we get sick, if we have pain, it is because of the spirits and the ghosts we have disturbed. If we disturb the spirits (*kaluluwa*), which are around – in the trees, below in the ground, in the sky – and if we do anything to disturb them, we will fall sick. It is related to our health. Sometimes, the doctor cannot explain everything.

Illness in this view is caused by a disturbance to the spirits. The belief in spirits among these nurses, and the excitement with which they tell me about faith healing, reveals that, even as they present themselves as pioneers of biomedicine, biomedicine is not sufficient in dealing with their own experiences of illness. Their scepticism of pills as cures and their awareness of complications in surgical operations, suggest that their own nursing expertise is not what they would necessarily choose when they themselves need care. Grace, when saying that Singaporeans only believe in pills, suggests that there are shortcomings in the social and moral fabric of Singapore.

Both Ella and Grace, though telling me about the *hilot*, are also devout Catholics who attend church regularly in Singapore. *Hilot*, as faith healing, is not purely a 'folk' healing practice, but one entangled intimately and in hybrid ways with Catholicism in the Philippines (Cannell, 1999). Faith healing (which encompasses the practices of *hilot* and more) is where divine intervention, called upon through prayer, heals an ailment. When Ella and Grace meet Catholic patients, they feel they can connect to them on a different level, compared to non-Catholic patients, because of this broad belief in faith healing. Healing is bound with questions about how one ought to care for the self and one's family in times of illness and pain. That Ella can go beyond the call of 'biomedical duty', and offer spiritual support to her patients, she says, leads to a different bond; a relationship where religion transcends ethnicity or nationality. In these moments, nursing, with its religious inflections, can foster a sense of openness to others transcending national boundaries (even if new boundaries are raised between Catholics and those of other religions). Many nurses express surprise to see Catholics of so many different nationalities in Singapore; the novelty of seeing Chinese, Tamil and

Eurasian Catholics in Singapore gives them a wider sense of belonging to their religion. Ella once told me:

> Sometimes I see patients who believe, especially Catholics. It is really touching to see patients with belief. You can really speak to them about God, but for those who don't believe, you cannot say God does these things, you cannot tell it to them. But you can really talk about it to Catholics. Once I had a neurosurgery patient, a Singaporean but devoted Catholic. She was quite ill. By her bed, she had all the pictures of the saints; she offers prayers to them, the devotion books, prayer oils, water. Her daughter is crying because she thought she is the reason why this happens to her mother. Her mother had been telling her, I know you are so busy, but please make time to go to church. Then the daughter still never goes and her mother falls ill. So she is crying because she understands that these things happen for us to seek God. God has a plan. So really it's true. If something happens there is a reason.

Ella indicates that it is difficult for her to speak to non-Catholic patients about God and in fact there is a concerted effort made by Filipino nurses to self-censor and to be 'politically-correct' in Singapore, out of fear of offending patients of a different faith. It is perhaps for this reason that nurses do not seem to be aware about non-Catholic beliefs in healing (not based on biomedicine) widely existing among Singaporeans. My informants often view non-Catholic Singaporeans as cold, disenchanted people who do not have a spiritual and moral world beyond their faith in taking pills. What is puzzling, however, is that when I ask them if they have spoken to other patients about say, beliefs in healing in Buddhism or Taoism, they often deflect the question by saying, 'Oh I don't know anything about those other beliefs', or 'in the hospital, we don't allow any Chinese medicine'. The observation among nurses that Singaporeans do not have beliefs beyond biomedicine does for instance not fit anthropological explorations of Chinese spiritual beliefs.[9] It might also be a case of deliberate misrecognition; a way for some of my informants to hold a position of moral superiority with their spiritual Catholic subjectivities, in contrast to those who they believe put them in shameful positions.

---

9. Toulson (2009) and Ju (1983), for instance, have written about Chinese spiritual beliefs in Singapore, while Manderson (1996) wrote on medical pluralism in colonial Malaya and the encounters between local healing practices and biomedicine.

Social Critique

The example of faith healing shows how spiritual and religious orientations can foster a sense of openness to others that transcends national
boundaries *within* the community of Catholics that they encounter.
However, Filipino nurses' other observations about the morals in
Singapore's society remain negative and they often provide sharp social
critiques of Singaporean forms of sociality. The work of nurses puts
them into direct interaction with notions of care; they witness the ways
in which Singaporeans care for their family members, which in turn
spurs them to ask themselves what it means to care for others.

Nurses comment about the absence of morality in many spheres of
their Singapore lives. One nurse, Alyssa, would remark that the Chinese
are always sick in the hospital because of the manner in which they live
their lives, always stressed and complaining and suggested that they
ought to have smiling classes (which indeed they already do in the hospital orientation programme). What Alyssa suggests is that Singaporeans
do not know how to live with others and that this also manifests itself
physically in illness.

Discussions about the family are also central in these social critiques.
The absence of relatives in hospitals, for example, is perplexing to many
nurses who argue that 'they [Singaporeans] don't even know how to
take care for their family. In the Philippines, the relatives are always there
in the hospital. If it is your mother in the hospital, how can you just leave
her?'[10] Aurelie and Remy, two nurses who work as operating-theatre
nurses, mention that one of the things that struck them the most about
Singapore is how the elderly are treated. 'In the Philippines' Aurelie says,
'we will always take care of our family. The Chinese especially, they don't
have anyone with them. They are all alone. We notice the Indian and
Malay families are there more. The work, work, work culture, it makes
me sad.' Remy adds, 'we are raised with different values. Here it is the
culture to put in the nursing home right?'

The medical workers in the nursing homes had similar sentiments.
The occupational therapist Jeff, says:

---

10. Datta *et al.* (2010) also write about how migrants involved in care labour in
    London develop social critiques about the lack of care they observe, comparing it
    to an ethic of care in their own countries. A 'feminist' ethic of care is broadened to
    a 'migrant ethic of care', where care is given national character.

I feel sad. They all have kids, most of them. Then you just imagine how they have tried to put them in education, they work so hard for them. Yet they still understand why their kids put them there. They say my son or my daughter is very busy. But you can hear from their stories … you hear how hard they worked for their kids before. For me family ties are so strong in Asian culture, so how come? If you put them in the nursing home, it is all there, easy. Then the relatives just fade away.

Jeff suggests that Singaporeans are 'too Western' in their orientation to family and are not 'Asian enough'. He continues, 'many things about here surprised me. They are Asian but they are trying to be like the West in the way they live'. Migrants' surprise is accentuated by the fact that they are in another Asian society, where they do not expect such behaviour within the family. These are the very debates that occupy the public sphere in Singapore, with statements from the government about the decline in 'family values' and 'filial piety'. Nurses are thus implicitly engaging with these anxieties, positioning themselves as migrants who know better how to care for elderly members of the family (New Paper, 2010; National Family Council; Straits Times 2009a; Toulson, 1999; Hill and Lian, 1995). The irony here is that migrants critique a population whose state has long trumpeted the care of family as a core Asian (and specifically Confucian) value in contrast to the moral vacuum of the materialistic West (Barr, 2002). Migrants not only mirror this Singapore state discourse which homogenizes the vast West in terms of 'their' values (glossing over the possibility of any diversity within the West they imagine) but they also begin, with surprise, to align Singapore with those very values.

In all these cases, care is reclaimed as a distinctive and naturalized trait of Filipinos. It is in these encounters with patients' families and in witnessing their apparent lack of care, that Filipinos distance themselves to any kind of 'Western' identification (even if in other spheres, for instance, in speaking English, in their Catholicism, or in their aspirations for onward migrations, their identifications are more ambiguous). Migrants speak in binary terms about their encounters with another Asian nation in which they feel dislocated because it lacks Filipino virtue. Interestingly, however, this binary between Singapore and the Philippines is occasionally interrupted when migrants reveal that by Singaporean they mean Chinese, and that Malays and Indians can at times share in these Filipino values; a sign of the subtle dynamics between inclusion and exclusion that migrants negotiate in Singapore. Even here, however, assertions are not always consistent. At one moment, I hear about how Malay-Muslims are just like Filipinos in their culture and ways of life when it comes to caring for the family. At other times, I hear the same nurse warning me not to travel anywhere south of the central Philippines on my research trips there because 'those Muslim people' live there. They thus shift from identifying with shared Asian values in some moments, to constructing values as distinctively Filipino (and Catholic) in others.

To proclaim care for one another as Filipinos, is how migrants fashion themselves – for their families, their nation and for God – into virtuous overseas citizens of the Philippines in the face of more stigmatizing labour experiences. My informants cope with the shameful experiences of their labour by asserting a form of citizenship and subjectivity that gives them a sense of moral superiority in comparison to 'the others' they encounter in Singapore. However, their discussions of shared Filipino values and solidarities remain rhetorical. In practice, there is a whole range of class and status related tensions between Filipino nurses and their domestic worker compatriots overseas.

Self-Reflection

Migrants do not necessarily arrive in Singapore with clearly articulated ideas about Filipino or Asian cultures, values, norms and moralities. Rather, I suggest they start to articulate these identifications upon encountering differences overseas, particularly when they encounter other Asian citizens in Singapore. Though they begin with a sense of openness to others, mutual forms of prejudice and exclusive self-definitions sit in contradiction to this initial imagined openness.

The experiences of Filipino medical workers who deal with care and caring relations on a regular basis are particularly well placed to bring such questions about cultural identifications to light. Moreover, migrant engagements with care in a plural landscape provide them with an opportunity for self-reflection and the expression of their views on how to live. Such encounters with difference and the accompanying self-reflections, take on distinctive dynamics in this migration story within Asia. Asia – and its 'other', the West – are categories which migrants use frequently to make sense of their experiences of crossing borders. On the one hand, they express pan-Asian sentiments when speaking about their journeys to Singapore, while taking advantage of this sense of familiarity in developing close friendships with others (such as that between Grace and Aunty). But more commonly, my Filipino informants debate what 'Asian values' really mean, while articulating the distinctions, in hierarchical and judgemental terms, between different kinds of Asians. Expectations and assumptions about Asian moralities are both reinforced and undermined through these encounters. In discussions of family values and care, migrants are particularly critical of Singaporeans who they assumed would be more Asian. 'The strategic character' of self-essentialism is most evident, as is its instability (Herzfeld, 1997: 26), in the way that it emerges in the inter-Asian encounters of migrant nurses in Singapore. Meanwhile, migrants continue to dream of futures in the West, underlining again how the postcolonial economic, political, military and cultural power of the West still lures, even if ambivalently (Young, 2001: 5). Even if migrants critique a homogeneously imagined West, they still aspire to move on to the countries they associate with it.

It should be said that while migrants express this notion of virtuous Philippine values, this unified voice does not always reveal itself as such in practice. In their own practices of sociality, medical workers often distance themselves from fellow Filipinos, particularly those in domestic work, in an attempt to assert their own definition of the overseas Filipino citizen. It is hence too simplistic to argue that a sense of Filipino national identity strengthens abroad, because the cultural identifications expressed by migrants do not always sit comfortably with their identifications of class and status. In fact, their own experiences complicate the uses of such categories and point to the limits of conceptualizing the world in these terms.

CHAPTER SIX

The Boundaries of Migrant Sociality

In the walk towards Lucky Plaza, one already hears the sounds of Filipino. Filipinas are sitting outside the mall on benches, in the entrance hall of the mall, along the staircases, picnicking, chatting, taking photos with friends in a bustling atmosphere where people are making a claim to this public space in the heart of Singapore's shopping street. Shops are doing a thriving business catering to the large Filipino migrant community in Singapore; remittance agencies and cargo shops have queues snaking around the mall, sari-sari (variety) stores sell cosmetics and groceries from the Philippines, beauty salons are full, many of the stores are named after specific regions of the Philippines, such as Bicol stores and Panay stores. There are the smells of Filipino food as I walk past the eateries, reminding migrants of a feeling of home through their senses.

Excerpt from field notes

T he question of how migrant medical workers from the Philippines confront, negotiate and challenge what it means to be a Filipino citizen in the world has been a central and recurrent one thus far in this ethnography. They negotiate different cultural definitions of care labour, what it constitutes and who is expected to perform it, as well as the moral debates surrounding care and intimacies in culturally plural spaces. These questions re-emerge in the socialities of different Filipino migrants in Singapore. Particularly, I explore how relations between different kinds of Filipino migrants are central to understanding the social lives of Filipino medical workers and how some of migrants' concerns raised in previous chapters manifest themselves in the forms and boundaries of migrant sociality. The actual practices of sociality call into question this notion of the 'blood of a Filipino' (mentioned in the Introduction).

The excerpts from my field notes opening this chapter describe Lucky Plaza, widely known as the mall synonymous with Singapore's Filipino community. It appears as a form of transnational community in the truest sense: Filipino migrants gathering, eating Filipino food together, speaking in a mix of Filipino and English (or in other regional languages of the Philippines such as Ilonggo or Cebuano, depending on where they are from), shopping in Filipino stores and sending money and boxes home. It is a landscape demonstrative of the oft-cited characteristics of transnationalism as, 'a social morphology, as a type of consciousness, as a mode of cultural reproduction, as an avenue of capital, as a site of political engagement and as (re) construction of "place" or "locality"' (Vertovec, 2009: 4). Yet further exploration of the social lives of Filipino nurses revealed that the image of a cohesive transnational community in Singapore does not hold. What this ethnography illuminates instead is a far more intricate landscape of migrant sociality where the construction and negotiation of boundaries, particularly *amongst* the large number of Filipino migrants in Singapore, influences the forms which migrant social lives take. Questions of occupation, class, status and aspiration are the main lines along which boundaries form and dissolve.

This chapter is concerned with two key points. First, it examines the quiet lives of Filipino migrant nurses, an observation that took me by surprise. Migrant nurses are not engaged with the wider Filipino migrant community in a public manner, nor do they engage significantly with Singaporeans. Rather nurses' friendships are restricted to smaller groups of friends, often Filipino flatmates, small groups of colleagues, or online social connections with relatives and friends elsewhere. These social connections are often intimate and private – based on shared aspirations, religious experiences, living arrangements and labour identifications – rather than forming a public collectivity with a common goal. This chapter argues that these nuanced forms of belonging are not necessarily captured within the labels of either a 'transnational migrant community' or a 'host society'. There is perhaps a need for a rethinking how we make sense of the plural forms of migrant sociality, and to reconsider in novel ways the idea of community in the lives of migrants.

Secondly, and relatedly, this chapter argues that in order to understand the social practices of nurses and the boundaries of inclusion and exclusion that they draw implicitly and explicitly, the stories of Filipina domestic workers in Singapore must be brought in as a point of comparison. Domestic workers' long-standing presence in Singapore has made them, in the minds of many Singaporeans, representative of migrant workers from the Philippines. A number of Filipino migrants I met – both domestic workers and nurses – are confronted with this pejorative image of the Filipino worker and often seek to move beyond it. The relation between domestic workers and nurses, moreover, is particularly important given that both are involved, broadly-speaking, in care labour. As we have seen, anxieties over the overlaps within the category of care labour manifest themselves in migrants' social practices beyond the workplace, in the divisions and distinctions that appear between domestic workers and nurses. I suggest reasons for why the socialities of domestic workers and nurses appear so different and explain how concerns with profession, class and citizenship feature in their attempts to construct boundaries. Yet there are also moments where the boundaries are not so stable and that these two groups are more proximate than they initially appear. This chapter demonstrates that 'nurse' and 'domestic worker' are categories that become more firmly established through the migration process, with the daily work of 'boundary maintenance' becoming a key preoccupation (Barth, 1969), though there are also certain exceptions to the patterns that I observed. It is nonetheless important to look at the processual character of sociality and identification rather than starting with pre-conceived categories or static understandings of 'community' and 'identity' (Hall, 1994; Cooper, 2005).

The Quiet Lives of Nurses

In my early days of fieldwork, I spent much of my time either at Lucky Plaza or attending events organized across Singapore for the 'Filipino community'. These included concerts, special Filipino movie screenings and beauty pageants. I remember that one 'Philippine Idol' concert I attended consisted mostly of professionals working in managerial roles and in information technology, and a handful of domestic workers. I also remember attending a special service for the annual 'International Day of Migrants' at a Catholic church, where most of the Filipino migrants at the service were domestic workers. As I began to speak to people at these events, I was surprised by a marked *absence* of nurses. As I got to know nurses better, I found that they rarely go to Lucky Plaza, apart from a monthly visit to remit money and perhaps eat some Filipino food. It is not a social or public gathering space for nurses in the same way that it is for domestic workers on Sundays.

Generally speaking, nurses spend most of their time in Singapore at work or at home in their neighbourhoods. They work six-day weeks on shifts, which means that their day-off is not fixed on a particular day of the week. Time off is often spent chatting with family (who live in the Philippines and elsewhere) online on *Skype* or *Yahoo Messenger*, playing computer games, watching *The Filipino Channel* (TFC) and doing household chores, such as laundry, cooking and ironing. When my nurse informants occasionally go out to shop, it is most likely to be at a convenient neighbourhood mall frequented by other Singaporeans rather than Lucky Plaza. Most of my informants, being Roman Catholic, go to church regularly, at least once a week in a small group together with their Filipino flatmates or family members (if they are in Singapore). However, they do not actively participate in church life beyond attending Mass, apart from a couple of nurses I met who sing in.the choir of a Catholic church through which they developed an intimate group of choir friends. Occasionally, nurses gather to celebrate someone's birthday. Sometimes, non-Filipino colleagues and neighbours are invited, whereas at other times, they tell me how they wish they could invite their 'Indian' and 'Muslim' friends, but because Filipino food has a lot of pork, they 'do not want to offend' them.

Whenever I visited Até Ella on her day off, she was at home with the children. Her routine on her day off is typically to wake up late, to cook lunch, *merienda* (an afternoon snack) and dinner, play with the children, take naps and spend time with whichever visiting relative who was around (as there was always a relative from the Philippines there to help look after the children since both Ella and her husband Joel work). Occasionally, she takes the children to visit Joel at his workplace (a hotel bar), or to go swimming or to the zoo during school holidays. Time off is therefore quality family time and rest, rather than time spent connecting with the wider Filipino community in public spaces. I also recall visiting

Alyssa one afternoon when I made the mistake of ringing the doorbell instead of knocking softly. The rest of her flatmates were asleep as they had been on night-duty, including her husband, who works night shifts at a food court in a shopping mall. Alyssa was the only one awake that afternoon and was watching a variety television programme ('*Wowowee*') on TFC with the volume turned down, while hanging up the laundry. During the time that I was there, a few flatmates walked out bleary-eyed to cook lunch, making little conversation with each other. Others were at work. It was rare, Alyssa said, for them all to be at home at the same time, which is why it did not feel as if ten of them were sharing a three-bedroom apartment. I would always meet Alyssa in her flat or in the McDonalds in the shopping mall beneath her flat. When I met Grace, it was often at the shopping mall closest to work, where she would have something to eat after her shift in the food court. When visiting Grace at home (in a small room she was sharing with one other Filipino nurse), she was usually obsessed with playing *Farmville* on Facebook, a game which requires one to manage a farm, employ workers and barter produce. As she played, she would give me running commentary on her different strategies and giggle when she noticed that other players of the game around the world were also incidentally Filipino. She and these other Filipino strangers would chat to each other on the *Farmville* platform in Filipino. Sometimes, she would tell me how she longed to go out dancing to rock music, but then reminded herself that she is not so young anymore, that she is now a family girl and that her husband would not like her going out dancing. Meanwhile, Nelia told me that she often spends her weekends browsing web forums about migrating to other countries, while chatting online with her husband and son in Manila. I found that these kinds of routines filled up my field notes recurrently. It is difficult to write about social events in the lives of Filipino nurses given that much of their free time is based on routines and even have somewhat of a mundane quality. The majority of nurses live their lives in Singapore quietly and privately.

Often recurrent observations stand out when one encounters an exception, such as when I met a group of evangelical nurses who diverged from this picture I have painted, and to whose stories I shall return. For now, I will briefly mention Jessie, a flatmate of Alyssa, whose lifestyle did not fit the 'norm'. Jessie works as a junior nurse in the same hospital as

Alyssa. A single mother, Jessie came to Singapore to support her daughters and to live her own adventure. In contrast to most other nurses, Jessie tends to spend her evenings going to pubs and discotheques with Singaporean men she meets on Internet chat and dating websites. She would meet them at night after her shifts, returning home in the early hours of the morning, according to Alyssa. Jessie once mentioned that her Singaporean lovers often would buy her new clothes, make-up, shoes and in one case, a plane ticket home to the Philippines to visit her daughters. Jessie also dresses differently to other nurses and wears more make-up than the typical nurse. Alyssa often talked to me about Jessie, and was a little disturbed about how she was living her life in Singapore. Jessie's life, as an exception, revealed that certain distinctions made between service workers ('nurse', 'sex worker', 'caregiver') are at times blurred. It also reaffirms the norm of the quiet lives of the majority of nurses I met. Their (not-always-conscious) cultivation of an image of a righteous, modest, career-oriented, family-oriented self was one that appeared to hold in the experiences of many nurses working in Singapore.

Nurses retreat on days off and spend time at home or with small circles of friends. Given my initial assumption that nurses too are a part of the identifiable 'Filipino community', the fact that they live private lives away from the community in Singapore was a surprising finding. This observation brought to light the fact that the Filipino community exists for some Filipino migrants and not for others. The patterns of nurses' social lives highlight the need to look beyond relations between migrants and the host society, for not only is there great variety within these categories, but migrants also define the boundaries of their social lives in relation to other migrants. Nurses' social lives are a marked contrast to other accounts of transnational migrant or diasporic community life, which typically refer to a collective sphere for fellow migrant nationals to debate moral and political issues at home and abroad, to share cultural expressions, or to build relationships, organizations and projects across borders in order to connect their lives and networks abroad to their home countries (Werbner, 2002: 251; Gilroy, 1994; Basch, Glick-Schiller and Szanton Blanc, 1994: 246–248). However, I did not find that nurses generally identified with a transnational community in this sense of the term. In the case of my informants, 'not belonging' to the Filipino migrant community is their own choice, rather than the deliberate exclusion by others. In another sense, however, they form their own micro-communities: intimate and private familial or friendship groups. I use the idea of a micro-community in a loose sense, in order to capture the contingency and small scale of nurses' chosen social connections. Transnational *connections* are, however, important to them as they use *Yahoo Messenger* to stay in touch with the Philippines and participate in web forums with Filipinos in countries further afield, but they do not engage much with a Filipino public in Singapore. Neither do they actively cultivate relationships with Singaporeans beyond those with their patients or immediate neighbours. In a sense, their social lives have the quality of being liminal, just like other aspects of their lives. Rather than an explicit political, public and moral engagement with the transnational community, they concentrate privately on their family and future-oriented selves. However, I suggest that a micro-politics of sociality is where migrants negotiate and construct their own vision of how a Filipino ought to live and behave whilst abroad. The moral and political engagement with issues concerning the transnational Filipino migrant in the world is not visible, but certainly not absent.

The quietness of nurses was accentuated when I compare it to my interactions with domestic workers during fieldwork. I now turn to look more closely at their social experiences.

Lively Domestic Workers

The reserved comportments of many nurses were a striking contrast to the comportments of domestic workers I met. As mentioned earlier, domestic workers often occupy the spaces of Lucky Plaza on Sundays. On those days, it is bustling with Filipina domestic workers dressed up on their day-off, having picnics, reading community magazines, going shopping, sending money home, and meeting migrant workers from other countries who also enter this lively space on Sundays. It is a moment of release from a week of working and living within the confines of their employers' homes. From this point of view, they are more publically visible as they gather with other Filipinos, attend events for Filipino migrants and participate in transnational and translocal activities. However, I also met domestic workers in a range of other spaces across Singapore, for instance, at churches, at local NGOs and at Sunday skills classes. While spending time in Filipino community groupings, many overtly display the cosmopolitan knowledge they have picked up in Singapore about other cultures, languages and religions from their wider interactions. Particularly memorable was the open manner in which domestic workers interacted with me as an anthropologist. At a Sunday skills class that I went to observe, the students were keen to chat with me from the moment I stepped into the room, welcoming me into the class and asking me many curious and friendly questions. When they heard that I could speak some Filipino, they tested what I knew with great delight and listened intently to my stories of travelling in the Philippines. One student, Melissa, asked me 'Are you Indian by race? Which part of India?' 'Chennai', I say. She stamps her feet in excitement. 'I know someone from Chennai, my friend Ms Priya. She takes me to Little India for vegetarian food. Are you vegetarian? I eat the masala there! The language in Mumbai and Chennai is different right?' she says proudly. The women communicate with pride their knowledge about the 'other cultures' they have encountered in their migrant lives. While we wait for the class to begin, Jennifer, another student, pulls out photographs of her own children in the Philippines and photographs of the American children she cares for in Singapore, telling me how old they are and how much she loves them.

The Filipina domestic workers I met were far more open than most of the nurses I knew. This was a common observation I made among most of the domestic workers that I met, in spite of the range of experiences captured within the category of 'domestic worker'. Ironically, they are the most restricted of Filipino migrants in Singapore, yet the most visible and experimental.[1]

I turn now to the stories which a domestic worker, Lilibeth (Lili), recounted to me in order to illustrate this.

---

1. When writing about domestic workers, I am not including those who are not given a day-off. Rest days are on Sundays, but in some cases employers only give domestic workers this free time every fortnight or every month. At the time of my fieldwork, a weekly day-off was not a mandatory condition in domestic workers' contracts. However, since 2013, as a result of the advocacy efforts of migrant organizations, a minimum day-off per week is now mandatory, though employers still have the option to pay domestic workers compensation instead of giving them a weekly day off.

The first time I met Lili was at the skills class for 'Care for the Elderly and Special Children'. She was sitting in front of me wearing a bright yellow outfit with a matching headscarf, and was the only Filipina Muslim in the class (and the only one I had encountered during the time I was conducting research). She was one of the students who immediately started chatting with me in a very friendly manner. We met again a few weeks later at 7:30am at the McDonalds in Lucky Plaza, on her weekly day-off. When Lili arrived, there were just a few minutes of small talk, after which she launched into her story without any inhibitions. She simply prefaced her story by saying, 'I love to talk and talk, but my story is a sad one - I forgot to bring tissues'.

She first told me about her upbringing in the Philippines. Losing her mother at a young age and raised by her father who gambled away family wealth, Lili as the eldest child was left to care for the family and for herself, dealing with family quarrels with relatives who were after their land and who wanted to see her family 'low, like rats'. She could not afford a college education, so instead worked in a restaurant where she met her husband-to-be. Before the age of 20, she married a '"5-6" ... an Indian'.[2] They had two children together but what followed was a messy marriage, with her Indian husband going back to India and never contacting her again. She took over his money-lending business in the Philippines, but Lili said it was just about 'luck or lose'. What is more, 'when people don't pay you back, it really makes you talk bad to other people. I don't like how I am becoming'. 'I had no hope' she said, left with little money and two children to support. Lili continued:

> At that time, I had a good friend in Singapore. Her name is Marla. She told me to go to Singapore to work, she arranged the agency for me. I had to sell all my jewellery and everything to go to Singapore. She asked me are you sure you can deal with it? You have to be a helper. I was scared because I have never washed, ironed - in my place, we always have a helper. But then I became a helper.

---

2. In the Philippines, people of Indian origin are often referred to as '5-6' or Bhumbais. The '5-6' refers to the money-lending businesses which many Indians (of primarily Punjabi origin) in the Philippines operate in cities as well as in small provincial villages ('they come in the morning to lend "five" and return in the evening to collect "six"', as one informant explained of their interest rates) – it has pejorative connotations.

And so she ended up in Singapore, changing employers a few times when she was not happy with the conditions of work. One of her former employers worked in a private condominium where she fell in love with the Malay security guard working there. He was already married with children, but Lili said, 'you know Singapore men, they can find prostitutes so easily, but he is a good Muslim so I know he is serious'. Lili and this man, whom she calls 'my husband Abang' only meet on Sundays, as he spends the rest of the week with his wife and family. Lili believed his promise to leave his wife for her one day. She told him that she would convert to Islam for him. She does not wear the headscarf every day; it depends on how she feels. Lili explained that she sometimes goes to Catholic Mass with friends in the morning, before attending a class for converts to Islam later in the day. Lili's religious practice is flexible. As she related, 'I am raised in a Catholic family, but for me there is one God, doesn't matter if it is Allah, God, Jesus. Sometimes I go to church in Singapore if my friends invite me. In the Philippines I used to go every Sunday. But for me religion is you don't lie, you don't steal, doesn't matter which God'.

Other migrant workers from India and Bangladesh, Lili explained, are apparently very curious about why a Filipina wants to be Muslim.

> Some are curious. They ask me, "are you Indonesian?" In my Koran class, I also have other Filipina friends; they are also Catholic but convert to Muslim. But for me I am the one who chooses to be Muslim, I love to wear *hijab* [headscarf]. But some Filipinas who converted and wear this *hijab* are still wild. Allah tests if what you say is true.

Lili aspires to learn the Koran and to change her comportment towards modesty ('I want to behave myself') and piety, as her story was peppered with utterances of 'Insha'Allah'. She does not tell her employers about her Muslim identity on Sundays, while her family tells her that if she wears the headscarf when she is in the Philippines, people will think that she is a terrorist. Meanwhile, she aspires to fulfil her childhood dream of being a nurse by taking these classes at the skills centre. On Sundays, she spends time at classes, with Abang and also with her Filipina friends at Lucky Plaza.

A few weeks later, I accompanied Lili, Abang and two of her friends Marla and April (also working as domestic workers in Singapore) to the Jurong East Swimming Complex. It was Abang's treat for Lili's birthday.

Along the way in Abang's car, Lili and her friends teased Abang, listened to Singlish jokes on the phone, and imitated accents. We spent the day taking photos, sitting in the sun eating the Filipino food that Lili proudly prepared, and swimming. 'This place is so beautiful … *ang saya saya* [such happiness]', Marla sighed. I remember them looking wistfully around at the water slides, at the floats and at the families. 'Tomorrow work. Today we enjoy, we free'. Later on, Lili started to question Abang again about when he would leave his wife. The mood was dampened briefly as a reminder of the transience of the fantasy-like experience at the swimming complex.

Distinctions

Why are Lili's story and the social lives of domestic workers important for an understanding of Filipino migrant socialities in Singapore?

I was struck by my encounters with domestic workers given how different they were to my encounters with nurses. The process of contacting nurses and the challenges getting them to open up to me was a gradual process of negotiation and building trust. Domestic workers, however, were immediately eager to tell me stories of the risks they take and the melodramatic occurrences of their migrant lives. I was drawn by the manner of these encounters and it became a methodological observation, which shed light on notably different patterns of sociality and on the relationship between nurses and domestic workers. Nurses were always more guarded – 'why Filipinos?' they would often ask with a hint of suspicion. They related their stories to me initially in a muted manner, with the deeper layers of their stories only emerging over the course of several meetings.

Lili's story is especially memorable from the dramatic and candid way in which she recounted it, the range of the characters in her stories and the immense level of detail she revealed to me, a near stranger. It was a sad story of vulnerability, recounted in a mood of suffering, while simultaneously being a story of optimism, adventure and pride. Lili's story, it appears to me, captures in true spirit the notion of 'the working-class cosmopolitan'[3] as she cultivates relationships with a range of others, takes risks, asserts her agency in changing her employers, experiments

---

3. 'Working-class cosmopolitans' are working-class migrants who '[open] up to the world' and who 'familiarize themselves with other cultures and know how to move

with religious practices and with the freedom she does not have in the Philippines (Werbner, 1999). Lili's story speaks to some of the more recent research on domestic workers which has gone beyond a purely political-economy approach to demonstrate, alongside experiences of vulnerability and immobility, their more creative social engagements, aspirations and self-transformations.

The comparison between nurses and domestic workers is also important because of earlier discussions on the ambiguity of care labour in Singapore, and the domesticized character of nursing. The experiences of nurses in Singapore must be seen as relational to those of domestic workers, and vice versa, since they often compare themselves to each other. The domestic worker has a high visibility in academic discussions, in the media, and in worldwide perceptions of the Filipino migrant. The public discourse in Singapore on Filipina migrants often has a sensationalized or moralistic tone either highlighting cases of abuse and victimization, or criticizing their behaviour in public spaces. This image is taken up by the migrants themselves and challenged.

I can offer a few possible explanations for why there are differences in the social lives of nurses and domestic workers. I suggest, however, that even with the prevalence of such distinctions, there are many overlaps.

Firstly, it is important to remember that many nurses feel that they are in transit in Singapore. The majority of nurses that I met do not intend to settle in Singapore. From the start their lives are geared to move on to North America or Europe. The social lives of nurses are consistent with their spatial and temporal orientations. Singapore is perceived as a place to work rather than a place to build a life; time off is spent speaking to the people they have left in the Philippines, with those whom they happen to live with and planning ahead for a future elsewhere. It is not surprising that many discussions among nurses centre on studying for exams, looking into opportunities abroad and filling out applications to work in other countries. The idea of temporariness is therefore relevant to understanding the patterns of nurses' socialities, which I shall deal with in more detail in the following chapter. Domestic workers also aspire to continue their overseas adventures in Spain, Canada and Italy (and some do). However, I speculate that domestic workers in their time

---

easily between cultures' (Werbner, 1999: 18-20). This idea challenges the belief that only 'elite' migrants are 'cosmopolitan'.

off, regardless of whether they have intentions to move on elsewhere or not, still cultivate social relationships in Singapore more willingly given their relative isolation during the week in their workplaces. I also suggest that the process of finding job opportunities in other countries for domestic workers is slower and more difficult, given that they have less time off and limited access to resources to plan onward journeys. They also lack the medical professional networks that nurses deploy, which makes moving on a more concrete dream for nurses, and a more distant dream for domestic workers.

Secondly, the difference between domestic workers' and nurses' socialities can be explained in part by their different mobilities in Singapore since they often do not hold the same type of visa. The rhythms and structures of the lives of nurses and domestic workers mean that they rarely occupy the same spaces across Singapore, and are out and about at different times of the week. As explained in Chapter 2, the work visas for junior and staff nurses (the 'S-Pass') and the work visas for domestic workers (the 'work permit') come with a different set of rights which enable or disable certain forms of mobility. Domestic workers are required to live in the homes of their employers and are often prevented from going out during the week. Sunday, for those who get a weekly day off, is the one day per week when they go out and express themselves with friends, outside of their working environments. It is a day of release from a week of relative immobility and constriction in the household and its surrounds. Meanwhile, nurses work six-day weeks, mostly on shifts. Their work involves dealing exhaustively with several kinds of people on a daily basis (patients, relatives, doctors and other nurses). When they finish work, they retreat at the end of the working day, staying home for rest and peace – they have their own private and independent spaces to go home to, even if these are in shared apartments. Domestic workers do not really have a space or a home in which to retreat, since they live in their places of work, in their employers' homes and often in very cramped conditions. The rhythms of their lives are therefore significant: nurses retreat, while domestic workers go out to express themselves. Nurses and domestic workers do not necessarily cross paths often. It is relevant to mention my interactions with Joy, a student in the skills class who was keen to share her story with me but who was not given time off by her employers apart from a few hours every fortnight to attend the class. She wanted to help me with my research and therefore decided to post me a handwritten letter telling me about her life in Singapore.[4] It revealed a lot about how different the mobilities of certain domestic workers compared with nurses and other professionals are. It is also notable that the growing number of NGOs in Singapore advocating for migrant workers' rights focus largely on domestic workers (alongside male construction workers). Some domestic workers seek humanitarian and legal help from these organizations; some of them are also empowered into action and advocacy in association with these NGOs and they therefore also develop relationships of trust and support with Singaporeans in this capacity.[5]

Finally and importantly, I shall explain the different forms of migrant sociality as inextricably linked to anxieties about the image of the Filipino in the world today. In response to the dominant stereotype that stigmatizes overseas Filipinos as low-skilled, vulnerable and victimized workers, the question of how to (re)define what it means to be a Filipino abroad is a recurrent preoccupation of migrants, both nurses and domestic workers. I suggest that such preoccupations are also linked to the varying possibilities for obtaining citizenship or residence rights in the countries to which they migrate, and to a politics of class in the Philippines.

Citizenship, Empowerment and Aspirations

I have previously outlined how care evokes a sense of shame among Filipino medical workers. Seeing themselves as professionals, yet being confused with maids or caregivers is something that many medical workers resent. A part of this resentment manifests itself in the social lives of migrants. Some nurses make it a clear point that they are superior to domestic workers. Many nurses emphasize that they deliberately avoid Lucky Plaza on Sundays because 'It is always so crowded with those DH'.[6] Ana, for example, is quick to say,

> I don't like to go to Lucky Plaza. Some of the maids, I know they prostitute themselves; some of them do have this underground business.

---

4. See Appendix C for Joy's letter.
5. Nurses facing exploitative working conditions can also approach these NGOs but are perhaps less aware of them given the different social networks they inhabit.
6. 'DH' stands for 'domestic helper'.

And then those men from I don't know what countries, they come and then you see these Filipinas with them, you know they want something else.

Her frank comments demonstrate her scorn of the intimate relationships that some Filipina domestic workers have with Bangladeshi men. The 'Filipina–Bangladeshi' relationship is scorned by both professional Filipinos and also by Singaporeans, who see their anxieties about migrant sexualities displayed in these relationships. Such moral panics are closely linked to the view held by the Singapore state and the general public that contract labour migrants are labour commodities whose only role in Singapore is to work. In comments that nurses make about these intimate relations, they are 'absorbing the dominant society's racially stigmatized definition of Filipinoness … middle-/upper-class professionals are among the most sensitive to the underclass image of their nationality in Singapore' (Aguilar, 1996: 123). I also remember some offhand comments made by nurses expressing irritation with maids who show up in church 'indecently dressed' and who are so 'noisy' (*maingay*). Nurses feel themselves belonging to a different class in the way that they ('modestly') dress and in the way they talk and carry themselves (even if this is not always consciously asserted). I reiterate the story told at the very beginning of the book when my Filipino teacher Ms Cherry told me that one can easily identify a Filipina nurse from the way she dresses and the way she carries herself. It is related to the habitus that a nurse cultivates. Nurses present themselves in Singapore as a different kind of Filipino citizen. They see themselves as having higher morals than the domestic workers who might give the nation a 'bad reputation' and they simultaneously pity these domestic workers as they reassert their higher social position.

Domestic workers, meanwhile, note the snootiness of some nurses they meet, well aware that nurses make it a point to assert their superiority. I remember the story a former domestic worker, Mary (now married to a Filipino man and in Singapore on a dependent's visa), told of being in hospital and the haughty treatment the Filipino nurse gave her, immediately asking, 'what is your work here?' Mary also spoke of how the nurse never smiled, did not respond to the call bell promptly and did not bother to come and talk to her, 'even though we are both Filipino. I don't know why she is acting like that'. Many nurses are also 'PRs' (permanent residents) in Singapore. Resentment is often expressed among Filipinos who are not PRs towards those who have PR status. Marla, Lili's friend, spoke about her employers as snobbish PRs, 'now I have Filipino employer – but not good'. Abang, Lili's husband then asked, 'I thought if Filipino they would be more understanding?' Marla responded, 'not like that brother, even now Filipino have so many differences. Those PR, I never imagined Filipino can be like that. They are so high and superior, like we are just nothing'. Marla then mocks the way they speak with their pretentious accents, much to the amusement of the others in the car, '"Marla, have you done this? Marla where are you going, Marla you come home by 7pm, ok"'. I also remember a Lucky Plaza beautician complaining about 'those Filipino PRs' being the ones with 'the biggest attitude,' who think they have everything and feel the need to show it off to the rest.

One's official residence and visa status and the extent to which one has rights, or potential rights, of citizenship in Singapore is something to flaunt. It is used to demonstrate that one is not at the bottom of the hierarchy of migrant workers but someone who can settle and have an identity apart from that of the OFW. It proves they are desirable enough by the state to be granted residence or even citizenship (though ironically, this is not always what nurses want). Nurses' quietness is a statement of citizenship showing how to be 'well-mannered' Filipino neighbours but not in a public or demonstrative way. Nurses also turn defensive when they find this status threatened in Singapore. In inhabiting micro-communities, they do not aspire towards a public engagement with neither the Singapore nor the Philippine state.

Although nurses may have PR status, it is domestic workers who are more politically engaged in Singapore, making claims as active Filipino citizens about their labour rights and seeking to participate more in the society, even as they are denied legal and citizenship rights in Singapore. These formal exclusions, however, do not serve as an absolute barrier to rights activism and engagement. They themselves attempt to redefine the stereotypical image of the Filipino migrant by participating with NGOs in advocacy, campaigning for better working conditions, utilizing their networks and expressing themselves through music and dance within the framework of Singapore's constrained political society.[7]

---

7. Robyn Magalit Rodriguez's (2011) work on Filipino transnational labour activism in Saudi Arabia is a parallel example of activism for recognition even in the absence

Domestic workers also participate in activities which are not directly associated with political advocacy, but which give them a greater sense of belonging. There are many domestic workers who do not see their current lack of PR-status or citizenship rights as a hindrance for feeling a sense of belonging in Singapore, or in potential future destinations. There are different ways in which they demonstrate this. Some domestic workers may participate in beauty pageants attended by large crowds of domestic workers where the contestants – parading their national costumes and evening outfits – are presented as follows: 'This is Rose from Ilocos Norte. Her dream is to be a nurse, she hopes she can study more and realize her dream'. The next contestant 'believes most of all in the value of education'; another 'hopes she can go to Denmark or Canada'. During the question and answer section, a typical answer followed the lines of: 'I want to do my best and be compassionate; caring for others. I want to help others', to the loud cheers of their friends. My nurse informants would never go to such an event, yet the beauty pageant illuminates the kind of success and glamour some domestic workers aspire towards. Many domestic workers also take practical steps to achieve this, by enrolling in skills classes on Sundays, to improve themselves and their prospects. I now return to the scene of a Sunday morning class set up for domestic workers on 'The Fundamentals of Nursing Aide'.

On a Sunday morning at 9am, sixty Filipina students – and a few Indonesian and Burmese students – gather in a small classroom in a private school in central Singapore. The tables and chairs are tightly packed together. There is much excitement, gossip and laughter as these women meet their friends after two weeks. Over their Sunday fashion clothes, the students wear uniforms: white t-shirts with the school logo printed on them. This is a training school set up by a Filipino pastor in a Baptist church to provide 'upgrading courses' for domestic workers. The women who enrol spend a good part of their day off every fortnight attending these classes.

The class begins with Mr Ken, the teacher (a nurse by training), coming in and asking his class: 'What is nursing? We all have our own concepts of nursing. So what is nursing to you?' One student puts up her

of citizenship and labour rights.

hand and reads the definition in her textbook: 'Sir, nursing means holistic care'. 'What else?' Mr Ken asks again, but this time there is silence in the room. 'A certificate to go to Canada or Denmark huh?' he jokes with his students, 'see, for some of you, this is what nursing means!' as the class erupts into giggles. Over the next three hours, there are discussions about the fundamentals and definitions of nursing; about anatomy, ageing, symptoms of illnesses and discussions about care, including care for the self. The latter is taught through a model of 'Maslow's hierarchy of needs', where the various stages are explained with reference to love, family and financial concerns, all of which affect migrants' daily lives. At one point in this discussion, a student in the front row stands up and says, 'how can you take care or help others if there is something lacking in yourself, right Sir?', arguing her point that nursing is not just about taking care of sick people. Mr Ken then tells the class that:

> Self-esteem is your inner self. I know, when we go to the Philippines, our self-esteem is *very high*. That is reality right? Don't deny! You have come from Singapore; abroad we earn dollars *not pesos*. So when we are there we boost ourselves, we see those who are not working, we have the feeling that we are helping them.

The students nod in agreement. He continues with self-actualization: 'How many have reached this stage? ... If you have reached self-actualization, you would not be in my class,' he states plainly. During the rest of the class, the students eagerly volunteer answers to the questions Mr Ken poses them. Teaching is interspersed with jokes to keep the students engaged. The students are also told: 'as a caregiver, see your purpose, they [nursing homes] might absorb you, when you get your training certifications'. He also warned them: 'don't play with your profession. I don't want to shock or scare you, but this is the reality, the life of nurses. Soon you will be a part of the nursing family. You must discipline yourself. I will mould you as professional nurses here'.

The skills class consists of a group of domestic workers who try to set themselves apart from the rest, challenging the image of the domestic worker as exploited, victimized or engaged in illicit activities. In their aspirations for self-transformation, they hope to possess slightly more than the average domestic worker. Some of them mirror the discourse among nurses about Lucky Plaza, saying that they try not to spend too much time with other domestic workers there. Many of these domestic

Figure 6: Domestic workers performing at an event on their day off (author's photo)

workers are fashioning themselves to display a comportment similar to those of nurses. In this case, they are studying to become certified caregivers and nursing aides, in an attempt to professionalize their work. At the end of their course, I accompanied the students to a weekend in a nursing home where they worked as volunteers in white uniforms. According to the course organisers, two of the students were hired by this nursing home, enabling them to change their job title from 'domestic worker' to 'nursing aide' (Straits Times, 2009b). There is in fact a 'continuum of sites for caring relationships' and boundaries between the different forms of care work are not always so clearly defined (Zelizer, 2005: 163).[8] Even if taking skills classes does not lead to an actual change in occupation, it reveals how hierarchies can be negotiated. Domestic workers imagine themselves moving on to better things, even though they are the most restricted migrants in policy and legal terms

8. In future journeys, nurses and domestic workers may find themselves under the same 'Live-in Caregiver' scheme in Canada, see Geraldine Pratt on 'From Registered Nurse to Nanny' (2004).

Figure 7: Lucky Plaza, the 'Filipino' mall (author's photo)

and are also subject to the greatest degrees of discrimination. These activities are not always about negotiating power and hierarchies though. In Lili's case, it is also about curiosity and experimentation, converting to a new religion and attempting to be a pious Muslim wife. Domestic workers too want to cultivate a moral sensibility of being virtuous and respectable, similar to the way in which nurses see themselves. The distinctions articulated between the two groups are thus shaken at times. Though each group may occupy different spheres of life in Singapore, they often have similar social aspirations, part of which is to challenge the image of, and the possibilities for, Filipino migrants in the world.

The Boundaries of Class

It may appear as though I speak of 'domestic workers' and 'nurses' as if they are distinct and neatly bounded categories. However, it must be emphasized that migrants are not *defined* by their work in a static manner, nor are they naturally pre-existing groups. 'Domestic worker' and 'nurse' as occupational identifications do not necessarily map directly or in any clear-cut manner onto distinct social classes. In fact, the irony is that domestic workers and nurses may not necessarily come from so different socio-economic backgrounds in the Philippines. The contingency of class boundaries in the Philippines follows migrants on their journeys overseas.

Some domestic workers in Singapore may have been graduates in accountancy in the Philippines; it is not so unlikely that they come from a similar social background to someone who studies nursing.[9] To provide an example, Liza, whom I mentioned in Chapter 3, has three sisters. One works as a domestic worker in Singapore and the other two work as caregivers in Canada. All four sisters had a relatively modest upbringing and achieved the same level of education. Their parents invested in the higher education of all daughters, despite financial hardship. Liza chose nursing by chance because her aunt suggested it would be a good course and is now the daughter who is seen to hold the greatest promise for social mobility in the family. There are many other examples demonstrating that nurses and domestic workers may not come from such different backgrounds. For example, Lili revealed that she had her own 'helpers' in her Philippine home, thus suggesting that a Filipino domestic worker in Singapore is someone who might not ever be a domestic worker in the Philippines. Another example is Grace's cousin, who expressed interest in working in Singapore as a

---

9. Parreñas (2001) speaks of 'contradictory class mobility', where those who go overseas as domestic workers and caregivers experience downward mobility: many, for instance, are college graduates but can earn more working abroad than they can in office jobs in the Philippines. However, the fact that they are 'overseas migrants' simultaneously gives them an elevated status.

domestic worker, to offset the loneliness of being a widowed housewife in the Philippines. Furthermore, when I went to visit Ella on her day off from the hospital, her friend Mary would sometimes be there. Mary and Ella met at church and get along very well. They come from similar social backgrounds in the Philippines and jointly laugh at other 'sosy' (*sosyal*, or posh)[10] Filipino migrants in Singapore. Yet in spite of this connection, when Ella discovered that Mary used to be a domestic worker in Singapore, she was taken-aback. The label of being a domestic worker carries with it associations that nurses do not want to share in. The distinctions that nurses make between themselves and domestic workers therefore emerge from *assertions* of distinction though in reality they may actually not be that different.

Michael Pinches (1999) writes about the growth of the middle classes in the Philippines as a part of a process of capitalist transformation in Asia. Many of those in the new middle classes have a high level of education and skills, which are obtained for the advancement of one's professional career; this includes a number of salaried professional and technical workers who seek social status and social mobility through acquiring educational and professional qualifications. (King, 2008; Mulder, 1998; Johnson, 2010; Earl, 2014). Nursing is a profession, which might be associated with both the traditional middle class – a 'genteel' profession, which led many to successful careers as nurses in the United States – and the new middle class. The latter contain those with upwardly mobile aspirations, who perhaps come from lower-income backgrounds but who have succeeded in their nursing careers. The boundaries of the new middle class are fragile as are the boundaries of once more distinct social classes in the Philippines. As Pinches (1999) argues:

> Until a decade ago, the most common language of social stratification simply distinguished between rich and poor, or *burgis* (bourgeois) and *masa* (masses), with only limited reference to a middle-class ... [Now, however,] there are new and substantial layers of people in between ... their collective existence is becoming important ... there is also the perception of new opportunities for social mobility.

The 'new middle-classes' nowadays thus encompasses a whole range of people from different socio-economic backgrounds and occupations

---

10. *Sosy*, which comes from *sosyal*, is a translation of 'social'. It generally pertains to those who act as socialites, displaying 'classy' or posh sensibilities.

and might include both migrant nurses and domestic workers (King, 2008). In these in-between positions, the new middle class is, 'split between the déclassé and the upwardly mobile' (Crompton, 1998: 153; see Bourdieu, 1986).

Bobby Benedicto (2009) suggests that the instability of these class boundaries is further accentuated by the process of migration and especially by the category of the migrant nurse. He argues that the category 'migrant' encompasses a wide range of people of diverse socio-economic backgrounds and that the special OFW queue in the Ninoy Aquino International Airport (NAIA) in Manila is illustrative of blurring class boundaries. Benedicto (2009: 293) describes NAIA as a space, 'where the privileged and the marginal all pass through' and 'that this shared space, the site where the borders of the nation are crossed, is also the site where the borders of class difference drawn across the city begin to unravel'. In contrast to other accounts I encountered among aspiring lower middle-class migrants in my own fieldwork who see the overseas nurse as someone to emulate, the nurse is 'an acquaintance to be hidden' from the point of view of the people featured in Benedicto's ethnographic work, who perceive themselves as 'privileged' or 'elite' members of society (2009: 296). Nursing is thus a category that is intertwined with class politics. On the one hand, the nurse in the white uniform is someone on a pedestal. Yet, the more 'elitist' view is that the nurse acts as a threat to their status. Given that it is now a way out for everyone – as the recruitment agent in Manila told me, 'everybody wants it, the rich and the poor' – nursing encompasses people from a wide range of backgrounds. Moreover, the blurring of boundaries is accentuated by the fact that a whole spectrum of workers from professional licensed nurses, to caregivers, nursing home assistants, all fall under the umbrella of subservient feminized care labour (Benedicto, 2009: 296). Mark Johnson (2010: 428) observes a very similar pattern among Filipinos in Saudi Arabia, where professional Filipinos simultaneously distance themselves from domestic worker compatriots while offering them support from a position of status. He explains that:

> ... it is precisely the proximity of middle class professionals to the social and material worlds and circumstances of their working-class compatriots, as well as the tenuous and precarious nature of their attempts to achieve and stabilize a middle class existence in the diaspora

that informs the reproduction of the stereotypes mobilised to reinforce and maintain the distinctions between them (Johnson, 2010: 445).

Migrant nurses in Singapore similarly hold a very precarious status as they experience discrimination in their Singapore environments.

We therefore see great complexity in these slippery categories of 'middle-class', 'nurse' and 'migrant'. The overlaps between the people within these categories – and the threat of misrecognition– are, I argue, what drive people to assert a sense of distinction further; that the quest for distinction is most hard-won among people of very proximate social classes (Bourdieu, 1986). As Bourdieu (1986) famously explained in *Distinction*, fundamental to this process of distinction are practices or markers that demonstrate one's class and level of 'cultural capital': how one conducts oneself, how one dresses, what one eats and who one chooses to socialize with. These cultural forms denoting class, are precisely what are deployed by nurses to distinguish themselves from domestic workers. Class is not about what one was born with – we see that nurses and domestic workers might have similar origins – but about the performance of a certain status.

Religious Communities: An Exception

I have painted a picture of Filipino migrants in Singapore divided between open and engaged domestic workers and nurses who retreat. No doubt, there are exceptions to this general picture. One notable exception is a group of nurses I met at an independent, non-affiliated church towards the end of my fieldwork. This was a group of nurses whose lives were very different from those of the nurses I had known until then. My informants until then had been Roman Catholic and were not very active in church life. Although they practise their religion devotedly and attend church regularly, they do so in a private manner. I was presented with a contrast upon meeting this new group of nurses whose lives are contrary to being quiet. These nurses belong to a church in Singapore that calls itself an evangelical 'movement', a movement that is a part of the global spread of evangelical and charismatic movements (Weigele, 2005; Cruz, 2009; Robbins, 2004; Liebelt, 2008; Coleman, 2000). The rapid rate at which the church is growing and the attempts of church members to transform other (predominantly Catholic) family members, friends and communities in the Philippines, suggest that this phenomenon – in which the migration process enables the religious imagination to thrive – is pertinent. I will suggest that even as this group of nurses is different from my other nurse informants, the boundaries between nurses or professionals and domestic workers are also inscribed in these forms of religious sociality.

My first encounter with *Faith Church* was when the Filipino congregation marked its anniversary. The event was held in a large hall in a shopping mall, with a capacity to hold several thousand people. With festive orange clappers, party whistles and deafening cheers, the service got off to a rousing start. It was like a rock concert, extremely loud and full of energy, with people dancing and jumping in front of the stage. Technology was used to show photo montages of church members bonding over food and prayer and projecting lyrics of the songs. The Singaporean pastor delivered his sermon in Singlish to a largely Filipino audience, relating one's relationship to God to anecdotes about marriage difficulties, job searches, lying, jealously and greed, shopping, travel and pop culture. During the service, people were in joyous celebration and dancing, and in prayer with their heads bowed down, some crying. This service was a sharp contrast to the orthodox Roman Catholic services I attended. Nurses in Catholic churches, I found, did not speak to me so openly about the importance of religion in their lives (apart from simply stating how important it was to pray), whereas the nurses at *Faith Church* were ready to tell the story of the church and to talk about their religious experiences and transformations.

The openness with which these nurses spoke of their religious experiences and their willingness to welcome me in their activities, again departed from the norm. The nurses I met in this church were very sociable and invited me immediately to join their services, for meals and 'care group' meetings. No doubt, their openness had to do with their evangelical aims to 'share the word of God' with others, myself included. The church congregation is largely Filipino, though not exclusively so. The pastors are Chinese-Malaysian and Singaporean and there are some members of the congregation who are not Filipino. My relationship with these nurses was ethically challenging. It was evidently a relationship with two-way interests: I was curious to hear more about their rich religious lives in Singapore without the will to be a part of them, while they were keen to make me a part of their religious community.

Maricel, a new member of *Faith Church*, for example was extremely warm towards me from the moment I met her at the anniversary. She invited me, along with other visitors to the church from China and Burma, to a small dinner gathering afterwards. After exchanging phone numbers with Maricel, I began receiving text messages from her regularly, an example being: 'You r a blessed person wd an important role to play in lyf and GOD is watching over u wd LOVE & concern. Be d best u can be. For God's purpose ... Morning! God bless! ☺'[11] Maricel, a 22 year-old nurse joined *Faith Church* soon after her arrival to Singapore. A member of the church who began inviting her to church events approached her in a shopping mall. 'Evax', or evangelizing, Maricel explains with a giggle, is a key part of the church activities. This means constantly cultivating new relationships with others in the hope they will join the church. Maricel says, 'I'm so thankful, because really my faith is deeper here in Singapore. We have so much bonding in the church, it's a lot of fun, excitement'. She explains how in the Philippines, she was 'quite naughty' but that in Singapore, she became very different, sending 'Godly SMS' to her family everyday. She alludes to the pull of obligation she feels in reciprocating the kindness of her fellow church members, 'I really want to do something for them', she says, 'that's why I ask you, I ask my other friends also to come and join us. People will see how happy everybody is, then they will be happy also if they join. Of course, we have to be very dedicated'.

Maricel then invited me to a weekly care group session. Care groups are micro-communities within the congregation, scattered across Singapore, which meet once a week for food and prayer. They are held in flats shared by church leaders. The session started off with a homecooked dinner of Filipino-style spaghetti, and we then went around the group of about twenty people, introducing ourselves. There were nurses, pet stylists, draftsmen, architects, accountants, hotel workers and teachers. The evening started with team-building exercises, followed by a gathering in one corner of the flat in order to sing religious songs along with a guitar. Maricel was moved to tears, while the care group leaders read pas-

---

11. Text messages from nurses were often composed with this shorthand style, e.g. 'u' stands for 'you', 'wd' for 'with'. Using this shorthand to communicate with nurses during fieldwork often enabled a sense of closeness and equality, whereas complete English sentences appeared distant and overly formal.

sages from the Bible. Others were in a trance-like state with their hands up in the air. It was clearly a very intense and emotional experience for many. This session was then followed by a group discussion of the Bible. Leah and Charis, two of the leaders, lead the discussion, making reference to how Filipinos have left their country to serve others: 'We have passion, conviction, perseverance, belief, heart and grace … we are here to become better people. We are away from our families. But this is our family'. The group discussion focuses on the topic of how to re-build the care group with commitment, fellowship, family, love, warmth and care. The care group, they say, should be fun, happy, joyful:

> And JOY is Jesus first, others second, you last … the purpose of this is to surpass the self, to live for a greater purpose. We have all seen how we transform. We start with resistance, many of us do not think we have time, we do not know why these people from the church are always "SMS-ing" us, and then we move from resistance to love.

Another member jumps in, smiling, with a glint in her eyes:

> It's like being in love – you can't wait to meet the person again. You leave home in the morning, what will God have in store for me today. You cannot help but come back. This is how we want people to feel. Your love will overflow; others will feel your love; they will want to feel the same. When we come here we are people, we are human again! After the whole week, we work and we don't even feel human sometimes. Nurses, we are very busy. But really, we have a lot of time; it is about time management. If you love God – it is not a chore.

The group reacts nodding earnestly, taking in the words being spoken.

> How do we feel when we are here and we miss our families? We weep, we cry. How do we care for those of our care group who cannot make it? We call them – just tell them one word, *parang okay na* (just like, it's okay). We need someone who can encourage us. We want to have the love, closeness - warmth of the group. The more ready we are, the more we can sacrifice. What I really want to see is commitment.

The care groups are crucial to sustaining the feeling of belonging that migrants have to the church and its members. Those who work as nurses to care for others, care for each other and for themselves in these intimate care groups. They become so close that there is almost a fear of letting others down if they do not show up, or contribute to the church through evangelical activities in their free time. Commitment requires a great deal of time management and sacrifice, given that the majority of Filipino migrants in the congregation are professionals; many are nurses performing shift-work with demanding working schedules. Yet nursing seems to be incidental to the lives of these migrants, the church being at the crux of their Singapore lives. The desire for self-transformation is powerful and immediate. The care groups are one part of a much larger, imagined religious landscape. To become 'a better person' and 'to put God first' are all notions which the members of the congregation espouse. In a sense, the lives of these nurses turn the notion of service on its head. As 'servants of God' who serve God and the world through their faith, they believe themselves to be far removed from the degrading characterization of Filipinos as 'servants of globalization'.

Yet the collective fashioning of this group is still very much linked to their class subjectivities. In the specific case of *Faith Church*, the collective religious community is also a professional and classed one, as there is a clear appeal to the concerns that Filipino migrant professionals face (Serrano-Cornelio, 2008; Cruz, 2009). In *Faith*, Filipino professionals form the congregation: the services are in English and the leaders are Chinese–Singaporean. The church targets professionals, with a particular focus on nurses. I asked why domestic workers only constitute five per cent of the congregation. I was told that it was because they do not have time. A prime expectation for belonging to the church is committing a significant amount of time to it. There is also an expectation that members will contribute financially to its growth and a belief that professionals are better placed to do this. Most of these nurses' free time is spent on church activities several times a week and they go to fellowship retreats every few months. 'Not having time' is not seen as a legitimate enough excuse to frequently miss gatherings or Sunday services (though this does not stop those who cannot attend regularly from forming their own faith groups). Belonging to this religious community of professionals, means belonging to an 'internationalized' class of people in 'noble' professions who willingly contribute financially to the church and who devote time to evangelism. The boundaries of exclusion are subtle; it is implied that domestic workers are not worth the evangelical efforts since they cannot contribute much time or money to church activities. Moreover, the fact that there are many nurses and other professionals who are a part of the congregation makes it easier to draw others of similar occupations since they identify with other professionals.

Apart from the few domestic workers in the *Faith* congregation, most others that I met attend Roman Catholic Mass on Sundays. A number of domestic workers in Singapore have also joined the charismatic Catholic movement *El-Shaddai* in Singapore, an increasingly popular religious movement in the Philippines that appeals to the poor while it preaches a 'prosperity gospel' (Cruz, 2009; Wiegele, 2005). In Singapore, the *El-Shaddai* congregation is made up mostly of domestic workers. Their main activities take place on Sundays and domestic workers play a major part in the church as stewards, choir members and church leaders. When meeting with a pastor, he spoke of alleviating the suffering of domestic workers as a key focus of this church's activities. The division between nurses and domestic workers and their perceived class and status differences is therefore also inscribed the spaces of religious sociality in Singapore.

Diverse Socialities

This chapter has illuminated the variety of practices of sociality among Filipino migrants in Singapore, with the boundaries among Filipino migrants just as salient, if not more, than those between migrants and Singaporeans. A key distinction that emerges recurrently is that between domestic workers and nurses. While domestic workers appear more open to new relationships, more cosmopolitan and more expressive, nurses generally retreat into quieter, private lives at home, spending more time maintaining transnational connections with families, resting, doing household chores and preparing for future journeys. The boundaries between domestic workers and nurses are formed deliberately, in some instances, informed by a politics of class, status and citizenship among Filipino migrants in Singapore. The boundaries are formed implicitly in other instances as a result of the different mobilities and rhythms, which their working lives permit. Even in the exceptional case of the lively evangelical nurses, their congregation's collective identity is based on a sense of cosmopolitan professionalism, largely excluding domestic workers. What is important is that even where a sharp distinction is drawn between nurses and domestic workers, there are overlaps between them. The overlaps might emerge from common socio-economic backgrounds in the Philippines, from shared aspirations to challenge the dominant image of the Filipino citizen in the world, and from the ambiguities within the category of care labour.

Migrant sociality, and the formation of groups and boundaries, is a dynamic process. Migrants form groups, they do not pre-exist. The social formations I observed, particularly among nurses, also shed light on how the public transnational community or sphere is not a space that all migrants choose to engage with. One point briefly made in this chapter is that many nurses expect Singapore to be a transit city and that this in part influences the kind of lives they lead in Singapore. It is a life-in-transit while they plan for a new home and life of stability further afield, whilst maintaining transnational connections with the Philippines. These spatial and temporal questions are powerful in nurses' lives, as they grapple with obstacles in their attempts to reach other destinations, alongside a desire to find a sense of belonging and home.

CHAPTER SEVEN

The Elusive Search for Home

T he question asked by Aguilar (2002): Are Filipinos 'at home in the world?' speaks powerfully to the realities of Filipino migrants. Many Filipinos suggest that this is a part of what it means to be Filipino, that a feeling of home moves with them as they travel, work and settle in places across the world. This chapter examines the spatial and temporal dimensions of migrant experience, as migrants reflect on the question of home; what are their imaginaries and expectations of home and how does this change along the way? A home is something that migrants yearn for and the spatial and temporal orientations of Filipino medical workers in Singapore significantly affect their everyday life priorities and activities. There is a sense of anxiety about where they can settle and develop a sense of future and belonging. Home here refers both to the practical possibilities of settling and build-ing a life (where one can get a longer-term visa or residence rights, for example) and the more subjective dimensions of where one feels a sense of belonging. What home constitutes is thus a question that produces much ambivalence, and it is not self-evident what this means to those who are on the move. The idea of being 'at home in the world' is far less stable than it initially appears (Constable, 2002; Aguilar, 2002: 24).

Typically, before their departures, migrants imagine leaving their homes in the Philippines to work in an indeterminate location in the West, where they plan to build a new home embodying material wealth and social and economic security. Many potential migrants also claim that they will eventually return to the Philippines, their original home - the place where they belong. The realities of their journeys and their changing relationships with the idea of home present quite a different story, particularly as they pass through Singapore, which they see as a transit city or stepping-stone. Their experiences of life and work in this transit city play an important role in shaping, reinforcing and reconfiguring their future plans and orientations.

Migrants move from one place to another, with yet other places also on their mind. Their journeys do not involve a simple binary between a place of origin and place of destination as is often assumed in studies of transnational migration. As Liebelt (2008: 568) reiterates in her ethnographic work with Filipina domestic workers in Israel:

> Many Filipina migrants move *on and on* rather than back and forth. They do so within a global hierarchy of desirable destination countries, ranked according to the differences between nation-states with regard to salaries and the legal entitlements migrants can claim, the costs and risks migrants have to take in order to enter, and these countries' overall subjective and imaginative attractiveness.

The idea of 'moving on' is significant to the lives of my informants, while at the same time notions of home and abroad also shift constantly. Concepts such as 'rootlessness' or 'homelessness' are often used in academic and public discourses about migration and the diaspora to capture a condition of displacement, a feeling of a lost home or a destabilization of the self from one's roots. Yet these processes of displacement also occur simultaneously with those of emplacement (Glick Schiller and Caglar, 2016) with the notion of 'travelling homes' or 'routes' (rather than just roots) also fundamental to the experiences of those on the move (Malkki, 1992; Clifford, 1992). Home, in practice, is not essentially bound to one place, but rather a state of mind.

In light of these questions which challenge the existence of a singular place called home, this chapter considers three moments and orientations in migrant medical workers' lives; of moving on and ahead, of turning back and of staying put. Firstly, in the section 'Moving On', I look at the lives of migrants in Singapore waiting to move on; those who stop in Singapore to gain a few years of experience while applying for jobs in other countries along with the delays and uncertainties that are a part of the process of waiting. This moment centres on a search for a new, more distant home further afield. In 'Returns Home', I focus on the act of going home to the Philippines, the place which migrants have left for overseas experience and its changing role from a place to escape from, to a temporary place to escape to. I explore these dynamics through an ethnographic account of following a nurse on her trip home to the Philippines for a family reunion during a festive occasion in her village. This section explores the socialities that emerge during the reunion, and in particular, the tension between the romanticization of the Philippine home and the fact that it is an unliveable home. Finally, in the third section, I share the experiences of a few nurses who slowly, gradually and unexpectedly stumble upon a feeling of home in the transit city, Singapore. This final section is a story of how constructions of home develop in states of relative transience. Here I look at the condition of being 'in transit' to an elsewhere, the dilemmas and reflections about home which this condition generates and the different possible scenarios that could emerge from it. The question of home unites these three distinct yet interconnected, spatial and temporal moments. As the ethnography ahead demonstrates, home is a relation between a self and a place, so as either or both change, so too does the relation. The notion of home is a hybrid, changing its own rules as it migrates in time and space (Minh-ha, 1994; Bammer, 1992).

Moving On

I now turn to the first of three scenarios: the transit mentality of my informants. The idea of moving on is almost an inherent part of most migrant nurses' mentalities at the outset of their journeys to Singapore. Singapore is a transit city, where migrants continue planning their journeys to other countries. I speak of transit as a period of a few years, a short period of time in the bigger scheme of migrants' imagined trajectories. Very few of my informants see Singapore as their destination, or contemplate the possibility that it would become a home for them. Migrants regard the disenchantment they experience in Singapore as temporary, and cope with this disenchantment by planning future journeys and cultivating connections elsewhere. Nurses spend much of their time (when not at work) studying for exams, contacting recruitment agencies, putting in visa applications to other countries and speaking to members of their global network of friends and family. They spend a lot of time in virtual spaces building connections to reach their future home elsewhere, browsing web forums about overseas life, chatting with friends and family. It was almost as if their home, for this period, was located in these virtual spaces rather than in any concerted practices of home-making with others in the city. There is a pervasive sense of anxiety at the same time as there is a yearning for a home and stability in the future. Home is imagined elsewhere, not here in the transit city.

As with potential migrants in the Philippines, in Singapore too, the elsewhere is always in people's stories. Most of my conversations with nurses automatically moved to the topic of 'where next?' particularly when they spoke about their discontentment with their Singapore lives. My own biography as a migrant researcher, moving between countries, was intimately connected to nurses' interests and I was often asked much about life abroad. I received detailed updates from them – in a routine and regular manner – on how their efforts to move on were taking shape (or not).

To illustrate how the idea of temporariness features in nurses lives, I turn to Alyssa's story. She had just arrived in Singapore when I first met her at the orientation for new nurses. Deeply disappointed by her Singapore experience, Alyssa was talking about moving on soon after her arrival in Singapore. 'I don't want to go back to the Philippines, I want more experience', she would say. Alyssa was not content with the people in Singapore and the absence of warmth in everyday life. Alyssa's husband, who previously worked in Malaysia, joined her after about one year. When he got to Singapore, he found a job working in a 24-hour food court chain, doing night shifts in a branch quite far away from where they lived. Alyssa, meanwhile, continued with her rotation shifts in the emergency department of the hospital. Alyssa and her husband live together in Singapore, staying in the living room of a shared flat, but they hardly see each other. Alyssa also points out that in her view, a flat in a high-rise building could never be a home. Several of my informants echo this sentiment, highlighting the physicality of living arrangements as another aspect of Singapore life that makes it feel temporary. Migrants often pondered on how an apartment could be a home. Migrants perceive home – in the Philippines and elsewhere – as constituted by land (*lupa*): a place with a territorial sense of rootedness.

Each time I saw Alyssa in her worn-out state, she would tell me that she and her husband had contacted an agency about going to Canada. She showed me a print-out of an advertisement that she had found online which stated that: 'even though many major countries are experiencing an economic slowdown, Canada is still looking for migrants to help build the country and boost the economy ... Now may be the perfect time to consider making the move!' The advertisement indicated that nurses' skills were needed and that this agency would advise and assist all aspiring applicants with assessments and papers. Alyssa gave me regular updates on what they had paid, on what documents they needed to obtain and on how long they had been waiting. The hope of Canada, it seemed, would solve their temporary state of dislocation and overwork in Singapore , which does not allow for a life beyond work. It is almost as if Canada is a coping mechanism; speaking about it, sending in documents, waiting with the hope of something different, keeps them going in Singapore. The idea of moving elsewhere also impacts the way that nurses live their lives in Singapore; they reside without attempting to settle, or without much intention to develop enduring friendships or ties to others.

Another nurse, Ana, had been working as an operating-theatre nurse for six years in Singapore. She started as a junior nurse and has since worked her way up, being selected to assist in difficult surgeries and to accompany teams of doctors on medical missions abroad. Over the years, Ana always had the intention to work in the US. She saved a lot of money to take NCLEX exams in Hong Kong and Australia, since there are no exam centres in Singapore. It is an expensive process in terms of time, money and mental energy. Having failed the exams twice by the time I met her, she said that she is searching for the will power to continue trying. Ana's life in Singapore is characterized by work and study with the ultimate goal of passing these exams and moving to the US. Ana's husband, a physiotherapist, also works in Singapore but they have left their son in the Philippines with Ana's parents looking after him. The promise of them reuniting and settling in the US keeps her going. A lot of the desire to move on is also about image. I remember once when Ana and I took a photograph together, she said, 'oh no, I can't upload this to Friendster, I already uploaded photos of me wearing this blouse, my friends will think I can't afford to go shopping in Singapore'. Comments like this about how their lives appear to others, gossip about friends and colleagues moving on to other places, and discussions about the application and recruitment process are commonplace and routine in conversations with my informants, rather than extraordinary. Temporally, the future is more present than the present itself.

Alyssa and Ana's stories are typical among nurses and such aspirations are widespread before they even leave the Philippines. However, in practice, the process of realizing these aspirations is often fraught with uncertainty. I now turn to recount Nelia's story of trying to obtain a British visa, revealing how this period of waiting, of simultaneous hope and disappointment, can at times lead to a sense of apathy.

Nelia has been working in Singapore for the past four years in the geriatric wards of a government hospital. All this time, Nelia has also had a visa application to migrate to the UK where her sister and cousins work as nurses and carers. Over my fieldwork period, I followed Nelia's plans and her application to the UK. Nelia often spoke excitedly about joining her many relatives in the UK, along with her husband and son who live in Manila. However, the application process starkly revealed the practical uncertainties and frustrations which accompany, and hinder, the dreams that many nurses have.

Nelia's application to the UK was put in at a time when there were changes to the UK's nursing recruitment policy which placed restrictions on the hiring of non-EU nurses (Duffin, 2008; Guardian, 2011; Buchan and Seccombe, 2009). Thus, Filipino nurses attempted to enter the UK on student visas instead. A typical scenario is that a nurse will be registered with a vocational college on paper, but will instead work twenty hours a week or more in a care home. Nelia similarly planned to work in a care home in Leeds, where her sister lives, and commute to London periodically to attend the college. Her initial visa application was rejected on the grounds that her plan was not feasible. She later appealed the decision, with the help of her relatives in the UK who appeared in court to defend her case, and was successful in doing so. When she finally sent her passport to the British High Commission in Singapore to obtain the visa, it was held for a further six months. Nelia did not receive any information about why it was being held for so long. She finally discovered that the college to which she applied had been suspended and was under investigation by authorities doubting its credibility. Her plans to go to the UK are thus postponed indefinitely.

The insecurity that accompanies this state of waiting can be draining. I remember Nelia once calling me to say that she wanted to talk to someone about her UK visa situation. When we met at the hospital cafeteria a couple of days later, she told me that she had called the British

High Commission several times to find out what had happened to her passport and visa. She complained that there was:

> So much delay, delay, delay. They are just delaying and delaying and delaying. In July I already sent it to them, then you call and they say they will call back - they never call. Then they told me; I can submit the passport. Why did she tell me I can submit my passport if not everything is okay? I think this lady [in-charge of Nelia's case] has some kind of dementia. She never call and inform or update us anything. It is disgusting, that is how they deal with people.

She was then silent for a few minutes before saying in a resigned manner: 'I am so tired of waiting … Meg, I'm so worried about my visa. Why it takes so long? So long I'm waiting already'. Clearly exasperated in that moment, she called the High Commission again. Nelia asserted her annoyance and in the end received the same answer, with the same condescension, 'you have to wait'. Nelia complained, 'I cannot do anything. I cannot book my flight, I cannot contact my school in the UK to arrange my starting date, I cannot see my son in the Philippines, I miss him so much, I cannot give my resignation, nothing because I don't have my visa, I don't have my passport'. At one point, the anger and resentment led Nelia into a period of withdrawal, as she stayed at home, did not eat regular meals and sat in front of the computer playing *Farmville* all day from morning until night on her days off. To make matters worse, her relatives in the UK seemed to have given up on her case too.

A few months later, Nelia looked back on that period of withdrawal, saying: 'I was so depressed. I lost faith. Maybe I am unlucky. So many bad things were happening to me, I felt the whole world is weighing on my shoulders. I am still hopeless now. Until now I am waiting for my visa'. At the time Nelia resigned and gave up going to the UK in the near future, I had to return to the UK after my fieldwork. Nelia is still in Singapore and she now tells me, on *Yahoo* chat, that she might look at Australia instead. Dreams still keep her looking ahead. I recall the time towards the end of fieldwork when I met Nelia at Lucky Plaza. She bought two medium-sized *balikbayan* boxes,[1] which she would fill

---

1. The word *balikbayan* refers to migrant returnees (literally, *balik* means 'to return', while *bayan* means 'town'). As Rafael (2000: 206) argues, 'being a *balikbayan* depends on one's permanent residence abroad. It means that one lives somewhere else and that one's appearance in the Philippines is temporary and intermittent'.

up with things to send home to Manila. After that we walked over to a nearby department store and wandered around in the kitchen section where Nelia introduced me to Corelle tableware. 'I want to see this Corelle', she told me before saying to the sales assistant, 'I don't have enough cash', as the sales assistant tried to sell her a set of Corelle tableware for $199. Nelia proceeded to speak dreamily and ecstatically about this tableware: 'We use that in my mother's house. I bought it last year, $99 for 16 pieces'. She whispered that she has another set, which she hides in her locker at home. Nelia was delighted about the plates: 'See, they are so light, you can hit it three times; it still won't break. Made in the USA. You can heat your food in the stove, in the microwave. This is my first love. I am so in love ... with Corelle', she giggles. 'I come here whenever I am sad, homesick, depressed, and then I see all these beautiful things and I feel better. Someday ...', she sighs. Nelia related how her husband always rebukes her, 'why do you like to look so much at these things, you don't even have a house!' The yearning for home is linked to certain desired practices of consumption and material cultures embodying a feeling of home (Miller, 1998). In this particular case, the desire for more Corelle plates cannot be fulfilled without a physical home or a lifestyle to match it.

Nelia's story illuminates a number of important points. It highlights once again the in-between position that medical workers are in. On the one hand, they are very much in-demand in hospitals across the world, and their professionalism opens up possibilities for mobility that are not open to 'low-skilled' workers. On the other hand, it is clear from this story that nurses are also significantly affected by state regulations and changes in immigration policies, which is a reminder of the structural constraints of migrant experience. This is not to say that migrants do not attempt to get around such structural constraints, as can be seen from how Filipino nurses enter the UK as student caregivers. Alongside these negotiations are the aspirations of migrants: the desire for a home and the desire to be settled in a place they perceive to be better for themselves and their families. These desires continue to flourish and

---

Balikbayan boxes are cargo boxes full of goods from overseas sent back as care packages to the family in the Philippines.

configure migrants' spatial orientations. However, Nelia's story cautions that no matter how far-reaching the dreams of these nurses are, the role of the state and the policing of borders are significantly consequential in determining whether or not these dreams materialize. Often, such dreams are delayed or thwarted, leading to moments of insecurity or resignation. Politics is never far away from subjective and imaginative constructions of home and the multiple meanings which migrants give them.

Returns Home

I now turn to the second spatial and temporal moment: of returning home to the Philippines. While I have demonstrated that migrants' transnational connections are not limited to the binary of origin and destination, the Philippine home left behind is still important in the lives of my informants and they maintain a strong orientation to it as an anchor, often uttering that, 'there is no place like home'. It does not exist in isolation, but remains deeply connected to multiple other locations across the world that feature in migrants' imaginaries and maps. However, migrants have a complex and ambivalent relationship with this Philippine home, both in terms of their own perceptions of the Philippines after some time abroad, and in terms of how family and village members perceive them when they return. Most Filipino medical workers in Singapore are able to visit the Philippines once or sometimes twice a year, given the relative proximity of the Philippines to Singapore and the availability of affordable flights on budget airlines. That said, heavy work schedules in Singapore sometimes prevent migrants from going home. A number of nurses have family members in the Philippines including young or teenaged children who are being looked after by siblings or by the children's grandparents. Sometimes one parent is in the Philippines while the other is working in Singapore, or both may be overseas (e.g. it is a fairly common scenario that a mother is working as a nurse in Singapore while her husband works as a seafarer). Migrants in Singapore make trips home to maintain regular contact with their children. Hence, they plan their trips to coincide with their children's summer holidays or exam periods.

Even when migrants do not physically go to the Philippines, this home is very much present in their Singapore lives, reiterating how translocal relationships are cemented in the migrant way of life. Many medical workers reminisce about the Philippines on a regular basis, beginning stories wistfully with: 'In the Philippines ...'. They also talk at length about their families; for example, about how their sister is not well, about how their son's graduation is coming up, about how they are missing a Philippine Christmas once again. *Skype* and *Yahoo Messenger* are always open on migrants' computers. Familial relations may also pose constraints. Che, a nurse in a private hospital in Singapore, for instance, spoke often about missing her husband and spent a lot of time on *Yahoo Messenger* chatting with him. But she also felt constrained by the frequency of these communications, protesting to me about her husband's demands to know where she is going every evening and with whom. Even as new technologies may have a transformative impact on increasing the possibilities and means for transnational communications between migrants and their families, the continuous nature of on-line contact may also lead to new tensions arising within transnational families (Madianou and Miller, 2012).

Following Grace to Layan

I now turn to the time when I had the chance to accompany Grace home to the Philippines for the holidays. She was going home at the peak of the Philippine summer for the *Fiesta* period in her village, Layan, on Panay Island. *Fiesta* is a time when the village celebrates the patron saint, comes together through social events, prayer and hospitality. It was a particularly special year to visit, Grace told me, because after a four-year absence from the Philippines, three of her sisters (along with their husbands and children) were coming home, one from the UK and the other two from Canada, where they work as nurses. Grace's aunt Tita Novy, who works as a nurse in Texas, had not returned home for fifteen years and her American-born son, Mark, who had never visited the Philippines before, would be there too. Grace's son would come from Manila, and her husband would come back from many months of working at sea. It was to be a rare and large family reunion of a truly global Filipino family.

Following Grace home enabled me to see first-hand the important place of home that is always present in migrants' stories. Going to the Philippines, I saw the layers of social relations in which Grace is embedded. This provided an additional dimension to our meetings in Singapore at the nursing home and in shopping malls. Grace claims her heart belongs to the Layan home. Returns home bring together family members and friends with different biographies, who have been through different migrant journeys. It demonstrates how expectations, transformations, denials and conflicts exist within a global migrant family returning to the Philippine *barrio*, also involving those who have not travelled abroad. I now go into the world of a trip home, an intensive few weeks of fun, reunions, eating, drinking and parties with family and friends. The stories ahead – and the elements that remain unspoken – point towards the tensions between a longing for a romanticized home left behind while recognizing that this is not a home to live in.

Meeting at the airport one Tuesday morning in May, Grace arrives telling me that she had been so excited that she could not sleep. We take a morning flight from Singapore on the Philippine budget airline *Cebu Pacific* to Manila and bring along Grace's overweight luggage full of gifts for her friends and relatives. Before we take off, she calls Auntie, her patient and friend from the nursing home to say goodbye. Along the way, Grace teaches me some Ilongo, the language spoken in Iloilo, explaining that it is very *malambing* (sweet and soft).

Upon arrival in Manila, we are picked up by Ricky, Grace's husband, who takes us to Grace's cousin Tess's house near the airport. We spend the first afternoon and night in Manila with Tess, eating a home cooked meal, wandering around the Mall of Asia and then sharing a seafood dinner at Manila Bay. We also picked up Grace's aunt, Tita Novy, and cousin, Mark, who had just arrived from Texas. Novy, who is in her late 50s, has been living there for years, and her son Mark, who greets everyone in a strong Texan accent, is in the Philippines for the first time to meet his extended family. That night, the three ladies spent time dying Novy's hair, 'to make [her] young and beautiful again for the Philippines,' while gossiping and giggling. Only briefly do they talk about their lives abroad when Novy asks Grace how her plans are going for moving on, 'still waiting?' she asks. Novy looks upset and shakes her head, 'you see what they make us go through,' she tells me. Meanwhile, the men go out drinking and come back just before we are to leave for our early morning flight to Iloilo. Mark says, 'I love Manila! Woohoo!' Novy, Grace and Tess are howling with laughter – 'he is already enjoying, and he just arrived! Don't worry you can enjoy some more in Iloilo'. The intensity of these few hours in Manila after our arrival – the sheer excitement of these reunions, of different generations coming together after years apart, of eating out, laughing, banter, drinking and bonding, was a mere taster of what was to come in the following days in Layan.

We arrive at 7am in Iloilo on a hot, sunny morning. We slowly move off the highway and on to a bumpier, dustier, pot-holed road with bright green rice fields and sugarcane plantations surrounding us, leading up to Barangay Layan, Grace's village. 'Megs, this is Layan! We are in Layan now!' she says barely able to contain her excitement. We pass a number of different kinds of houses along the path, some concrete and tiled, some smaller and made of thatch (*nipa*) materials. We finally pull up to Grace's house. 'Are you serious?' Mark exclaims, 'this is like the Whitehouse of Iloilo!' It is a large and imposing con-crete two-storey house painted in light yellow, in a walled compound, complete with a tall red gate and a large patio in which a jeep and a car are parked. It is clearly one the largest and most impressive houses in the *barangay* that we had seen until then. It is situated in the centre of the village, next to the elementary school where many village gather-ings take place in the courtyard. We get out of the van and see a boy running towards us saying 'Mama'. He runs to Grace's sister in a mo-ment of confusion. Grace then gets out of the van and puts her arms out saying, 'that's my son' and goes to him with her arms stretched out, giving him a kiss on the head. He looks shy and turns his head to one side. We go into the house and loud shrieks are heard as four sisters and several cousins are running forward to give hugs to Grace, Novy and Mark. We immediately sit down to a breakfast of garlic fried rice, *longganisa* sausages and *lapu-lapu* fish. '*Kaon na!*' (Let's eat!) Grace's sister insists. Grace's uncle and aunt walk in and there is another round of screaming. The uncle puts on the karaoke machine on the TV and starts singing 'Besame Mucho'. This uncle has been living in the US for decades and from the attention he commands, it is clear that he is an influential member of the family.

After breakfast I wander around the house and compound. Along one side of the house there are benches under mango trees and a door leading to the indoor kitchen. At the back, there is a wooden hut where the two *katulong* (domestic helpers) live. Next to that is the outdoor kitchen, where Grace's mother spends most of our week there cooking, to make sure there is enough food for the family and for the whole host of visitors expected during the *fiesta*. Around the other side of the house, there is a family hall. Inside the house, the bedrooms have parquet wooden flooring, the bathrooms are equipped with modern WCs and shower stalls, the living room is done up with white tiles and wooden panelling on the ceiling. There is a sofa set upholstered with dark green floral velvet, rugs, coffee and dining tables, and a large TV, DVD player and big speakers. There are also display cabinets for glasses, crockery, photo albums and the daughters' school trophies.

Each day during our stay, we awaken to the sounds of Spanish influenced Filipino folk music. The *fiesta* atmosphere is in the air. We hardly sleep much in any case. Throughout the stay, Grace's sisters tell me, 'we Filipinos love to eat, so just go ahead and help yourself. Don't be shy, just eat like we all do'. Days are spent playing mahjong from morning until night, particularly among the older aunts and uncles. The men hang around outside on the patio, sitting on the benches, idle, making jokes, drinking San Miguel beer and watching basketball matches taking place next door. The children play outside all day and the ice-cream man comes in the afternoons to scoop out mango ice cream. There is a lazy, slow feel to these days spent outside. Meanwhile, the kitchen and dining room are places of intense activity and preparation. The women – Grace, her sisters and cousins – are cooking around the clock, as well as getting the children washed and dressed in the morning. The days revolve around breakfast, lunch, *merienda* and dinner. On top of that, preparations had to be made for Grace's Uncle Ceasar's 70th birthday, the *bisperas* (the day before the *fiesta*), and most importantly, the *fiesta* day itself. All kinds of desserts are prepared, in addition to the folding of empanadas, the marinating of fish and chicken, preparing shrimp and crab, and the peeling of mangoes. Two pigs are brought in one afternoon on a tricycle, one waiting to be slaughtered the next day. Roasted pig – *lechon* – is a delicacy, and providing it on occasions like these is a symbol of wealth and hospitality. For Uncle Ceasar's 70th birthday, *lechon* was the centre of attention, people saying, 'come come, let's have *lechon*!' Photos are taken with the *lechon*, and it is shared around. One evening, we wander to Grace's cousin's house to watch the pig slaughter. The relatives are less well off than Grace's family, their compound consisting of a dusty yard, one concrete, unpainted house without windows and a *nipa* hut. Sharing the pig slaughter with others is clearly a big event for this family. We sit down on chairs, which are laid out, to watch. Jayvee sighs as we sit there, 'aaah, village life, this is the happiest time of my life'. Usually he is on a ship sailing all over the world.

Each day in the run-up to the *fiesta*, there are more emotional re-unions between Grace, her siblings, aunts, uncles, cousins, and other distant members of the extended family who live in the village and who come to visit the overseas returnees. During the *fiesta* period, there are many village activities: the basketball tournament, the parade for children, the evening festivities and the all-night disco, which all take place at the elementary school yard next to the house. During the day, Grace's sisters occasionally pass snacks and drinks over the fence to fellow villagers who are gathered for the activities in the schoolyard. They are clearly the primary household offering hospitality to other villagers.

One day, we drive to Iloilo city to check on the small house, in a large, landscaped private residential compound that Grace and Ricky bought. This is a new development pitched to overseas Filipinos and the 'new rich'. The company's slogan is: 'Philippines' First Middle-Class Mass Housing Community'. Grace and Ricky own a small plot of land in this compound, a model of American suburbia. The small house is currently empty, but Grace explains to her son that it is for him when he grows up.

Fiesta day starts with the Philippine national anthem at 6 a.m. The first event of the day is the Mass at church. Clothes are ironed and everyone dresses up. The service brings the whole village together in the small and cosy Layan Catholic Church. When we return from church, relatives are already at the house and all the food is set up outside, along with crates of soft drinks, tables and chairs for the guests. People come in and out all day. During the day, I meet a cousin who used to work as a caregiver in Singapore, moving from there to Canada where she has been living happily for the past sixteen years. I meet a ten-year old girl living with her grandma, while her mother is away working as a nurse in Saudi Arabia. I meet several others working as nurses with the hope to go overseas, some successfully passing the board exam, others failing and having to work as volunteer nursing assistants. Uncle Ceasar keeps

Figure 8: 'The Whitehouse of Iloilo'

Figure 9: Elementary school courtyard, where village activities are held during the fiesta

coming to practise his English with me, saying that maybe one day he can go to the UK to visit his daughter in the Isle of Man.

In the evening, there is a beauty parade. Children are introduced to the community, dressed in their finest dresses and suits. During the parade, special mention is made of *balikbayans* – migrant returnees – including to Grace and Ricky. The *balikbayan* families and children are presented to the rest of the village and revered. It goes as follows: 'This is the son and daughter of Mr and Mrs ... she dreams of being a nurse one day ... he wants to be a nursing aide ... he wants to be a seaman ... her dream is to become a teacher'. It was also a time for a congressman to make a speech, promising development in the village in the run-up to the Philippine elections. After the parade, the *fiesta* continues at home with everyone staying up late, drinking beer, and sitting out on the patio.

The experience up until this point gives the impression that this Philippine home, which Grace had romanticized in her stories in Singapore, really exists. Home appears to live up to its 'mythic status' (Bammer, 1992). The idea of nostalgia in the diaspora for a home left behind is certainly not new, with earlier works also highlighting how migrants romanticize and imagine home as a place where they will be welcomed eagerly and joyfully by family and relatives upon their return and where village life continues in virtuous and harmonious ways (see Khater, 2001; Striffler, 2007; Wolf, 2006; Parry 2003). However, Jonathan Parry (2003: 221), powerfully captures these moments as a kind of 'flickering nostalgia', because it quickly becomes apparent what this nostalgia conceals. In the specific case of this trip there are things beneath the surface that are unspoken in the Layan home. Amidst the fun, there are moments of suppressed tension. A couple of these moments emerged towards the end of the trip.

Our trip ends with a large family visit in two big vans to Boracay, the beach resort island off the coast of Panay. In Boracay, Grace and the other overseas family members, sponsor everyone's stay in beach huts, pay for large family seafood dinners and island hopping excursions. That night, sitting by the beach with Ricky, Grace's brother-in-law Kuya

Benny, and a few cousins, was one of the only times during the trip when I heard frank remarks about life overseas. Benny says to Ricky about Boracay, 'there is no money, these restaurants are expensive'. Benny lives in Edinburgh with his wife Ruth (Grace's sister) and their six-year old daughter. He works as a train steward in first class compartments of Virgin trains in the UK. He never sees the family because his shifts and Ruth's nursing shifts alternate so that someone is home to look after their daughter. 'It's okay', he says, 'but how long am I supposed to do this kind of work'? Trained as an architect, Benny applied everywhere but did not find a job that would allow him to practice his profession in the UK. He sighs, 'Hazel [his daughter] is good at drawing, maybe one day she will be an architect and fulfil my own dream … but there our rental is 650 pounds per month, so expensive, *walang pera eh* [there is no money]'. Their apparent ease with money when they return home for these holidays – spending and enjoying – is more an illusion than a reality, Benny implies.

We then meet Novy who is wandering through the Boracay night markets. 'The Philippines has changed a lot, so many buildings, I can't recognize them. I feel like I am lost in the country of my birth. I am scared to be alone'. When I ask if she is thinking about retiring in the Philippines, she shakes her head honestly and decisively, scrunching up her face. 'I've been there [in Texas] for so many years; I think it's better. Do I look healthy? I have a heart problem. If you have this problem here without insurance, it's impossible; insurance is so expensive here. The insurance is better there. It's better if I just come back for vacation – like now. We are enjoying'.

These moments illuminate two key points. The first that Benny's story highlights has to do with the status of overseas migrants and the expectations that those 'left behind' have of their migrant relatives. Grace tells me that her great grandfather had been a senior government official under the Spanish, although her own father lived a more humble life with a small fishing business. Her grandfather was well respected and for a long time, their house has been the centre for family gatherings. It used to be simpler, but since her uncles and aunts went to the US, they have sent money back to Grace's mother to renovate the family house.

This explains how and why their house is the centre of village life. It is the house that provides hospitality and it is now the house of highly educated nurses living successful lives abroad (in the eyes of other villagers). The very fact of being overseas – even when they are not doing well financially, as Benny's story reveals – is enough to give the impression of wealth. Migrants who return home have an obligation to give money and presents on their sojourns home, and there are expectations among villagers that they will. A great deal of power and expectation comes with being a migrant, particularly a migrant nurse. Going home becomes an expensive trip, which is why such large reunions only take place every four or five years. Tensions and disparities exist within families over issues to do with care, duty, money and expectations. Deirdre McKay (2010: 334–335) illuminates these tensions in explaining how, 'overseas migrants can feel overwhelmed and express fear they will be "consumed" by the needs of those at home', with constant demands from distant kin and village mates who want a share of the perceived overseas success. The fears that migrants may have about giving money and presents to people at home were hidden during the vacation, I observed. It was striking how little conversation took place during the trip home among family members and friends about the details of their routine lives overseas. People generally did not ask much about details; for them, it was the simple fact that their relatives and friends are overseas that matters, as well as the fact that they return looking happy, healthy, wearing different kinds of clothes and displaying a different habitus. This reveals that life overseas is successful enough. It was only the conversation with Benny in Boracay which revealed how bare and unfulfilling a life overseas could be. Neither Grace nor her sisters spoke in much detail about the difficulties they face in their working lives, or living abroad. The trip is therefore not a time to sit and talk about the past years, but to re-enter Philippine village life as if no time had passed and no distances travelled. Migrants also have to balance their personal, familial and future aspirations and plans alongside keeping up the appearance of a successful migrant who meets social obligations and demonstrates conspicuous consumption (see also Osella and Osella, 2000; 1999).

The second point raised by Novy's comments, relates to the questions of home, security and the future. When she says: 'it's better if I just come back for vacation – like now. We are enjoying', she alludes to how the trip home embodies within it a sense of nostalgia for a happy Filipino life, of being together in the moment, playing mahjong, cooking, dancing and singing. It is also a time when migrants revert back to traditional gender roles, with the women cooking and putting the children to bed, while the men participate in pig slaughters, drink beer and go to the all-night disco. This is all seen nostalgically as harmonious familial conviviality and is captured in the phrase 'ang saya saya' (such happiness). However, Grace, Novy and other overseas relatives recognize that the Philippines is not a place where to spend one's working life, to raise children or to find adequate health security. The utopian Philippine experience is condensed into a period of two or three weeks. Home is longed for but no longer realistically seen as a place to live, even if migrants are not happy or successful overseas. Rather, home becomes a temporary space for the denial of the hardships of life overseas.

As a comparative example, Steve Striffler (2007) has written poignantly on Mexican immigrant workers and their search for home. What Striffler observes about Mexican migrants' trips home is strikingly paralleled by what I saw with Grace and her relatives. He relates that:

> Time spent in Mexico allows immigrants to forget their daily reality and to escape ... where, if only for a moment, they are not only unmarked by race, language, and occupation but also hold the elevated status of a successful migrant. [Yet at the same time] ... like a paternalistic pat on the back, the trip home reminds people that the decision to migrate was a good one; that they were a little more clever, a little smarter, a little more ambitious than those who stayed in Mexico; that the humiliation, hard work, and sacrifice were worth it. [He underlines how] ... narratives about the greatness of Mexico ... are quickly followed by rather pointed statements about corrupt governments, the economy, lazy Mexicans and the general unlivability of Mexico' (2007: 681–683).

Home is thus romanticized at the same time as it is pitied or scorned as a backward place. When migrants leave the Philippines, most say that the government does not care about them and their futures. The basis for many nurses leaving is the idea that the Philippines does not provide an image of progress, a stable future or one of security, rather, they associate their country with corruption. If we consider Novy who has been in the US for 25 years, she admits that the Philippines is not a place where she can rely on the state to provide for her health. The idea of return is thus postponed and if not explicitly denied, it fades into the background, not dissimilar to earlier studies of migration which spoke of a 'myth of return', referring to how diasporic groups continually speak of returning home upon retirement, but do not actually do so.[2]

The Philippines is still what migrants call home. Yet in practice, this home is now the most transient of all; a place for sojourns in which one can experience intensely yet briefly the feeling of home without actually settling or building a future there. I now consider the third moment, of how migrants may build a home in an unexpected location.

From Transit City to Home

We have seen how migrants make plans to travel on from Singapore, with all its challenges, while experiencing the Philippines as a home for short sojourns. What role, then, does the transit city play? What happens when plans change, along with expectations? I return to the story of Nelia who was waiting for more than a year for her UK visa, only to have her plans to move there halted. The period of waiting saw Nelia feeling helpless. She is now stuck in Singapore for longer than she imagined. Nelia has slowly resigned herself to the possibility of a life in Singapore, and will apply for PR status in Singapore, which will enable her to bring her husband and son over. Here, the role of state restrictions elsewhere makes Singapore more than a temporary stop. The third spatial and temporal scenario is not about moving on elsewhere, or returning back home, but about unexpectedly staying put. I share here a few exceptional cases of Filipino migrants and how they began, often by accident, to call the transit city, a home.

Home as Routine

Até Ella arrived in Singapore as a nursing aide and initially lived in Singapore on a work permit, the lowest category migrant visa. Ella did not have much working experience in the Philippines prior to that and therefore did not have much to compare her experience in Singapore with; she was consequently not as disappointed as other nurses I met. Over the years, she worked her way up through the ranks of nursing in a large government hospital. A few years into her work, she went back

---

2. See Bhachu, 1985; Watson, 1977.

home to marry Joel, a civil engineer, in her Ilocano village who then moved to Singapore to be with Ella (who by that time had an S-Pass and was eligible for permanent residence). The first time I went to Ella and Joel's flat was in the beginning of my fieldwork. I remember sitting at the kitchen table with Joel's mother who was chopping garlic while Ella and Joel were cooking Filipino dishes for their daughter's birthday party. She told me, 'my son, in the Philippines, he was civil engineer. Now waiter!', and then started laughing and laughing, as if someone had told the funniest of jokes. Joel too could not help chuckling at his mother's comments.

Ella and Joel, along with their three children, aged six, three and one, live together in a two room HDB flat. Their Chinese neighbours (called 'aunties') dote on the children, give them sweets and take care of them when Ella and Joel are at work. The children's birthdays are celebrated at home; colleagues of Ella and Joel are invited to eat in their flat. Ella would always say to me, 'I wish I could put nicer decorations in my home; the walls are so empty, I feel so ashamed sometimes [sigh]. Someday, I can have my own place, decorate it how I want, make it beautiful.' Nonetheless, in spite of the shame she feels, Ella and Joel see hospitality and entertaining guests on special occasions as crucial to their Singapore lives, which are otherwise fairly consumed by work, caring for the children and taking rests. Many of Ella and Joel's friends are Filipino, but at their house gatherings, there are also Indian, Chinese, Malay, Burmese and Korean friends who are colleagues or neighbours of Ella and Joel.

Over time, slowly but surely, they have made Singapore a home for themselves and the family. Their three children were born in Singapore. Ella never really expressed much interest in moving on to other countries. She reminisces about the Philippines, but does not express a desire to return there. Above all, Ella says that she feels fulfilled doing the work that she does in Singapore as a senior nurse; it is a job she loves, in spite of its daily stresses.

Not everything is rosy though. Joel struggles with work, not fulfilled working as a waiter for as long as he has been in Singapore. Ella tells me they are thinking of enrolling him into a nursing course in Singapore as an alternative career path. There were times when Ella seemed down; juggling her responsibilities as a nurse, and taking care of three young children and generally feeling exhausted. Most of the time, Ella and Joel have a relative from the Philippines visiting for a few months to help them take care of the children; over the year, I met Joel's mother and father and two of Ella's sisters.

This is a clear example of a Filipino family that has made Singapore a home; in spite of things not being completely stable, they have made peace with spending their working lives and raising their children there. They have made arrangements with family in the Philippines to have relatives visit and help care for the children, they have developed a diverse network of friends and neighbours and obtained permanent residence in Singapore. Their eldest child, April, is already in the local school and speaks English with a strong Singaporean accent, much to their amusement. On a subsequent visit a year after my main fieldwork period, I visited Ella, Joel and the family in a new flat, which they had just purchased; it is an HDB flat in a large estate with lots of open space for the children, playgrounds and barbeque areas. The flat itself is also bigger than the previous flat, and they were clearly proud of having a place of their own in Singapore. Through the busy routines of daily life – of work and taking care of the children, putting them in school, running a family household, cooking, getting to know neighbours – a feeling of home crept up on Ella and Joel.

Unlike Ella, who chose to stay in Singapore because of a fulfilling career and the establishment of a secure family life, Charis and Leah are two nurses who unexpectedly chose to make Singapore their home.

Spiritual Homes

The experiences of Charis and Leah are rather different to other experiences that I have described. Charis and Leah are nurses from *Faith Church*, a church that has completely transformed their sense of self and their priorities in life. Frowning upon their previous greedy selves, hungry to make more money overseas as nurses, they now step back to consider what 'accepting God' has done to change their moral compass of the world and their sense of belonging.

Charis was Roman Catholic when she arrived in Singapore but she later stumbled upon the evangelical church *Faith Church*. Charis's journey started off in a fairly typical manner as a career move to help the family; trained as a nurse in Manila, she moved to Singapore to work in a public hospital. However, her journey was then transformed into a spiritual one. She believes that her move to Singapore was fated so that she could 'discover God'. Within a month of arriving in Singapore, she 'received Christ' at *Faith Church* after some initial indecision, given her Catholic upbringing. Charis felt that the people from *Faith* were 'consistent in their sharing ... they would visit us, bring us food, teach us the Bible, spend time with us and pray for us ... then I understood my faith'. She began to share many stories about the 'sacrificial spirit' of the church members, making people feel that they belong to a family. However, it was difficult to balance her commitment to the church alongside her nursing career. She says, 'I was really thick-skinned (*kapal ng mukha*) at that time; I would take so many scoldings, mostly from my nursing managers. I had to change shifts all the time so that I can attend the church meetings'.

A few years later, the church offered her a full-time position and she quit her job as a nurse; she now calls herself a 'servant of God' working for the Church in their outreach programme. Charis has reached the point of saying, 'the church is really my life, that's what makes me stay here'. She continues, 'I now have confidence in the way I live my life. I don't have my own family ... but still I am so fulfilled'. When I ask her if she misses nursing, or if she would ever take up a nursing opportunity abroad, she gave me a very affirmative 'no'. She explains:

> My family, they encourage me to go overseas to work, but they understand what my life is here. I am serving God here and I will stay – this is what I want to do with my life, because I have received Christ and I want to serve and share his word. I would only go to other places on missions to help spread the word.

Other nurses that I encountered in the church appeared to be following similar trajectories, extremely active in the weekly services, group prayer meetings and evangelizing outings.[3] Leah, for instance, another nurse in the same church, recounted a similar story of changing her priorities from nursing to the church. She initially felt displaced like many other nurses arriving in Singapore; the kind of care in Singapore is different to what she was used to; nurses are not seen as partners

---

3. That said, most nurses I met were Roman Catholic. The smaller number that I met who are involved in Faith Church, however, are very active in church life and have different experiences of Singapore compared to my Roman Catholic informants.

of doctors but rather as maids. She cried to her mother several times about quitting and returning to the Philippines. But again, the church changed Leah's experience. She related how nurses from the church approached her at the bus stop after work; she was sceptical at first, but finally allowed them to visit her. 'Then', she said, 'that Sunday I went to *Faith Church*. It's mostly nurses at that time – you know, we really have something common, we are all Filipino nurses, you get a warm feeling, then you see there are some people the same like you'. In spite of some initial resistance, Leah later found herself leading the care group Bible discussions and playing the guitar at these group gatherings. Leah tells me that she used to be very shy and insecure, but suddenly opened up. 'I definitely changed so much since I came here', she said pensively. Leah said, 'I just have to thank them for not giving up on me. You didn't reply to their SMS and then still they welcome you, still they ask you to come'. She continues by explaining that 'my purpose is not to live for my own self. My purpose is to live for others, to serve God. You have to live for other people in your life, serve them, that is the purposeful thing'. During her first five years in Singapore, she was always thinking about other countries. Five years later, she no longer wants to move. Singapore is now home for her.

These nurses initially go to Singapore to pursue an in demand career, and instead find their calling, not in nursing, but as 'servants of God'. The stories of nurses in *Faith Church* reveal how transformations in religious practice and in self-practices can also transform aspirations and sense of place. Charis and Leah find their spiritual homes in Singapore, fundamentally linked to their feelings of being at home with themselves. Migrants embedded in these churches have to negotiate commitments to these new spiritual communities and families while also negotiating financial and emotional demands of those back home. As McKay (2010: 343) rightly points out, 'traditional village exchanges have not simply been extinguished by a Christian and individualized subjectivity'. This is once again a reminder of the constant entanglements between migrants' different homes.

Here, There, Elsewhere

Although most Filipino nurses arrive in Singapore with the intention to move away, a few do unexpectedly stay on: Nelia is stuck in Singapore for longer than she hoped; the routines of work and raising a family give Ella and Joel the semblance of home; while Charis and Leah discover new dimensions of themselves and change their life aspirations and priorities. The stories I have shed light on reveal how Singapore could, for some, become a home: a place with a sense of future.

The migration of medical workers to Singapore sees three spatial and temporal orientations: an orientation to the future, located beyond Singapore in the minds of migrants; an orientation towards the past, to homes in the Philippines with which they sustain significant connections, even if the nature of these connections change over time; and an orientation to the present, of living in a city of expected transience. These three states are linked together by the search for home as migrants yearn for stability in moments of displacement. Of course, all three orientations are connected within the life of each individual migrant. Negotiating between these orientations is a key feature of migrants' lives as they attempt to realize their aspirations and test the possibilities of their citizenship.

For the majority of migrants who orient themselves towards the future, there is a great sense of uncertainty, as they, generally speaking, connect only superficially with their present surroundings, while not being sure of whether, when and how future plans will materialize. The Philippines remains a strong point of connection and a moral, familial and territorial foundation for migrants. In spite of this anchor, the Philippines rarely resembles a home in a lasting or practical sense as my trip home with Grace revealed. The anxiety caused by the tensions between yearning for something ahead, and a 'flickering nostalgia' for something left behind, emerges powerfully in transit (Parry, 2003).

Cities like Singapore – and dozens of others in the Middle East, such as Doha, Muscat and Dubai – are rarely seen as settling points. They have often been places bringing together large networks of people in a melting pot, as they pass through from one place to another. Such cities represent only one stage in a longer trajectory of mobility, and hence migration and mobility have been central to the identities of many of these cities. Yet in Singapore, there has been a growing debate about which migrants can settle and which can only stay temporarily. In fact, very few Filipino nurses *want* to stay as being in another Asian city is not seen as prestigious, secure or desirable. 'Home-making' is not always a conscious process of active planning. An element of surprise can change people's notions of what or where home is, and this includes even those places perceived as temporary. There are many possible continuations of the stories of Filipino medical workers as they move physically and imaginatively between the Philippines, Singapore and the elsewhere.

CHAPTER EIGHT

Quiet Lives

I have explored the changing perceptions that migrant medical workers have of home, where places expected to be transient might unexpectedly end up feeling like home. This happens through, for instance, discovering new intimate communities of friendship and spirituality, and through career and familial stability. However, the more commonly narrated story that I found was one that held within it the thirst to move somewhere else. Plans and motivations were articulated in neat and linear narratives, yet, there was a certain unpredictability and restlessness in the lives of the migrant medical workers as they continued to imagine different futures and possibilities through their vast global networks of family and friends. McKeown (2001: 7) argues that 'many migration studies establish a polarization between concepts like push and pull, emigration and immigration, sending society and host society, or tradition and adaptation, which privilege the perspectives of nations that frame the two ends of migrant journeys'. In so doing, they tend to overlook the connections, circulations and 'in-between' spaces within which debates, dilemmas, and transformations unfold in the everyday lives of migrants. Beyond the two ends of the migration journey, of origin and destination, 'every voyage' as Trinh Minh-ha (1994:9) observes, 'can be said to involve a re-siting of boundaries ... between a here, a there, *and* an elsewhere'.

Getting to know my informants well over the course of fieldwork offered me a novel perspective on how relationships take shape in a location of expected transience. It made me think of how transit cities, and the varied forms of social life which exist within them, are highly relevant spaces to understand as people become ever more mobile on the one hand, and visa and border controls become ever more restrictive on the other. Albeit from a position of privilege (whereby my passport and research profession allowed me the opportunity to cross borders without much difficulty), my period in the field and my movements as an academic researcher, allowed me to empathize with a life in transit: both with the rich opportunities it offers, and with the challenges it involves, such as the difficulties of building bonds in places that one initially perceives to be temporary. However, as these ethnographic stories demonstrate, rather than seeing transit as empty in meaning, transit space is in fact a generative space within which migrants reflect on and modify self-definitions and orientations (Johnson, 2010; Lindquist, 2009). The idea of transience itself is not new – both historical and contemporary works have explored the sojourns of diverse migrants, as well as circular or seasonal movements (Harper, 1997; Parry, 2003; Shah, 2006; Gidwani and Sivaramakrishnan, 2003). Most of these studies also recognize the limits to this stated temporality in migrants' narratives when mobility becomes a way of life or a livelihood strategy over a longer-term and indefinite period. Less attention has been given to the condition of transience itself as productive or transformative of new aspirations and goals; or as a condition that permeates, often with anxiety, the rhythms and priorities of migrants' daily routines as they deal with both the present and the future. In this light, the places to which migrants move are not just backdrops or blank settings within which their lives play out. Instead, as Doreen Massey (1994: 154–155) has powerfully elaborated, place, 'is constructed out of a particular constellation of social relations, meeting and weaving together at a particular locus', and that these social relations far exceed the boundaries of that particular place. This is clear in the case of migrants whose lives are necessarily translocal and transnational, and where a sense of place 'includes a consciousness of its links with the wider world'. It is through these negotiations of locally situated relationships and the sense of the wider world that migrants attempt to build and inhabit a place and make it their own – particularly as the places in which they find themselves also shape them in powerful and often unexpected ways.

Among the migrant nurses I got to know, transience was dealt with in quiet ways. I recall the silences about the details of life overseas I observed among Grace and her sisters when they returned home to Layan for the family reunion and *fiesta*. The very act of keeping quiet – as Grace and her sisters did – echoes the tensions that have emerged throughout this book: of heightened expectations and alienating realities, of experiences of shame over dignity, of desires to move on versus obstacles that hold them back, and of not wanting to disappoint the family. Alongside the silences I observed on the trip home with Grace and her family, is a parallel quietness in many nurses' lives in Singapore. The quietness is not always explicit or calculated. It is in part a consequence of long shifts at work. It is also linked to the subjectivities that nurses wish to cultivate. Unlike domestic workers, it appeared that the majority of my informants' creative engagements and new friendships were not actively sought, but stumbled upon and gradually, subconsciously, developed. Furthermore, the overriding picture that emerged is that many Filipino nurses in Singapore in fact seek to 'inhabit norms' (Mahmood, 2004: 15). These are norms that we might associate with a secure middle-class life, which valorize neoliberal individual enterprise, flexibility and prosperity, as well as material security and so-called respectable and modest behaviour. They also spend much of their time nurturing connections with families at home or in other places in the world – where a digital and intimate co-presence with the family unit is preferred over going out late. Some spend their time watching Korean soap operas and music videos; others engage with a 'global Christian media', revealing their expansive imaginaries and engagements alongside their private existences in the city (Cruz, 2009: 130–131).[1] Through my fieldwork I found that nurses do not participate in the 'louder' and more visible collective gatherings in public spaces, more frequently associated with domestic workers. The quieter forms of nurses' socialities were for me a striking finding given the prominence of discussions of community in studies of migration. In this case, it is the very association with a defined community – Singapore's Filipino community – that nurses distance themselves from. Rather, it is within intimate social groupings and spaces that medical workers choose to cultivate their subjectivities, while attempting to realize personal and family life projects.

Transnationalism, belonging and the politics of citizenship

The quieter dispositions of the nurses I encountered sit in contrast to the idea of a transnational public sphere or community, and do not relate to initiatives or organizations that work collectively in advocacy

---

1. See McDuie-Ra (2012) for an interesting parallel with migrants from the Northeast of India in Delhi.

for migrants' rights or 'homeland' concerns and projects (Levitt and Waters, 2002; Basch, Glick-Schiller and Szanton-Blanc, 1992; 1994). In the case of transnational rights advocacy, it is domestic workers who are primarily involved in campaigns directed at the Philippine state's policy of labour export, or in campaigns for a minimum wage and decent working conditions in the societies to which they go (such as in the case of Hong Kong).[2] They use these platforms in the hope to improve their conditions of life and work, as they are the migrant workers most starkly excluded from residence rights and formal or substantive forms of citizenship. Beyond advocacy, they also engage in practices to challenge the image of a victimized and voiceless migrant worker through a range of socio-cultural practices. However, the nurses do not share in their struggles in any practical or immediate way, even if they feel pity or shame that their compatriots experience abusive situations.

On a related note, I was often curious about the fact that the nurses I worked with seemed little interested in politics: they rarely spoke about party politics in the Philippines or about activism in nursing unions.[3] While the fact that nurses are not active in unions in Singapore can partly be explained by the curtailment of union activity and public protest in Singapore's restricted political landscape, I noticed that nurses also did not seem to feel their absence. This could suggest that, in that particular moment of their lives, they held different ideas on where to invest their energies and pursue their goals. That said, while they were rarely explicit or public about politics, this book demonstrates that they did engage in forms of micro-politics in ways that permeated many aspects of their lives. One way this micro-politics manifested itself was through a politics of status with other Filipinos over how the Philippines ought to be represented abroad. Migrant medical workers seek social inclusion and distinction, even if achieving this depends on

---

2. The case of domestic workers in Hong Kong is distinctive in the region. It is one of the few cities in Asia where there are visible forms of public protest and activism among migrant domestic workers. Domestic workers get together in cross-national solidarity alliances to protest better labour conditions and rights. Anthropologist Nicole Constable has documented this activism in much of her work (see e.g. Constable, 1997 and 2010). Such forms of protest are less visible in the Singapore context, even if there are other ways through which domestic workers exercise their agency.

3. It is however, notable that Filipino nurses are very active in nursing unions in North America.

an accompanying process of exclusion and boundary making. Their specific point of contention is to counteract the image of overseas Filipinos occupying feminized and subservient sectors of the global service economy, particularly in the sphere of care labour. As such, they use a professionalized status to negotiate borders and hierarchies, which in the process, creates new ones. What one does becomes an important form of identification; labour categories affect how migrants perceive each other, and also affect how others perceive migrants; this take on a routine salience in this ethnographic context. Of course, these forms of identification are not pre-existing or rigid and there are attempts amongst nurses and especially amongst domestic workers, to find new creative engagements and forms of empowerment in which they are not exclusively defined by their labour (even if part of the advocacy for labour rights involves reconfiguring the meanings of their work and to have it recognized as work). Save a few important exceptions, a large part of the scholarship on migration has focused either on low-wage contract workers on highly restrictive visas, or 'highly skilled' migrant who cross borders with greater ease and freedom. However, the focus on two ends of the spectrum only tells a partial story given the importance of new mobilities that include middle-class and semi-professional migrants situated ambivalently in-between. This ethnography has highlighted how the negotiation of migration policies and of boundaries relating to profession, gender, class and race take place precisely in these liminal spaces.

Within such liminal spaces, we furthermore see how 'acts of citizenship' are variably articulated by different groups of Filipino migrants in Singapore (Isin, 2008). Rather than making claims on either the Philippine or Singapore state as transnational migrant workers, migrant nurses' acts of citizenship work to redefine the image of the overseas Filipino citizen through their *exclusions* of 'lower-skilled' compatriots from their spaces of sociability; a form of agency that is not necessarily inclusive. Isin (2008: 18) argues aptly that 'the enactment of citizenship is paradoxical because it is dialogical' and necessarily involves a moment of differentiation from the other. The other may include a range of people and groups, which are approximated or pushed away in particular moments. The migrants in this study shift from moments of solidarity and affinity to those of competition and hostility.

Caring for Strangers in Asia

Understanding the other in nursing is central to the profession, as one of my informants suggested. Central to this ethnography is how an understanding of the other takes place within a particular inter-Asian context. My informants who move from the Philippines to Singapore are crossing borders in a region that appears, at least on the surface, to be culturally familiar but in reality reveals a number of stark differences. The second form of micro-politics that nurses engage with therefore relates to an inter-Asian cultural politics. A renewed political, intellectual and public interest in the changing geopolitical and economic relationship between Asia and the rest of the world is also debated in and through everyday spaces of care bringing together citizens of different Asian countries. Told through the voices of migrants themselves, we see the anxieties and hopes that they express on regional transformations in economy, health, family and community within which they are embedded. In Singapore, nurses encounter assertions of living in the heart of global Asia through, for instance, the hypermodern technologies in the hospitals they work in, the rhetoric of efficiency and economic success that they hear, the wealthy medical tourists they care for and a modern urban lifestyle that offers a wide range of consumption possibilities. However, their actual encounters also shatter this coherent image and reveal the marginal and residual elements, where the substance beneath the image of capitalist success reveals a sense of social isolation and unease.

Filipino medical workers oscillate between asserting a cosmopolitan sensibility on the one hand, and deploying narratives of national homogeneity on the other. They narrate abstract ideals about caring unconditionally for other human beings. However, in practice, distinctions between self and other are drawn both explicitly and implicitly. Upon encountering prejudice and experiencing exclusion, they respond with sharp social and moral critiques of the forms of social and family life they witness in Singapore, which they view as morally lacking. This leads nurses to think about wider ethical questions on how one ought to live in the world. They represent themselves through nationalistic narratives that posit warm and virtuous Filipinos against cold, atomized and capitalist Singaporeans. These essentialized expressions of their cultural values are prominent and strengthened in and through the stresses of migrant life in postcolonial Asia.

There has been growing antipathy in Singapore with regard to its non-resident population, with mounting opposition to the ruling government's open door immigration policy and an explosion of xenophobic hate speech on online social media. Tensions between migrant workers, the resident population and the state were widely debated following the 'Little India riots' involving South Asian migrant workers in Singapore. It was the first riot in decades in Singapore, which exposed fissures in the image of Singapore's multicultural harmony and the potential consequences of restrictive migration policies that are oriented towards dividing rather than bridging diverse populations. In another case, a Philippine Independence Day celebration in 2014, to be held in the heart of Singapore's commercial district, had to be cancelled after organisers were taunted and harassed on online social media with hate speech claiming that migrants should not have the right to public space and cultural expression in Singapore. While there is some resentment towards migrant 'elites' (e.g. those in financial and managerial executive positions), most of it is targeted at lower-income contract labour migrants from the Philippines, Indonesia, China, India, Bangladesh, Burma, Thailand and Sri Lanka. The negative reception to their physical presence in Singapore is based on a perception of 'Third World' migrants as chaotic presences in the ordered 'First World', even though they enable the very functioning of this global city and state. Certain officials have put forward proposals to set up self-contained residences in the marginal spaces of Singapore so that migrants do not interact with Singaporeans in their neighbourhoods and residential spaces.

However, for migrant nurses and carers, a socio-spatial separation proposed by these exclusionary proposals is not possible given the very nature of their work which puts them in very close proximity to Singaporeans. Nurses and patients thus negotiate questions of self and other, as well as trust, in the intimate spaces of care, with all the tensions that this might involve in multiple directions. This ethnography has also shed light on how these tensions can be overcome, or at least balanced by relationships between nurses and patients that are based on respect. Some of these long-term caring relationships have the potential to generate new intercultural bonds through sharing and indeed, feeling each other's experiences across cultural boundaries. We see this through Grace's intimate rapport with Aunty and the silent yet supportive co-presence of nurses and nursing home residents. We also see this beyond institutional spaces of care in the neighbourly bonds forged between Ella and her Chinese neighbours who help to care for her children, whilst spoiling them affectionately with treats. It would appear to make far more sense to focus policy efforts on spaces and initiatives that enable people to interact and care for each other in close proximity and over time, so that they can jointly shape these urban spaces and neighbourhoods.

In these actually existing inter-Asian encounters, we see how these cultural exchanges between carers and cared for, neighbours and colleagues, strangers and friends, develop and take shape. Cultural differences are not fixed or static. Migrants modify their statements about their cultural selves as they engage with difference and it is often through wider interactions with others, that such self-understandings develop (Marsden, 2008). Such categories of fixed cultural difference should not be starting points in our analyses, for self-definitions, either exclusive or open, take shape and form through wider, dynamic interactions (Said, 2000: 577). These observations apply more generally in any context of intercultural encounter. In the case of Singapore, one can ask the question of why these more fluid understandings of culture are not dealt with, for instance, in educational curricula, in orientation courses and in policies relating to cultural diversity. At present, these still perpetuate a static understanding of culture as based on discrete cultural groups holding essential characteristics. Moreover, it is clear that these dynamics between self and other are not limited to 'host society' and 'migrants' since these also are heterogeneous categories and migrants too are agents of inclusion and exclusion, as we have seen. I recall for instance, how Filipino nurses simultaneously pity and disapprove of the behaviour of domestic workers and construction workers. We can learn much from paying attention to the spaces that express vividly the contradictions and possibilities of a 'globalization from below' (Hall, [2006] 2008; Mathews, 2011).

While the process of migration and displacement foster and provoke new understandings of others, we also see how it provides revisions of migrants' self-understandings, as suggested at the opening of this chapter. Aguilar (2002: 24) observes that: 'ubiquitous in the migration literature, "home" and "family" are words that appear self-evident but, on reflection, signal a domain of problematic assumptions, methodological complexities, and hegemonic discourses and ideologies ... magnified by processes of movement and displacement'. Aside from home and family, the notion of care in this ethnography has been central to different spheres of migrants' lives. We see this in how nurses care for those perceived as strangers even as it may contradict their own understandings of care: an example is when Filipina nurses discover unexpectedly that bathing patients is a part of their job description in Singapore, while in their own upbringing, it is understood to be a task performed by family members. Patients too may sense nurses' aversion to doing particular tasks, which may also affect them since they carry with them their own cultural expectations of care and look to nurses to care for them in particular ways. We also see how the unconditional care taught to nurses in their Catholic-oriented nursing education is called into question when they confront the conflicts and mundanities in the workplace; and the ironies of their critiquing absent family members in Singapore's nursing homes when they themselves are absent from their family members as migrants abroad (even if polymedia offers new ways of being present). Among the most striking empirical observations from this research is that care is not in any way a neutral or straightforward term: it has multiple meanings and changes as it crosses borders. In this book, care has been described through its different articulations as an aspiration, a value, a practice and a form of labour. For migrant nurses, it relates to the wellbeing of their patients, the wellbeing of their families and their own futures. Beyond this, the globalization of medical care has ethical implications and understanding in-depth these different cultural understandings of care, as it is articulated in different spaces and institutions, will be important for ensuring a sense of collective wellbeing more broadly.

While this book has focused on the experiences of Filipino migrant medical workers specifically, the questions it raises are universally pertinent in this particular moment of global social and demographic transformation. The globalization of healthcare is a phenomenon most commonly addressed in the fields of economics, demography and public health, which inform policymakers on addressing issues related to ageing populations and the governance of migration flows and labour markets. Equally fundamental and necessary are social and cultural analyses that seek to understand how care in all its inflections, is experienced by those who receive it and by those who provide it. Speaking of ageing and illness, Atul Gawande in his book *Being Mortal* (2014), poignantly explores the ways in which the practices of modern medicine and of medical professionals profoundly influence how people spend the last stages of their lives, in ways that take me back to the hospital wards of the chronically ill that I spent time in during my research in Singapore. He reflects upon the ethical questions at these stages, observing that:

> ... the waning days of our lives ... are spent in institutions – nursing homes and intensive care units – where regimented, anonymous routines cut us off from all the things that matter to us in life. [And in] ... lacking a coherent view of how people might live successfully all the way to their very end, we have allowed our fates to be controlled by the imperatives of medicine, technology, strangers (Gawande, 2014: 9).

But he also suggests that we now have an 'opportunity to refashion our institutions, our culture, and our conversations' in ways that make lives meaningful (Gawande, 2014; 243) and to reconsider how we approach the care for strangers and obligations to others in the future when such interdependencies will be increasingly common. Understanding the 'sudden, transient bonds' that are forged in these circumstances through the acts of listening and witnessing are worthy of greater contemplation and attention (Tisdale, 1987:66; 2016).

Towards the future

In a landscape of globalizing health in Asia, shaped by a politics of inequality and cultural difference, this book has followed the lives of migrant medical workers across borders, through a range of institutional, public and intimate spaces in which they live, work and dream.

For medical workers from the Philippines, nursing in particular offered a promising future overseas. Since the period after my field research – a time when there was much optimism about nursing education and international careers – a growing number of news reports and blog posts speak of a decline of nursing schools and fading dreams of nurses in the Philippines as its symbolic potential comes into question. In spite of this, there are still significant numbers going abroad and already living abroad in countries across the world.[4] Among the nurses I met during

---

4. See Appendix A.

my period of fieldwork, hardly any have returned home permanently or for long periods of time. Yet we can see how the structural linkages between nursing and the international labour market may suddenly change as it moves through different phases. Unfulfilled expectations and the difficulties in reaching the countries that migrants actually aspire to reach might make nursing less desirable. It makes me ask to what extent this field will still offer a channel for the global aspirations of this new generation of Filipinos. Will it continue to be a compelling career option, or will people turn to other kinds of salaried and professional employment as an alternative? Perhaps the answer will not be straightforward or linear for demographic change continues across the world and immigration policies are dynamic, with the constant 'opening' and 'closure' of particular destinations. Nursing has been important to the history of Philippine labour migration, and it is unlikely to fade away; at the same time, the possibilities for secure employment do and will matter in the decisions of families and youth.

It leaves the question of the future as open and nebulous. Articulations of future plans are at the heart of the narratives of the medical workers I met, even as there remains much uncertainty in the realization of these plans – this was captured most powerfully in the silences. I found that I was often made the subject of their discussions as they projected their own desires onto my future plans. They would delight in imagining a future for me and suggested repeatedly that I should hurry up and finish my research, make sure I get a good salary, and find someone to marry in Europe so that I could be happy there. 'Why', they ask, 'if you are already there, would you want to go come back to Asia?' In spite of their cravings for happy endings to their life projects, it is worth asking if they ever reach that point of resolution (Osella and Osella, 2006: 571–573). Whether they do or not, their expansive imaginaries and aspirations will remain a driving force in their lives.

Bibliography

Abinales, P. N. and Amoroso, D. J. (2005) *State and Society in the Philippines*, Lanham: Rowman and Littlefield Publishers Inc.

Acuin, J., Firestone, R., Htay, T. T., Khor, G. L, Thabrany, H., Saphonn, V., Wibulpolprasert, S. (2011) 'Southeast Asia: An Emerging Focus for Global Health', *The Lancet* 377, pp. 534–35.

Aguilar, F. V., Jr. (1996) 'The Dialectics of Transnational Shame and National Identity', *Philippine Sociological Review*, 44 (1–4) pp. 101–36.

——— (2002) 'Beyond Stereotypes: Human Subjectivity in the Structuring of Global Migrations', in F.V. Aguilar, Jr. (ed.), *Filipinos in Global Migrations: At Home in the World?* Quezon City: Philippine Social Science Council, pp. 1–36.

——— (2006) 'Experiencing Transcendence: Filipino Conversion Narratives and the Localization of Pentecostal-Charismatic Christianity', *Philippine Studies*, 54 (4), pp. 585–627.

——— (2012) 'Manilamen and Seafaring: Engaging the Maritime World Beyond the Spanish Realm', *Journal of Global History* 7, pp. 364–88.

Aguilar, F. V. Jr, Peñalosa J. E. Z, Liwanang, T. B. T, Cruz, R. S. I, Melendrez, J. M. (2009) *Maalwang Buhay: Family, Overseas Migration, and Cultures of Relatedness in Barangay Paraiso*, Quezon City: Ateneo de Manila University Press.

Alliance for Health Workers (2008) 'Migration of Health Workers & Professionals: The Philippine Experience'. Available from: http://iamr3.files.wordpress.com/2010/07/effectsofmiginhealth, accessed, 12 June 2011.

Almonte, J. T. (2004) *Toward One Southeast Asia: Collected Speeches*, Institute for Strategic and Development Studies, Quezon City: Inc. Philippines.

Amrith, S. S. (2011) *Migration and Diaspora in Modern Asia*, Cambridge: Cambridge University Press.

——— (2013) *Crossing the Bay of Bengal: The Furies of Nature and the Fortunes of Migrants*, Cambridge: Harvard University Press.

Anderson, Benedict (1991) *Imagined Communities: Reflections on the Origins and Spread of Nationalism*, London: Verso.

——— (1998) *The Spectre of Comparisons: Nationalism, Southeast Asia, and the World*, London: Verso.

Anderson, Bridget. (2000) *Doing the Dirty Work? The Global Politics of Domestic Labour*, London: Zed Books.

Anderson, W. (2006) *Colonial Pathologies: American Tropical Medicine, Race and Hygiene in the Philippines*, Durham. Duke University Press.

Appadurai, A. (1996) *Modernity at Large: Cultural Dimensions in Globalization*, Minneapolis: University of Minnesota Press.

Appiah, K. (1997) 'Cosmopolitan Patriots', *Critical Inquiry*, 23 (3), pp. 617–39.

Arnold, D. (1993) *Colonizing the Body: State Medicine and Epidemic Disease in Nineteenth Century India*, Berkeley: University of California Press.

Asperilla, P. F. (1971) *The Mobility of Filipino Nurses*, PhD dissertation, Teachers College, Columbia University.

Bach, S. (2003) 'International Migration of Health Workers: Labour and Social issues' *Working Paper 209*, Geneva: International Labour Office.

——— (2006) 'International Mobility of Health Professionals: Brain Drain or Brain Exchange', *Wider Research Paper*, 82, Helsinki: UNU-WIDER.

Ball, R. (2004) 'Divergent Development, Racialised Rights: Globalised Labour Markets and the Trade of Nurses —The Case of the Philippines' *Women's Studies International Forum*, 27, pp. 119–33.

——— (2008) 'Globalised Labour Markets and the Trade of Filipino Nurses: Implications for International Regulatory Governance', in J. Connell (ed.), *The International Migration of Health Workers*, New York: Routledge, pp. 30–46.

Bammer, A. (1992) 'Editorial', *New Formations: Journal of Culture/Theory*, 17, Special Issue on The Question of Home, pp. vii–xi.

Bangko Sentral ng Pilipinas (2015) 'Overseas Filipinos' Remittances'. Available from: http://www.bsp.gov.ph/statistics/keystat/ofw2.htm accessed 8 June 2016.

Barr, M. (1998) 'Lee Kuan Yew's "Socialism" Reconsidered'. *Access: History*, 2 (1), pp. 33–54.

Barth, F. (1969) 'Introduction', in F. Barth (ed.), *Ethnic Groups and Boundaries: The Social Organization of Culture Difference*, Bergen: Universitetsforlaget.

Basch, L., Glick Schiller, N., Szanton Blanc, C. (eds), (1992) *Towards a Transnational Perspective on Migration: Race, Class, Ethnicity, and Nationalism*

Reconsidered, New York: New York Academy of Sciences.

———(1994) *Nations Unbound: Transnational Projects, Postcolonial Predicaments, and Deterritorialized Nation-States,* New York: Gordon and Breach.

Bashford, A. (1997) 'Starch on the Collar and Sweat on the Brow: Self Sacrifice and the Status of Work for Nurses', *Journal of Australian Studies,* 21 (52), pp. 67–80.

Bayly, S. (2007) *Asian Voices in a Postcolonial Age,* Cambridge: Cambridge University Press.

Bello, W. (2004) *The Anti-Developmental State: The Political Economy of Permanent Crisis in the Philippines,* London: Zed Books.

Benedicto, B. (2009) 'Shared Spaces of Transnational Transit: Filipino Gay Tourists, Labour Migrants, and the Borders of Class Difference', *Asian Studies Review,* 33, pp. 289–301.

Bhachu, P. (1985) *Twice Migrants: East African Sikh Settlers in Britain,* London: Tavistock.

Biehl, J. (2005) *Vita: Life in a Zone of Social Abandonment,* Berkeley: University of California Press.

Borneman, J. (1997) 'Caring and being Cared For: Displacing Marriage, Kinship, Gender and Sexuality' *International Social Science Journal,* 49 (154), pp. 573–84.

Bourdieu, P. (1986) *Distinction: A Social Critique of the Judgment of Taste,* London: Routledge [translated by Richard Nice].

Brenner, S. (1998) *The Domestication of Desire: Women, Wealth, and Modernity in Java,* Princeton: Princeton University Press.

Buchan, J. and Seccombe, I. (2009) 'Difficult Times, Difficult Choices: The UK Nursing Labour Market Review 2009', *RCN Labour Market Review,* Royal College of Nursing.

Bulatlat (2004) 'A Sick Health Care System', *Bulatlat,* IV (37), 17th–23rd October 2004. Available from: http://bulatlat.com/news/4-37/4-37-sick.html, accessed 11 September 2011.

Cabañes, J. (2009) 'Pinoy Postings: On the Online Cultural Identity Performances of Young Filipino Professionals in Singapore', in I. Banerjee, and S. R. Muppidi (eds), *Changing Media, Changing Societies: Media & the Millennium Development Goals,* Singapore: Asian Media Information and Communication Centre.

Cannell, F. (1999) *Power and Intimacy in the Christian Philippines,* Quezon City: Ateneo de Manila University Press.

Caregiver (2008) Film, Directed by Chito S. Roño, Philippines, Star Cinema Productions.

Carsten, J. (2013) 'Ghosts, Commensality and Scuba Diving: Tracing Kinship and Sociality in Clinical Pathology Labs and Blood Banks in Penang', in S. McKinnon and F. Cannell (eds) *Vital Relations: Modernity and the Persistent Life of Kinship*, Santa Fe: SAR Press, pp. 109–31.

Cassell, J. (1998) *The Woman in the Surgeon's Body*, Cambridge: Harvard University Press.

Catholic Institute for International Relations (CIIR) (1987) *The Labour Trade: Filipino Migrant Workers Around the World*, London: CIIR.

Cheah, P. (2006) *Inhuman Conditions: On Cosmopolitanism and Human Rights*, Cambridge: Harvard University Press.

Chee H. L (2010) 'Medical Tourism and the State in Malaysia and Singapore', *Global Social Policy*, 10 (3), pp. 336–357.

Chee H. L and Whittaker, A. (2010) 'Why is Medical Travel of Concern to Global Social Policy?', *Global Social Policy*, 10 (3), pp. 287–91.

Choy, C. (2003) *Empire of Care: Nursing and Migration in Filipino American History*, Durham: Duke University Press.

Chua, B. H. (1995) *Communitarian Ideology and Democracy in Singapore*, London: Routledge.

——— (1999) '"Asian Values" Discourse and the Resurrection of the Social', *positions*, 7 (2), pp. 573–92.

Chua, B. H. and Kuo. E. C. Y (1995) 'The Making of a New Nation: Cultural Construction and National Identity', in B.H. Chua, *Communitarian Ideology and Democracy in Singapore*, London: Routledge, pp. 101–23.

Clark, P. F., Stewart, J. B. and Clark, D. A. (2006) 'The Globalization of the Labour Market for Health-care Professionals', *International Labour Review*, 145 (1–2), pp. 37–64.

Clifford, J. (1992) 'Traveling Cultures', in L. Grossberg, C. Nelson, P. Treichler (eds), *Cultural Studies*, London: Routledge.

Coleman, S. (2000) *The Globalization of Charismatic Christianity: Spreading the Gospel of Prosperity*, Cambridge: Cambridge University Press.

Connell, J. (2008) 'Towards a Global Health Care System?', in J. Connell (ed.), *The International Migration of Health Workers*, New York: Routledge, pp.1–29.

Constable, N. (1997) *Maid to Order in Hong Kong: Stories of Filipina workers*, Ithaca: Cornell University Press.

—— (2002) 'At Home But Not at Home: Filipina Narratives of Ambivalent Returns', in F. V. Aguilar Jr. (ed.), *Filipinos in Global Migrations: At Home in the World?* Quezon City: Philippine Social Science Council, pp. 380–412.

—— (2009) 'The Commodification of Intimacy: Marriage, Sex and Reproductive Labor', *Annual Review of Anthropology*, 38, pp. 49–64.

—— (2010) 'Telling Tales of Migrant Workers in Hong Kong: Transformations of Faith, Life Scripts, and Activism', *The Asia Pacific Journal of Anthropology*, 11 (3–4), Special Issue on Diasporic Encounters, Sacred Journeys, pp. 311–29.

Constitution of the Republic of the Philippines, Article 2 of 1987. Available from: http://www.chanrobles.com/philsupremelaw1.htm, accessed 19 September 2011.

Cooper, F. (2005) *Colonialism in Question: Theory, Knowledge, History*, Berkeley: University of California Press.

Copeman, J. (2009) 'Introduction: Blood Donation, Bioeconomy, Culture', *Body & Society*, 15 (2), pp.1–28.

Cornelio, J. (2008) 'New Paradigm Christianity and Commitment-formation: The Case of Hope Filipino (Singapore)', in A. Day (ed.), *Religion and the Individual: Belief, Practice, Identity*, Aldershot: Ashgate, pp. 65–77.

Crompton, R. (1998) *Class and Stratification: An Introduction to Current Debates*, Cambridge: Polity Press.

Cruz, J. N. (2009) 'A Spectacle of Worship: Technology, Modernity and the Rise of the Christian Megachurch', in F. K. G. Lim (ed.), *Mediating Piety: Technology and Religion in Contemporary Asia*, Leiden: Brill, pp. 113–38.

Datta, K., McIlwaine, C., Evans, Y., Herbert, J., May, J. & Wills, J. (2006) 'Work, Care and Life among Low-paid Migrant Workers in London: Towards a Migrant Ethic of Care', *Working Paper 6*, London: Queen Mary, University of London.

—— (2010) 'A Migrant Ethic of Care? Negotiating Care and Caring Among Migrant Workers in London's Low-Pay Economy', *Feminist Review*, 94, pp. 94–16.

Diamond, T. (1992) *Making Gray Gold: Narratives of Nursing Home Care*, Chicago: Chicago University Press.

Dimaya, R. M., McEwen, M.K, Curry, L.A. and Bradley, E. H (2012) 'Managing Health Worker Migration: A Qualitative Study of the Philippine Response to Nurse Brain Drain', *Human Resources for Health*, 10: 47, pp. 1–8.

Dingwall, R., Rafferty, A.M., Webster, C. (1988) *An Introduction to the Social History of Nursing*, London: Routledge.

Divinagracia, C. (2005) 'Policy Issues on Skilled Migration: The Case of Filipino Nurses', *Dr. Alfredo J. Ganapin Advocacy Forum Series III,* Quezon City: Center for Migrant Advocacy.

Dubai (2005) Film, Directed by Rory B. Quintos, Philippines, Star Cinema Productions.

Duffin, C. (2008) 'Immigration Changes Will Cause Staffing Crisis in Care Home Sector' *Nursing Standard,* 23 (2), p. 9.

Earl, C. (2014) *Vietnam's New Middle Classes: Gender, Career, City*: Copenhagen, NIAS Press.

Ehrenreich, B. and Hochschild, A. R. (eds), (2003) *Global Women: Nannies, Maids and Sex Workers in the New Economy,* New York: Metropolitan Books.

England, P. (2005) 'Emerging Theories of Care Work', *Annual Review of Sociology,* 31, pp. 381–99.

Espiritu, Y. L. (1995) *Filipino American Lives,* Philadelphia: Temple University Press.

——— (2002) 'Filipino Navy Stewards and Filipina Health Care Professionals: Immigration, Work and Family Relations', *Asian and Pacific Migration Journal,* 11 (1), pp. 47–66.

Eviota, E. (1992) *The Political Economy of Gender: Women and the Sexual Division of Labour in the Philippines,* London: Zed Books.

Faier, L. (2009a) 'Filipina Migrants in Rural Japan and their Professionals in Love', *American Ethnologist,* 34 (1), pp. 148–62.

——— (2009b) *Intimate Encounters: Filipina Women and the Remaking of Rural Japan,* Berkeley: University of California Press.

Falzon, M.A. (2005) *Cosmopolitan Connections: The Sindhi Diaspora, 1860–2000,* New Delhi: Oxford University Press.

Ferguson, J. and Gupta, A. (2002) 'Spatializing States: Towards an ethnography of Neoliberal Governmentality', *American Ethnologist,* 29 (4), pp. 981–1002.

Foucault, M. (1976 [2003]) *Society Must be Defended: Lectures at the Collège de France 1975–76,* London: Penguin [translated by D. Macey].

——— (1977) *Discipline and Punish: The Birth of the Prison,* London: Allen Lane [translated by A. Sheridan].

——— (1978) 'Governmentality', in Burchill, G. and Gordon, C. (eds.) (1991) *The Foucault Effect: Studies in Governmentality,* London: Harvester Wheatsheaf, pp. 87–104.

——— (1997) *Ethics: Essential Works of Foucault 1954–1984, Vol. 1,* London: Penguin [ed. P. Rabinow, translated by R. Hurley and others].

Frost, M. R. and Balasingamchow, Y. (2009) *Singapore: A Biography,* Singapore: Editions Didier Millet.

Galvez-Tan, J. Z., Sanchez, F. S., Balanon, V. L (2004) *The Philippine Phenomenon of Nursing Medics: Why Filipino Doctors are Becoming Nurses,* Philippines: National Institutes of Health.

Gawande, A. (2014) *Being Mortal: Illness, Medicine and What Matters in the End,* London: Profile Books.

George, S. (2000) '"Dirty Nurses" and "Men Who Play": Gender and Class in Transnational Migration', in M. Burawoy (ed.), *Global Ethnography: Forces, Connections and Imaginations in a Postmodern World,* Berkeley: University of California Press, pp. 144–74.

Ghosh, A. (1988) *The Shadow Lines,* London: Black Swan.

Gibson, K, Law, L., McKay, D. (2001) 'Beyond Heroes and Victims: Filipina Contract Migrants, Economic Activism and Class Transformations', *International Feminist Journal of Politics,* 3(3) pp. 365–86.

Gidwani, V and Sivaramakrishnan, K (2003) 'Circular Migration and Rural Cosmopolitanism in India', *Contributions to Indian Sociology,* 37 (1–2), pp. 339 – 67.

Gilroy, P. (1994) '"After the Love has Gone": Bio-Politics and Etho-Poetics in the Black Public Sphere', *Public Culture,* 7, pp. 49–76.

Giron-Tupas, A. (1961) *History of Nursing in the Philippines,* Manila: University Book Supply Inc.

Glick Schiller, N. and Caglar, A. (2016) 'Displacement, Emplacement and Migrant Newcomers: Rethinking Urban Sociabilities within Multiscalar Power', *Identities: Global Studies in Culture and Power,* 23 (1), pp. 17–34.

Government of Manitoba Immigration Department (2010) 'Premier renews memorandum of understanding for co-operation with the Philippines'. Available from: http://www2.immigratemanitoba.com/browse/news.html?item=3755, accessed 11 September 2011.

Government of Saskatchewan Advanced Education, Employment and Immigration Department (2006) 'Memorandum of understanding'. Available from: http://www.aeei.gov.sk.ca/memorandum-understanding-sk-vietnam-philippines, accessed 11 September 2011.

Guardian (2011) 'Nursing dream fades for Filipinos as UK jobs dry up'. Available from: http://www.guardian.co.uk/world/2011/feb/23/nursing-dream-filipinos-uk-jobs, accessed 12 June 2011.

Guevarra, A. R. (2009) *Marketing Dreams, Manufacturing Heroes: The Transnational Labor Brokering of Filipino Workers,* New Brunswick: Rutgers University Press.

Guinto, R. L. L. R., U. Z. Curran, R. Suphanchaimat and N. S. Pockock (2015) 'Universal Health Coverage in "One ASEAN": Are Migrants Included?', *Global Health Action* 8: 25749. Published Online 24 Jan. Available at: http://www.globalhealthaction.net/index.php/gha/article/view/25749, accessed 12 March 2016.

de Guzman, O. (2003) 'Overseas Filipino Workers, Labor Circulation in Southeast Asia, and the (Mis)management of Overseas Migration Programs', *Kyoto Review of Southeast Asia,* 3. Available at http://kyotoreview. cseas.kyoto-u.ac.jp/issue/issue3/index.html, accessed 11 September 2011.

Halili, S. D. Jr. (2006) *Iconography of the New Empire: Race and Gender Images and the American Colonization of the Philippines,* Quezon City: University of the Philippines Press.

Hall, S. ([2006] 2008) 'Cosmopolitanism, Globalisation and Diaspora: Stuart Hall in Conversation with Pnina Werbner', in P. Werbner (ed.), *Anthropology and the New Cosmopolitanism,* Oxford: Berg, pp. 345–60.

Hardt, M. (1999) 'Affective Labour', *boundary 2,* 26 (2), pp. 89–100.

Hardt, M. and Negri, A. (2000) *Empire,* Cambridge: Harvard University Press.

Harper, T. N. (1997) 'Globalism and the Pursuit of Authenticity: The Making of a Diasporic Public Sphere in Singapore', *Sojourn,* 12, pp. 261–92.

Helble, M. (2011) 'The Movement of Patients Across Borders: Challenges and Opportunities for Public Health', *Bulletin of the World Health Organization,* 89, pp. 68–72.

Herzfeld, M. (1997) *Cultural Intimacy: Social Poetics in the Nation-State,* New York: Routledge.

Hill, M. and Lian, K. F. (1995) *The Politics of Nation Building and Citizenship in Singapore,* London: Routledge.

Hochschild, A. R. (1983) *The Managed Heart: Commercialization of Human Feeling,* Berkeley: University of California Press.

——— (2000) 'The Nanny Chain', *The American Prospect,* 11 (4), pp. 32–36.

Holston, J. and Appadurai, A. (1996) 'Cities and Citizenship', *Public Culture,* 8 (2), pp. 187–204.

Hondagneu-Sotelo, P. (2007) *Domestica: Immigrant Workers Cleaning and Caring in the Shadows of Affluence,* Berkeley: University of California Press.

Ileto, R. (1998) *Filipinos and Their Revolution: Event, Discourse, and Histori-*

ography, Quezon City: Ateneo de Manila University Press.

Irving, D. R. M. (2010) *Colonial Counterpoint: Music in Early Modern Manila*, Oxford: Oxford University Press.

Isin, E. F. (2008) 'Theorizing Acts of Citizenship', in E.F. Isin and G. M. Nielsen (eds), *Acts of Citizenship*, London: Zed Books, pp. 15–43.

Johnson, M. (2010) 'Diasporic Dreams, Middle-Class Moralities and Migrant Domestic Workers among Muslim Filipinos in Saudi Arabia', *The Asia Pacific Journal of Anthropology*, 11 (3–4), Special Issue on Diasporic Encounters, Sacred Journeys, pp. 428–48.

Ju, S. H. (1983) 'Chinese Spirit–Mediums in Singapore: An Ethnographic Study', *Contributions to Southeast Asian Ethnography*, 2, pp. 3–48.

Khater, A. F. (2001) *Inventing Home: Emigration, Gender, and the Middle Class in Lebanon 1970–1920*, Berkeley: University of California Press.

King, V. T. (2008) 'The Middle Class in Southeast Asia: Diversities, Identities, Comparisons and the Vietnamese Case' *International Journal of Asia Pacific Studies*, 4 (2), pp. 75–112.

Kingma, M. (2005) *Nurses on the Move: Migration and the Global Healthcare Economy*, Ithaca: Cornell University Press.

—— (2007) 'Nurses on the Move: A Global Overview', *Health Services Research*, 43 (3, Part II), pp. 1281–98.

Kirk, J. M. and Erisman, H. M. (2009) *Cuban Medical Internationalism: Origins, Evolution, and Goals*, New York: Palgrave Macmillan.

Kramer, P. (2006) *The Blood of Government: Race, Empire, the United States & The Philippines*, Chapel Hill: University of North Carolina Press.

Lan, P. (2003) '"They Have More Money but I Speak Better English!" Trans-national Encounters between Filipina Domestics and Taiwanese Employers', *Identities: Global Studies in Culture and Power*, 10 (2), pp. 133–61.

Lee, H. L. (2009) 'Prime Minister Lee Hsien Loong National Day Rally Speech 2009'. Available from: http://www.nas.gov.sg/archivesonline/speeches/view-html?filename=20090826007.htm, accessed 6 December 2016.

Lee, K. Y. (2000) *From Third World to First: The Singapore Story, 1965–2000*, New York: Harper Collins.

Levitt, P. and M.C. Waters (2002) 'Introduction', in P. Levitt and M.C. Waters (eds), *The Changing Face of Home: The Transnational Lives of the Second Generation*, New York: Russell Sage, pp.1–30.

Li, T. (1989) *Malays in Singapore: Culture, Economy and Ideology*, Singapore: Oxford University Press.

Liebelt, C. (2008) 'On Sentimental Orientalists, Christian Zionists, and "Working Class Cosmopolitans": Filipina Domestic Workers' Journeys to Israel and Beyond', *Critical Asian Studies*, 40(4), pp. 567–85.

—— (2010) 'Becoming Pilgrims in the 'Holy Land': On Filipina Domestic Workers' Struggles and Pilgrimages for a Cause', *The Asia Pacific Journal of Anthropology* 11(3), Special Issue on Diasporic Encounters, Sacred Journeys, pp. 245–67.

Lindquist, J. A. (2009) *The Anxieties of Mobility: Migration and Tourism in the Indonesian Borderlands*, Honolulu: University of Hawaii Press.

Long, N. (2009) *Urban, Social and Personal Transformations in Tanjung Pinang, Kepulauan Riau, Indonesia*, PhD Dissertation, Department of Social Anthropology, University of Cambridge.

Long, D., Hunter, C. L, and van der Geest, S. (2008) 'Introduction: When the field is a ward or a clinic', *Anthropology and Medicine*, 15 (2), Special issue on Hospital Ethnography, pp.71–78.

Lorenzo, F. (2002) *Nurse Supply and Demand in the Philippines*, Manila: University of the Philippines Institute for Labour Studies.

Lorenzo, F. M., Dela, F. R. J, Paraso, G. R., Villegas, S., Issac C., Yabes, J. Trinidad, F. Fernando, G., Atienza, J. (2005) *Migration of Health Workers: Country Case Study*, The Institute of Health Policy and Development Studies, National Institute of Health, Philippines.

Lorenzo, F. M. E., Galvez-Tan, J., Icamina, K. and Javier, L. (2007) 'Nurse Migration from a Source Country Perspective: Philippine Country Case Study', *Health Services Research*, 42 (3), pp. 1406–18.

Madianou, M. and Miller, D. (2012) *Migration and New Media: Transnational Families and Polymedia*, London: Routledge.

Mahathir, M. (1970) *The Malay Dilemma*, Kuala Lumpur: Federal Publications.

Mahler, S. (1995) *America Dreaming: Immigrant Life on the Margins*, Princeton: Princeton University Press.

Mahmood, S. (2004) *Politics of Piety: The Islamic Revival and the Feminist Subject*, Princeton: Princeton University Press

Malkki, L. (1992) 'National Geographic: The Rooting of Peoples and the Territorialization of National Identity among Scholars and Refugees', *Cultural Anthropology*, 7 (1), Special Issue on Space, Identity, and the Politics of Difference, pp. 24–44.

Manalansan. M. (2008) 'Queering the Chain of Care Paradigm', *The Scholar & Feminist Online*, 6(3). Available from: www.barnard.edu/sfonline/immigration/manalansan_01.htm, accessed 4 August 2011.

Manderson, L. (1996) *Sickness and the State: Health and Illness in Colonial Malaya, 1870–1940*, Cambridge: Cambridge University Press.

Marcus. G. E. (1995) 'Ethnography in/of the World System: The Emergence of Multi-sited Ethnography', *Annual Review of Anthropology*, 24, pp. 95–117.

Marks, S. (1994) *Divided Sisterhood: Race, Class and Gender in the South African Nursing Profession*, New York: St. Martin's Press.

——— (1997) 'The Legacy of the History of Nursing for Post-Apartheid South Africa', in A.M Rafferty, J. Robinson and R. Elken (eds), *Nursing History and the Politics of Welfare*, London: Routledge, pp. 29–44.

Marsden, M. (2005) *Living Islam: Muslim Religious Experience in Pakistan's North-West Frontier*, Cambridge: Cambridge University Press.

——— (2008) 'Muslim Cosmopolitans? Transnational Life in Northern Pakistan', *The Journal of Asian Studies*, 67 (1) pp. 213–47.

Marshall, T. H. (1950) *Citizenship and Social Class: And Other Essays*, Cambridge: Cambridge University Press.

Massey, D. (1994) *Space, Place and Gender*, Cambridge: Polity Press.

Mathews, G. (2011) *Ghetto at the Center of the World*, Chicago: University of Chicago Press.

Matsuno, A. (2011) *Nurse Migration: The Asian Perspective*, Bangkok: International Labour Organization.

McDowell, L. (2009) *Working Bodies: Interactive Service Employment and Workplace Identities*, Chichester: Wiley-Blackwell.

McDuie-Ra, D. (2012) *Northeast Migrants in Delhi: Race, Refuge and Retail*, Amsterdam: Amsterdam University Press.

McKay, D. (2010) 'A Transnational Pig: Reconstituting Kinship among Filipinos in Hong Kong, *The Asia Pacific Journal of Anthropology*, 11 (3–4), Special Issue on Diasporic Encounters, Sacred Journeys, pp. 330–44.

——— (2012) *Global Filipinos; Migrants' Lives in the Virtual Village*, Bloomington: Indiana University Press

McKeown, A. (1999) 'Conceptualizing Chinese Diasporas, 1842–1949', *The Journal of Asian Studies*, 58 (2), pp. 306–37.

——— (2001) *Chinese Migrant Networks and Cultural Change: Peru, Chicago, Hawaii, 1900–1936*, Chicago: University of Chicago Press.

Mehta, K. (2002) 'National Policies on Ageing and Long-term Care in Singapore: A Case of Cautious Wisdom', in D. R. Phillips and A.C.M. Chan (2002) *Ageing and Long-Term Care: National Policies in the Asia-Pacific*,

Singapore: Institute of Southeast Asian Studies, pp. 150–80.

Miller, D. (1998) *A Theory of Shopping*, Cambridge: Polity Press.

Miller, D and Slater, D. (2000) *The Internet: An Ethnographic Approach*, Oxford: Berg.

Milner, A. (2001) 'What's Happened to Asian Values?' ANU Working Paper. Available at: https://digitalcollections.anu.edu.au/handle/1885/41912, accessed 6 June 2016.

Minh-ha, T. (1994) 'Other than Myself/My Other Self', in G. Robertson et al. (eds), *Travellers' Tales: Narratives of Home and Displacement*, London: Routledge, pp. 9–26.

Ministry of Manpower, Singapore (2016) 'Work Passes and Permits. Available from: http://www.mom.gov.sg/passes-and-permits, accessed 9 June 2016.

——— 'Employment of Foreign Manpower Act (Chapter 91A)'. Available from: http://www.mom.gov.sg/Documents/services-forms/passes/WPS PassConditions.pdf, accessed 21 September 2011.

Misra, J, Woodring, J. and Merz, S. (2006) 'The Globalization of Care Work: Neoliberal Economic Restructuring and Migration Policy', *Globalizations*, 3 (3), pp. 317–32.

Mol, A. (2008) *The Logic of Care: Health and the Problem of Patient Choice*, London: Routledge.

Monocle (2011) 'People Power – Manila', *Monocle,* Issue 40, February 2011, pp. 77–81.

Mulder, N. (1998) 'The Legitimacy of the Public Sphere and Culture of the New Urban Middle Class in the Philippines', in J. D. Schmidt, J. Hersh and N. Fold (eds), *Social Change in Southeast Asia*, Harlow: Longman, pp. 98–113.

Nakano Glenn, E. (2000) 'Creating a Caring Society' *Contemporary Sociology*, 29 (1) Special issue on Utopian Visions: Engaged Sociologies for the 21st Century, pp. 84–94.

National Family Council, 'Think Family' website. Available from: http://www.thinkfamily.sg, accessed 12 September 2011.

National Library Board of Singapore (2004) 'Speak Mandarin Campaign'. Available from: http://was.nl.sg/details/www.mandarin.org.sg.html, accessed 11 September 2011.

National Population Secretariat, Singapore (2009) 'Population in Brief'. Available from: http://www.nps.gov.sg, accessed, 25 February 2011.

New Paper (2010) 'National Family Council on Filial Piety Ad – "Idea was to Inspire Young"', *The New Paper*, 28th June. Available from: http://www.asiaone.com/News/Education/Story/A1Story20100628-224204.html, accessed 12 September 2011.

Ohno, S. (2012) 'Southeast Asian Nurses and Caregiving Workers Transcending National Boundaries: An Overview of Indonesian and Filipino Workers in Japan and Abroad', *Southeast Asian Studies*, 49 (4), pp. 541–69.

Ogawa, R. (2012) 'Globalization of Care and the Context of Reception of Southeast Asian Care Workers in Japan', *Southeast Asian Studies*, 49 (4), pp. 570–93.

Ong, J. and Cabañes, J. (2011) 'Engaged But Not Immersed: Tracking the Mediated Public Connection of Filipino Elite Migrants in London', *Southeast Asia Research*, 19 (2), pp.197–224.

Ortin, L. (1994) 'The Exodus of Filipino Nurses: An Action Agenda', *Asian Migrants* 4 (4), pp. 126–45.

Osella, C. and Osella, F. (1999) 'From Transience to Immanence: Consumption, Life-Cycle and Social Mobility in Kerala, South India', *Modern Asian Studies*, 33 (4), pp. 989–1020.

————— (2000) 'Migration, Masculinity and Money in Kerala', *Journal of the Royal Anthropological Institute*, 6 (1), pp. 117–33.

————— (2006) 'Once Upon a Time in the West? Stories of Migration and Modernity from Kerala, South India', *Journal of the Royal Anthropological Institute*, 12 (3), pp. 569–88.

Ozden and Schiff (2006) *International Migration, Remittances and the Brain Drain*, Washington DC: World Bank.

Paper Dolls [Bubot Niyar] (2006) Film, Directed by Tomer Heymann, Israel, Heymann Brothers Films.

Parreñas, R. S. (2001) *Servants of Globalization: Women, Migration and Domestic Work*, Stanford: Stanford University Press.

————— (2005) *Children of Global Migration: Transnational Families and Gendered Woes*, Stanford: Stanford University Press.

————— (2008) *The Force of Domesticity: Filipina Migrants and Globalization*, New York: New York University Press.

Parry, J. P. (2003) 'Nehru's Dream and the Village "Waiting Room": Long-Distance Labour Migrants to a Central Indian Steel Town', *Contributions to Indian Sociology*, 37 (1–2), pp. 217–49.

Philippine Nurses Association (2008) 'Nurses Cry Over Long Overdue Salary Increase'. Available from: http://www.pna-ph.org/mainframe.html, Press Releases, accessed 12 June 2011.

———(2008) 'Many Filipino Nurses Now Underemployed and Unemployed'. Available from: http://www.pna-ph.org/mainframe.html, Press Releases, accessed 12 June 2011.

Philippines Overseas Employment Agency (2013) 'Commission on Filipinos Overseas: Stock Estimate of Overseas Filipinos. Available from: http://www.cfo.gov.ph/index.php?option=com_content&view=article&id=1340:stock-estimate-of-overseas-filipinos&catid=134:statisticsstock-estimate&Itemid=814, accessed 8 June 2016.

——— (2010–2014) 'OFW Deployment Statistics'. Available from: http://www.poea.gov.ph/ofwstat/ofwstat.html, accessed 8 June 2016.

Pinches, M. (1999) 'Entrepreneurship, Consumption, Ethnicity and National Identity in the Making of the Philippines' New Rich', in M. Pinches (ed.), *Culture and Privilege in Capitalist Asia,* London: Routledge, pp. 275–301.

Pinto, S. (2009) 'Crises of Commitment: Ethics of Intimacy, Kin and Confinement in Global Psychiatry', *Medical Anthropology*, 28 (1), pp. 1–10.

Pollock, S., Bhabha, H., Breckenridge, C. and Chakrabarty, D. (2000) 'Cosmopolitanisms', *Public Culture*, 12 (3), pp. 577–58.

Porio, E. (2007) 'Global Householding, Gender and Filipino Migration: A Preliminary Review', *Philippine Studies*, 55 (2), pp. 211–42.

Pratt, G. (2004) *Working Feminism*, Philadelphia: Temple University Press.

Rabinow, P. and Rose, N. (2006) 'Biopower Today', *BioSocieties* 1, pp. 195–217.

Rafael V. L. (1997) '"Your Grief is Our Gossip': Overseas Filipinos and Other Spectral Presences', *Public Culture*, 9, pp. 267–91.

——— (2000) *White Love and Other Events in Filipino History,* Durham: Duke University Press.

Raghuram (2012) 'Global Care, Local Configurations – Challenges to Conceptualizations of Care', *Global Networks,* 12 (2), pp.155–74.

Rahim, L. Z. (1998) *The Singapore Dilemma: The Political and Educational Marginality of the Malay Community*, Oxford: Oxford University Press.

Robbins, J. (2004) 'The Globalization of Pentecostal and Charismatic Christianity', *Annual Review of Anthropology*, 33, pp. 117–43.

Rodriguez, R. M. (2008a) 'The Labor Brokerage State and the Globalization of Filipina Care Workers', *Signs: Journal of Women in Culture and Society*, 33 (4), pp. 794–800.

——— (2008b) 'Domestic Debates: Constructions of Gendered Migration from the Philippines', *The Scholar and Feminist Online*, 6 (3), Summer 2008. Available at: http://sfonline.barnard.edu/immigration/rrodriguez_

01.htm, accessed 7 June 2016.

———— (2011) 'Philippine Migrant Workers' Transnationalism in the Middle East', *International Labor and Working-Class History*, 79, pp. 48–61.

Romero, M. (1992) *Maid in the U.S.A.* New York, Routledge.

Romulo, C. P. (1941) 'I am a Filipino' [Reprinted from The Philippine Herald Aug 16, 1941], in L. Romulo (ed.) (1998) *The Romulo Reader*, Makati City: Bookmark Inc., pp. 1–5.

Rose, N. (1996) 'The Death of the Social? Re-figuring the Territory of Government', *Economy and Society*, 25 (3), pp. 327–56.

———— (2007) *The Politics of Life Itself: Biomedicine, Power and Subjectivity in the Twentieth-First Century*, Princeton: Princeton University Press.

Said, E. (2000) *Reflections on Exile*, London: Granta.

Sassen, S. (2000) 'Spatialities and Temporalities of the Global: Elements for a Theorization', *Public Culture*, 12 (1), pp. 215–32.

Sears, L. J. (2007) 'Postcolonial Identities, Feminist Criticism, and Southeast Asian Studies', in L. J. Sears (ed.), *Knowing Southeast Asian Subjects*, Seattle: University of Washington Press, pp. 35–74.

Severino, R. C. and Salazar, L. C. (2007) *Whither the Philippines in the 21st Century?*, Singapore: ISEAS.

Shah, A. (2006) 'The Labour of Love: Seasonal Migration from Jharkhand to the Brick Kilns of Other States in India', *Contributions to Indian Sociology*, 40 (1), pp. 91–119.

Sheridan, G. (1999) *Asian Values Western Dreams: Understanding the New Asia*, St. Leonards NSW: Allen & Unwin.

Silvey, R. (2006) 'Consuming the Transnational Family: Indonesian Migrant Domestic Workers to Saudi Arabia', *Global Networks*, 6 (1), pp. 23–40.

Singapore Department of Statistics (2015) 'Population in Brief 2015', September 2015. Available from: http://population.sg/population-in-brief/files/population-in-brief-2015.pdf, accessed 1 June 2016.

Singapore Nursing Board, 'Annual Report 2014'. Available from: http://www.healthprofessionals.gov.sg/content/dam/hprof/snb/docs/publications/SNB%20Annual%20Report%202014.pdf, accessed 8 June 2016.

Spivak, G. (1999) *A Critique of Postcolonial Reason: Toward a History of the Vanishing Present*, Cambridge: Harvard University Press.

Stoler, A. L. (2002) *Carnal Knowledge and Imperial Power: Race and The Intimate in Colonial Rule*, Berkeley: University of California Press.

Straits Times (1933) 'Letter to the Editor: Nursing Services', *The Straits Times*,

5th Oct, p. 17

——— (1950) 'The Asian Nurse', *The Straits Times*, 22nd Sept, p. 6

——— (1951)'The Nurse's Life in Singapore', *The Straits Times*, 28th July, p. 9

——— (1952) 'Muslim Women Become Nurse Conscious' *The Straits Times*, 28th Feb, p. 5

——— (2009a) 'Government May Act Against Children Who Dump Their Elderly Parents', *The Straits Times*, 17th Aug. Available from: http://www.pmo.gov.sg/content/pmosite/mediacentre/inthenews/primeminister/2009/August/govt_may_act_againstchildrenwhodumptheirelderlyparents.html, accessed 12 September 2010.

——— (2009b) 'Maids Turn Health-Care Attendants', *The Straits Times*, 21 December, p. B2.

——— (2011) 'Zero Tolerance for Violence at Nursing Homes', *The Straits Times (online)*, 11th June 2011. Available from: http://www.straitstimes.com/Singapore/Story/STIStory_678586.html, accessed 20 August 2011.

Striffler, S. (2007) 'Neither Here nor There: Mexican Immigrant Workers and the Search for Home', *American Ethnologist*, 34 (4), pp. 674–88.

Tadiar, N. (2004) *Fantasy-Production: Sexual Economies and Other Philippine Consequences for the New World Order*, Quezon City: Ateneo de Manila University Press.

Tagliocozzo, E. (2013) *The Longest Journey: Southeast Asians and the Pilgrimage to Mecca*, New York: Oxford University Press.

Tan, K.K. (ed.) (2004) *Beyond the Screen: Nurses' Reflections*, Singapore: Integrated Press.

Tan, T. (2003) 'Keynote Address by Singapore Deputy Prime Minister Dr Tony Tan at the Biopolis Opening'. Available from: http://www.nas.gov.sg/archivesonline/speeches/view-html?filename=2003102904.htm, accessed 6 December 2016.

Teo, P., Mehta, K, Thang, L. L., Chan, A. (2006) *Ageing in Singapore: Service Needs and the State,* London: Routledge.

Tisdale, S. (1987) 'We do Abortions Here: A Nurse's Story', Harper's Magazine, October 1987. Available at: http://harpers.org/archive/1987/10/we-do-abortions-here-a-nurses-story/, accessed 15 June 2016.

——— (2016) *Violation: Collected Essays*, Portland: Hawthorne

Today, 'Nursing Home Not Allowed to Take in New Patients', *Today Online,* 10th June 2011. Available from: http://www.todayonline.com/Singapore/EDC110610-0000065/Nursing-home-not-allowed-to-take-in-new-patients, accessed 20 August 2011.

Tolentino, R. (2001) *National/Transnational: Subject Formation and Media in and on the Philippines*, Quezon City: Ateneo de Manila University Press.

Toulson, R.E. (2009) *Pockets in Shrouds: Death and Desire in Contemporary Singapore*, PhD Dissertation, Department of Social Anthropology, University of Cambridge.

Trocki, C.A. (2006) *Singapore: Wealth, Power and the Culture of Control*, New York: Routledge.

Trouillot, M. R. (2001) 'The Anthropology of the State in the Age of Globalization', *Current Anthropology*, 42 (1), pp. 125–38.

Tyner, J. (2004) *Made in the Philippines: Gendered Discourses and the Making of Migrants*, London: RoutledgeCurzon

—— (2009) *The Philippines: Mobilities, Identities, and Globalization*, New York: Routledge.

Vertovec, S. (2009) *Transnationalism*, London: Routledge.

Watson, J. (1977) *Between Two Cultures: Migrants and Minorities in Britain*, Oxford: Basil Blackwell.

Weiss, M. (1997) 'War Bodies, Hedonist Bodies: Dialectics of the Collective and the Individual in Israeli Society', *American Ethnologist*, 24 (4), pp. 813–32.

Werbner, P. (1998) 'Exoticising Citizenship: Anthropology and the New Citizenship Debate', *Canberra Anthropology*, 21 (2), pp. 1–27.

—— (1999) 'Global Pathways: Working Class Cosmopolitans and the Creation of Transnational Ethnic Worlds', *Social Anthropology*, 7 (1), pp. 17–35.

—— (2002) *Imagined Diasporas among Manchester Muslims: The Public Performance of Pakistani Transnational Identity Politics*, Oxford: James Currey.

Werbner, P. and Johnson, M. (2010) 'Diasporic Encounters, Sacred Journeys: Ritual, Normativity and The Religious Imagination among International Asian Migrant Women', *The Asia Pacific Journal of Anthropology*, 11 (3–4), Special Issue on Diasporic Encounters, Sacred Journeys, pp. 205–18.

Whittaker, A (2008) 'Pleasure and Pain: Medical Travel in Asia', *Global Public Health*, 3 (3), pp. 271–90.

Wiegele, K.L. (2005) *Investing in Miracles: El Shaddai and the Transformation of Popular Catholicism in the Philippines*, Honolulu: University of Hawaii Press.

Wind, G. (2008) 'Negotiated Interactive Observation: Doing Fieldwork in Hospital Settings', *Anthropology and Medicine*, 15 (2), Special issue: Hospital Ethnography, pp. 79–89.

World Health Organization (2003) 'International Migration, Health and Human Rights', *Health and Human Rights Publication Series*, 4, Geneva.

——— (2011) 'The Philippines Health System Review', *Health Systems in Transition*, 1 (2). Available at: http://www.wpro.who.int/asia_pacific_ observatory/Philippines_Health_System_Review.pdf, accessed 12 June 2016.

Yeates, N. (2009a) *Globalising Care Economies and Migrant Workers: Explorations in Global Care Chains*, Basingstoke: Palgrave.

——— (2009b) 'Production for Export: The Role of the State in the Development and Operation of Global Care Chains', *Population Space and Place*, 15 (2), pp. 175–87.

Yeoh, B. S. A. (2004a) 'Cosmopolitanism and its Exclusions in Singapore', *Urban Studies*, 41 (12), pp., 2431–45.

——— (2004b) *Migration, International Labour and Multicultural Policies in Singapore*, ARI Working Paper, No. 19.

Yeoh, B. S. A. and Huang, S. (1998) 'Negotiating Public Space: Strategies and Styles of Migrant Female Domestic Workers in Singapore', *Urban Studies*, 35 (3), pp. 583–602.

Young, R. C. J. (2001) *Postcolonialism: An Historical Introduction*, Oxford: Blackwell Publishers.

Zelizer, V. A. (2005) *The Purchase of Intimacy*, Princeton: Princeton University Press.

Zialcita, F. N. (2005) *Authentic Though not Exotic: Essays on Filipino Identity*, Quezon City: Ateneo de Manila University.

Appendices

Appendix A: Top ten destinations and occupational categories

Table 1: Number of deployed land-based overseas Filipino workers by top ten destinations, new hires and rehires, 2010–2014

Destination	2010	2011	2012	2013	2014
Saudi Arabia	293,049	316,736	330,040	382,553	402,837
United Arab Emirates	201,214	235,775	259,546	261,119	246,231
Singapore	70,251	146,613	172,690	173,666	140,205
Qatar	87,813	100,530	104,622	94,195	114,511
Hong Kong	101,340	129,575	131,680	130,686	105,737
Kuwait	53,010	65,603	75,286	67,856	70,098
Taiwan	36,866	41,896	41,492	41,145	58,681
Malaysia	9,802	16,797	25,261	34,088	31,451
Bahrain	15,434	18,230	22,271	20,546	18,958
Canada	13,885	15,658	19,283	18,120	18,107
Total Destinations	**1,123,676**	**1,318,727**	**1,435,166**	**1,469,179**	**1,430,842**

Source: Philippine Overseas Employment Agency (POEA), 2014, http://www.poea.gov.ph/ofwstat/compendium/2014.pdf

Table 2: Number of deployed land-based overseas Filipino workers by top ten occupational categories, new hires

Occupational Category	2010	2011	2012	2013	2014
Household Service Workers	96,583	142,689	155,831	164,396	183,101
Nurses Professional	12,082	17,236	15,655	16,404	19,815
Waiters, Bartenders and Related Workers	8,789	12,238	14,892	14,823	13,843
Caregivers and Caretakers	9,293	10,101	9,128	6,466	12,075
Charworkers, Cleaners and Related Workers	12,133	6,847	10,493	12,082	11,894
Labourers/Helpers General	7,833	7,010	9,987	11,892	11,515
Wiremen and Electrical Workers	8,606	9,826	10,575	9,539	8,226
Plumbers and Pipe Fitters	8,407	9,177	9,657	8,594	7,657
Welders and Flame-Cutters	5,059	8,026	8,213	7,767	7,282
Cooks and Related Workers	4,399	5,287	6,344	7,090	5,707
Others	168,782	209,283	207,800	205,835	206,061
All Categories: Total	341,966	437,720	458,575	464,888	487,176

Source: Philippine Overseas Employment Agency (POEA), 2014, http://www.poea.gov.ph/ofwstat/compendium/2014.pdf

Appendix B: General structure of the nursing profession in Singapore

Director of Nursing

↑

Assistant Director
Advanced Practice Nurse (clinical)
Principal Nurse Educator (education)

↑

Senior Nurse Manager
Senior Nurse Clinician
Senior Nurse Educator

↑

Nurse Manager
Nurse Clinician
Nurse Educator

↑

Senior Staff Nurse

↑

Staff Nurse (also known as Registered Nurse)

↑

Enrolled Nurse (also known as Junior Nurse)

↑

Assistant Nurse/Nursing Aide

↑

Healthcare Assistant

Source: Adapted from a brochure by a public hospital in Singapore.

Appendix C: Joy's Letter

07-27-09

I recently leave in village whom my parents give birth and raise me up. My village is quite, not crowded mostly are farmer like us. Being a farmer is not easy, takes too long, waiting for many months to harvest but despite of these we learned that "poverty is not the hendrance to succee a strong determination in life, as my parents thought us and mold by saying "Since we are poor and we don't have any thing, so, importan all of you must finish and get good education...

I started my primary on public school in my village sad to know education in my village is too crowded and they can't occupy the need of students like materials. I am the eldest and we are all 7 person with 2 brother and 2 sister. My parents education is a high school graduate due to barrier of living they can't afford to pursue education in university. Our house is a bungalow type made of wood and bamboo. My father works as a farmer and b-4 and later on change as an ordinary worker then promoted as a foreman. My childhood dreams is to finish my education and have a good job with a happy family to live with and a successful POLICE WOMAN.

After I finish my primary I move on and enrolled my Secondary not far from my village but takes risk b-coz the bus are limited and population of passenger is so much... takes a lot of sacrifices, patient and always positive minded. I can't get the even during these period more tears I spend, a very complicated situation due to the risk and barrier. You know life up poor....

I spend my college or university in city. I took up BACHELOR OF SCIENCE and COMMERCE major MANAGEMENT ACCOUNTING...... aside from studying I am also WORKING to support my studies and luckily I graduated with that course and have a job for 7months working but I move on to other challenge. I work as a supervisor in a Multi shopping center for 4 years at the middle of that year I take a bar exam as a police license then its greet and god bless me I pass and get license but sad to know I can't go on 4 training due to I meet my coming husband and get pregnant then later we marry and I have now a kid its a boy now he is a 4 years old.

Date   No.

Now, why I choose in coming here in Singapore? is that because of my problem my marriage is not good and turn it worst. so, it took me in coming here. actually, I don't have plan going oversea b-4. Suddenly i came up to these to forget bot, I can't escape though Im here, still marriage in my mind. Its a complicated I choose a wrong destiny of life. I mean and late to realize, hard to accept, although you made all the adjustment but it doesn't work. . . . . But never mind at all, life is full of chances and I have an inspiration to move on and carry on its my son who give me strenght though were far but nud to be strong and determine life with prayer. . . . .

As I stay here, I encounter lots of values, depperent living and country, at first, it so hard to adjust my work, familiarization ... every thing and I can't cope the home, sickness, night and day I cry, but, thanks GOD he guide me till I adjust fully and cope.

Here in Singapore I don't have close friends but, I have some like and seldom we talk all are busy. Since working are always in a hurry. I don't know exactly bout them .. but, I think they are nice and good ...
I been here for 2yrs. and more months I think its the same I never change bat a little bit of progress about learning. About moral and conduct its the same because every now in then, I always look back and remind my self all my hendrances ....

I decide to enroll school as to upgrade myself and fully don't want to waste time during my off day. Now class mean to me a bridge of my knowledge, a way of helping needy by enhancing my services and most of all preparation for my future .. 10 yrs. from now, Hope God grant me to have a good job. I mean change my job, I don't like fever like these. Since, I have studied also, I have strong faith to help myself with prayer, If not here hope in other country. I choose oversea than my country coz of Economy.

DURABLE

Index